Handmade
for Profit!

Handmade for Profit!

Barbara Brabec

M. Evans and Company, Inc
New York

M. Evans and Company, Inc.
216 East 49th Street
New York, NY 10017

Library of Congress Cataloging-in-Publication Data

Brabec, Barbara
   Handmade for profit: hundreds of secrets to success in selling arts & crafts / Barbara Brabec
      p.   cm.
   Includes index.
      1. Handicraft industries—Management. 2. Selling—Handicraft. I. Title
   HD2341.B713   1996
   745.5'068—dc20   96-22960

Design by Evan Johnston

Printed in the United States of America

9   8   7   6   5   4   3   2   1

Contents

Chapter One

The "Creative Cash" Market

Throughout North America, thousands of people are experiencing "craft encounters of the closest kind" as they suddenly discover they have a creative streak or artistic talent.

Thanks to the many books, magazines and Web sites that offer how-to projects and patterns, the average person can easily learn any art or craft technique of interest. And people everywhere do have a great desire to practice an art or craft themselves. This trend was first documented in a 1975 survey conducted by the National Research Center of the Arts, which also revealed that 75 percent of the public thought it was important to have a community center where one could learn arts and crafts.

Crafts and hobbies became big business in the last decade of the 90s, with consumers spending over $10 million a year on craft supplies and related products. Since the turn of the century, however, spending has exploded, according to Susan Brandt, Director of Communications for the

1

Hobby Industry Association (HIA). "Consumers are now parceling out $23 billion each year on items they use to make as gifts, decorate their homes, wear on their persons, celebrate their holidays, and otherwise fulfill their wishes for fun and creativity," she says. "Ironically, the very technology that has speeded up our lives and increased our need to indulge in relaxing and fulfilling activities has created craft products that are easier to use, quicker to complete, and result in more professional looking projects. All of this has helped to alter the perception of crafts—once somewhat questionable in nature—to a much higher level."

Also being altered these days is the perception of a crafts business at home. Once viewed as a nice way to make a little extra cash on the side, today's craft professionals are serious business people who earn substantial annual incomes. Often, whole families become involved in such homebased businesses, adding a kind of richness to life that the average wage-earner can only envy.

Like many of the people I've written about through the years, I know the joy that can come from taking a creative idea and running with it as fast as you can go. How sweet it is when you see that it's actually possible to make a living doing what you love most! My interest in crafts ultimately led me to self-sufficiency as a professional writer and publisher, and I wrote my first book in 1979 at a time when craft businesses were enjoying new popularity. I titled it *Creative Cash*, using a phrase I had coined for the kind of money one can earn by using their creative mind and hands. In fact, many of the people featured in this edition of *Handmade for Profit* used my *Creative Cash* book to get started in business. I now have a special family of successful home-business owners who have contributed information and advice to my various books, so I hope you'll read all of them to get their combined advice, and mine, too. (See the Resource Chapter for a directory of Web sites owned by everyone mentioned in this book.)

Like *Creative Cash*, this book has its own unique content, with a special focus on how and where to market handmade/handcrafted products at the retail level through dozens of different outlets, many of them in your own backyard. This new edition of *Handmade for Profit* will help you grab a share of today's "creative cash market" simply by doing things you enjoy most and may already do best. With this book in hand, you can start making money from your art or craft hobby *right now.* Or, if you're already selling what you make but not making as much money as you had originally hoped, this book will help you figure out what you're doing wrong while also giving you hundreds of tips on how to increase both sales and profits.

Crafts' Importance to the Economy

It has long been known that America's handcraft industry was making a significant contribution to the American economy, but there were no statistics to prove it until early 2001, when the Craft Organization Directors Association (CODA) released the results of its landmark study. It confirmed what many industry leaders knew instinctively all along: Craft businesses are truly important to this country's economy, contributing nearly $14 billion a year (see details below).

The first clue about the size of this economy came in 1995 after HandMade in America, a nonprofit organization, made a study of 22 counties in western North Carolina and learned that crafts were contributing $122 million annually to the economy of that part of the state. Later, a similar study in Kentucky revealed that craft artists were contributing more than $52 million to that state's annual economy. These findings encouraged CODA to do the first major national study on the size and scope of the crafts industry.

Over 84,000 surveys were mailed directly to craftspeople who earn all or part of their living from the sale of handmade products, and CODA released the results of its study of 7,500 completed surveys on April 1 at the CODA 2001 Conference in Asheville, North Carolina. Here are some surprising facts and figures:

- There are 106,000–126,000 craftspeople working in the United States today.
- These business owners (79% of whom are homebased) are generating sales of between $12.3 to $13.8 billion per year.
- The average gross sales/revenue per craftsperson is $76,025.
- Income from craft activities comprises 47% of household income on average, and 22% of craft households derive all of their income from craft.

- Retail sales account for 52.9% of annual sales, with just over one-half of these sales being made at craft fairs.
- The average craftsperson derives 27% of annual sales from wholesale, and 11.2% from consignment to galleries.

"Armed with this economic impact survey, CODA is moving forward to obtain an appropriate NICS code (formerly called SIC codes) to have the federal government recognize the craft industry and validate it as an industry," says Barbara Arena, Director of the National Craft Association (NCA) and a CODA member. "This is all made possible by everyone who took time to participate in the CODA survey. I think the artisans realized just how important this was for the craft industry."

In summary, the CODA study findings have validated the crafts industry as a vibrant and growing network of small American businesses, while drawing added attention to small and homebased businesses in general. These statistics are expected to prove to business and government leaders that craft is a viable and sustainable industry worthy of investment and support. They also draw attention to the important relationship between crafts and cultural tourism. Now, states armed with accurate statistics will be able to partner with economic development agencies to encourage growth and development of this important sector of homebased businesses. If used by craft business owners, these statistics may also be useful when applying for business loans.

Who's Crafting and Why

In looking at who's crafting and why, we have information from two segments of the crafts industry: the general crafts consumer industry, represented by the Hobby Industry Association (HIA), which tracks the expenditures of hobbycrafters, and CODA, which is tracking the earnings of professional artisans. Both studies agree that far more women than men are involved in crafts.

More specifically, CODA statistics reveal that 64 percent of craftspeople are female and 41 percent are between the ages of 46 and 55. Nearly 80 percent of all professional craftspeople work in a studio located on or in their residential property, and 78 percent of them are members of a craft organization.

According to HIA statistics, except in the area of woodworking, where about two-thirds of the participants are male, hobbycrafters are far more likely to be female than male. According to HIA spokesperson Susan Brandt, there is at least one crafter in more than half (54%) of U.S. households. These crafters are involved in needlecrafts (34 percent), painting and finishing (27 percent), floral (16 percent), and general crafts (37 percent). The five most popular activities are cross stitching (16 percent), home decor painting (13 percent), cake decorating and crocheting (both 12 percent), and scrapbooking/memory crafts (11 percent). Apparel sewing and floral arranging (both 10 percent) come next, followed by craft sewing, art and drawing, wreathmaking, beading and woodoworking (all 9 percent). Craft and hobby participants, compared to nonparticipants, are more likely to be married with children under 18, more educated and with higher incomes. Women in these households tend to be younger and employed part time. HIA statistics aside, I believe most of America's crafters fall into one of four categories:

1. Hobbyists who craft just for the fun of it

2. Those who sell occasionally (or want to)

3. Part-time crafters who earn a substantial amount of money from their crafts, yet may not feel they are really "in business"

4. Craft professionals (called "professional crafters," "procrafters" or "PCs" by some) whose primary goal in selling is to earn a part- or full-time living.

Because there are hundreds of different arts and crafts, individuals who work with their hands tend to think of themselves in specific terms, such as stitcher, quilter, painter, woodworker, stained glass artist, jeweler, potter, folk artist, weaver, spinner, basketmaker, dollmaker and so on. Some of these people are "craftsmen" and some are "craftswomen," but because of the sensitivity many people have expressed about sexist language, it is now common for writers to refer to groups of creative people as "artists," "craftspeople," "artisans," "crafters," and so on. If you are a needleworker or home sewer, or someone who practices an unusual craft, please don't feel left out when I use these broad terms. If you make anything by hand, you are part of the huge and steadily growing arts and crafts industry. (NOTE: In their zeal to make sure no one is offended, some editors ask writers not to use the word "craftsmanship," but I think it would be a shame to let such a beautiful word fall from our language. Whether politically correct or not, this word cannot easily be replaced. Fine craftsmanship is, and always will be, the hallmark of a successful craft producer.)

Since more women than men craft, it follows that more women than men start homebased craft businesses. Supporting this statement are figures I got from Linda Coomer at Coomers craft malls. Some six thousand crafters sell through these stores, but only 20 percent or so are male, she says. In the past thirty years, I figure I've received over two hundred thousand letters and e-mails from people who were interested or involved in arts and crafts, and I'd guess that about 95 percent of this mail has been from women. For some reason, men don't search out or share information the way women do. (Humorously speaking, I think this has something to do with the fact that a man, when lost, will drive for hours before he will ask anyone for directions, while a woman's first instinct is to pull into the nearest gas station for help.) It should not be surprising, then, that most of the tips and ideas in this book have come from women.

"What This Book Will Do For You"

This book contains all the information you need to get started selling at the retail level and keep growing. It is a collection of some of the best crafts marketing tips you will ever find. All of them have come from professional crafters in my network, developed over thirty years of writing about creative people who make money from home.

One of my columns, "Selling What You Make," ran in *Crafts* magazine for more than twenty years, setting a record for being the longest-running column of its type. While that column provided the foundation for the first edition of *Handmade for Profit*, this edition is filled with many new tips, ideas and success stories of crafters I have met since the first edition was published. It also contains a new chapter on selling on the Web, plus a Resource Chapter of both print and Web resources. It is the real-life experiences of all the real people featured in this book that gives it authenticity and excitement! If you will read it carefully and *apply the information it offers,* I guarantee it will

- Show you how to start making money right now from something you love to do;
- Increase your sales and profits if you're already selling;
- Encourage you to get more serious about the business side of crafts;
- Prompt you to set exciting new life goals.

Notice the emphasis on "apply the information"? You know that old saying about leading a horse to water. While I can give you all the information you need to successfully sell handmade items of any kind, I can't force you to get out and do this. I can only try to prompt you to action with words and encouraging examples of how others have done this. With all the crafts writing I've done, I figure I've helped launch more craft businesses than Helen of Troy launched ships. With this new edition of *Handmade for Profit,* I hope to help launch thousands more.

Your "GET READY" Recipe for Success

To start making money from your arts and crafts talents, follow the steps in my "GET READY Recipe for Success":

G et it together! As soon as your home begins to share space with a money-making venture, everything changes. You will save time and stress by getting your home and personal life organized before you begin to sell your handmade creations.

E ducate yourself to your possibilities for financial profit from selling handcrafts and related products and services. Attend craft conferences, small business workshops, join art or craft organizations, get involved on the Internet, and read, read, *read!*

T alk to other creative people who share your enthusiasm for crafts. Browse craft fairs and network with all the interesting people you meet in person or on the Internet.

R esolve to give your new endeavor your best effort. Remember these four Ps of accomplishment: Plan purposefully, Prepare prayerfully, Proceed positively, and Pursue persistently.

E mulate but do not copy the products, designs, and selling methods used by others. You are unique, and God has given you special gifts or abilities that no other person has. Your challenge in life is to discover and develop them. (Tip: Generally, these are things that come easy for you, things you seem to have a natural "bent" for.)

A nticipate that you will have problems. *Everyone* has problems. Fortunately, this book offers solutions to the most common problems you're likely to encounter in starting a crafts business at home.

D evelop a written plan of everything you need to do to get started selling. As a wise man once said, "If you don't know where you're going, you might miss it when you get there."

Y OU are the most special ingredient in this recipe, so begin by remembering that you can do anything you set your heart on doing. If there is no one else around to do it, it's okay to pat yourself on the back each time you achieve a new goal or do something you didn't know you could do.

There has been a well-established professional arts and crafts community since the mid-60s, and dozens of print and online periodicals and organizations now serve the small business needs of North America's professional artists and crafters. Hundreds more cater to the interests of hobbyists in this field. According to the HIA surveys, sales of supplies in 2000 were $23 billion. Of this amount, professional crafters spent about $72 million (according to surveys conducted by *ProCrafter* magazine, formerly known as *Craft Supply Magazine*)

At this time you still may be learning or working to perfect a particular art or craft. As you make one new handmade creation after another, you may find yourself thinking, "This is great! I didn't know I could do this!" Your friends and family may be showing signs of amazement, if not outright envy, and you can hardly wait to try that new idea you got this morning.

As exciting as it can be to just make things, it's doubly exciting when you begin to sell what you make and get positive feedback from appreciative buyers. As soon as you take this step, I guarantee all kinds of interesting things will happen. You will gain self-confidence and poise. You will get ideas you could not have envisioned before getting out in the public as a seller. While selling at fairs and shows, you will meet people you never would have met otherwise. Shop owners may approach you, asking if you could sell to them at wholesale prices, and someone from your local paper may want to interview you. If you are featured in the paper, your spouse will be amazed, your family will be proud, your friends and neighbors will be impressed, and you will be so excited you can't sleep.

You will never know where your talents and ideas might take you if you don't give them a chance to grow and develop. Where arts and crafts are concerned, ordinary people often accomplish the most extraordinary things. Don't you agree the possibilities ought to be explored?

So Many Crafts, So Many Possibilities!

Have you ever thought about the many things that people do
in their homes for fun and profit? Well, I have, and so should you.
Today a living room is apt to share its time and space
with equipment used to make things for the busy marketplace.

Here yarns are spun and weavings done for sale to stores or shops,
and with work like this in progress, all normal housework stops!
In cozy little offices in rooms once used for dining,
more than one ambitious person will be writing or designing.

Creative people don't just sleep in rooms that hold a bed;
they may be doing needlepoint and quilting there instead.
The bathroom also doubles as a workroom now and then,
where people go to dye their yarn or dip batik again.

These days the rec room isn't used for pool or cards or darts;
it's now a little factory where the craft production starts.
Dad and Mom and all the kids may go there after dinner
to manufacture something that is sure to be a winner.

And think of all the cars without a roof above their hoods,
'cause garages aren't for parking, they're for crafting arty goods.
Like wooden toys, ceramic work or things made out of glass,
or metal sculpture, furniture or objets d'art en masse.

And the kitchen? Ah, the kitchen, it is such a busy place,
but the things that are a cookin' won't end up inside your face.
Take bread dough for example, it's not what you bake and eat,
it's something that you bake, then paint, *in colors nice 'n' neat.*

Do you begin to see the point poetically I'm making—
That "arts and crafts" (now household words) are sometimes overtaking
entire households, stem to stern, disrupting normal living . . .
yet sometimes satisfaction is the only thing they're giving.

If this is true with you, my friend, you ought to do some thinking.
Perhaps it's time to sell the crafts you spend so much time making.
Because you give your arts and crafts their very sustenance,
Don't you agree it would be nice if they helped pay the rent?

More Help on Library Shelves

Thousands of new books are published every year, some of which are bound to be on your favorite art, craft or hobby. If you're on the Internet, it's easy to find new books of interest. Simply browse over to Amazon.com or BarnesandNoble.com. If you're not yet online, check the library for *Books in Print,* an annual directory that is supplemented with periodic editions of *Guide to Forthcoming Books.* Look under subject categories of interest to turn up new book titles and pertinent information regarding each book's publisher, publication date, price, etc. When you've listed all the books that sound exciting to you, check to see if they are on library shelves. If you can't locate a particular book in a bookstore, and it's not on library shelves either, remember that most libraries can obtain hard-to-find books through their Inter-Library Loan program. While browsing in the library, also take a look at these problem-solving reference directories:

- ▼ *The Standard Periodical Directory* and *Ulrich's International Periodicals Directory.* These directories are helpful if you know the name of a magazine or newsletter but lack its address. These two annuals describe thousands of consumer magazines, trade journals, newsletters, government publications, directories, yearbooks and other periodicals in both the United States and Canada. Listings are arranged alphabetically as well as by subject matter.
- ▼ *Encyclopedia of Associations.* There are organizations for just about every art and craft you can name, and many publish periodicals or sponsor conferences and trade shows to help members get ahead. This directory will help you connect with them. Membership in an art or craft organization may enable you to buy more affordable health insurance and obtain merchant status for your business. Many organizations also offer discounts on

office supplies and raw materials and publish a member newsletter or directory.

▼ *The Thomas Register of American Manufacturers*. Its twenty-three volumes profile more than 150,000 companies with a description of over 50,000 individual product and service headings and 112,000 trade and brand names. Very helpful when you're trying to locate raw material suppliers, wholesale supply sources, or the owners of brand names and trademarks. Companies are listed alphabetically and by type of product.

Recommended Reading

See the Resource Chapter of this book for my favorite craft business books and other helpful small business and crafts marketing resources on the Web. In addition to books available in bookstores and libraries, there are a growing number of downloadable eBooks you can buy on dozens of Web sites devoted to the sale of electronic information. One of the best of these sites, which features home business books on many different topics, is BizyMoms.com, which coincidentally published my first eBook, *Money-Saving Tax Strategies for Homebased Entrepreneurs*.

Other self-published books and magazines are available only by mail from individual homebased publishers, many of whom now have Web sites that are included in the Resource Chapter.

Chapter Two

Building Confidence and Setting Goals

If you feel fearful and insecure, it's not because you lack courage or self-confidence, only that you've locked them inside you for so long that they can't get out. What you have to do is find the key that unlocks the door.

*I*f you have not yet begun to sell the things you make, look around your home and tell me what you see. By any chance, have you reached what I call the "crafts saturation point"? That is, are you now making so many things you can't give all of them away? I went through this phase myself back in the 60s, and my real motivation to sell came the day my husband walked into my hobby room and said, "Your crafts are nice . . . but what are you going to do with all this stuff?"

I knew then that I had to do one of two things: stop producing or start selling. Every serious crafter eventually reaches this point and almost has to start selling if only to pay for supplies and make room for new creations yet to come. In time, even those who craft only for fun will begin to entertain the idea of selling when friends begin to comment, "Your work is lovely! Have you ever thought about selling it?"

Although many people will never find the courage to plunge into the marketplace, the idea of selling may lurk in their minds like a cat waiting for a mouse to make its move. Once a person has been bitten by the "selling bug," many questions automatically arise. Where are the markets? What selling methods are best? Where do I get the information needed to turn a hobby into a business? Once a few things have sold, a crafter may begin to look for ways to improve sales and ask, "How do I get into big-time selling?"

Although I will occasionally touch on the topic of wholesaling, "big-time selling" is not what this book is about. It's about how to get started selling directly to consumers at the retail level in ways that beginners find most comfortable. It's about developing talents and skills, exploring new territory, branching out and moving on. It's also about *business.*

Why do I keep talking about *business* when all you're interested in is making money? Ah, there's the rub! *You can't have one without the other.* You may sell your crafts and say you're not "in business," but in the eyes of the law, you are also subject to a variety of local, state and federal laws, rules, regulations and taxes. (You'll learn more about this in Chapter Three.)

If you do not have a business background or a job that has encouraged your entrepreneurial instincts in the past, you may be resistant to the idea of starting a homebased crafts business. If this scares you now, don't worry about it. Just slip this idea into your subconscious mind and let it rest there awhile. The more of this book you read, the more you'll learn about the personal and financial advantages of turning your hobby into a genuine homebased business. By the time you've finished this book, the idea of a real crafts business may feel as comfortable as an old pair of shoes.

An "Analyze Your Excuses" Exercise

No matter what we attempt to do in life, the hardest part is just getting started. Here are some of the excuses I've heard from people who said they wanted to sell their crafts but just couldn't seem to get started. Which of these "roadblocks" are preventing you from following your dream?

❏ It's hard to decide what to sell.

❏ I'm not good at selling.

❏ I don't know how to find buyers.

❏ I have no business experience.

❏ I don't know how to price my products.

❏ I'm too old (or too young).

❏ I don't have enough time.

❏ I have no start-up money.

❏ My family might complain if I got too involved.

❏ I'd look like a fool if I tried and failed.

❏ I don't know anything about taxes, laws, or bookkeeping.

With a list of excuses like this, it's no wonder so many craft businesses never get born! If you see yourself in the above list and wish you knew how to get past the hurdles in your path, try the following exercise. It will help you expose your fears, decide what you do best, and set some new goals. You'll need three sheets of paper.

1. *Expose Your Fears.* On the first sheet, complete this sentence: "I have not gotten serious about a craft business because . . ." Be honest with yourself—identify what scares you most. Once identified, fears can be killed, one by one, through self-study and experience. Above all, don't fear failure itself. Successful businesses, like successful lives, are built not only on one small success after another, but on one small failure after another. Each small failure is a new learning experience that illuminates for us the things that won't work and teaches us to avoid larger failures of a similar kind. Thus, each small failure automatically leads to a small success somewhere along the line.

2. *Identify Yourself.* On the second sheet, write a description of who you are and what you do best. Examples: "I am a needleworker who creates patterns for other stitchers," or "I am a folk artist who paints on weathered wood," or "I make contemporary furniture and accessories." Giving yourself this kind of formal identity will do wonders for your ego and help you target customer prospects.

3. Set Some Short-Term Goals. On the third sheet, list three things you will do this month to get moving on your craft business. For example, you might start checking the kind of handcrafted merchandise being sold in local shops or craft malls. You might list six things you've made that buyers might view as a coordinated product line. Another goal might be to get together with a creative friend who will listen to your ideas and give you practical reactions to them. It doesn't matter what three things you do—pick anything that makes you feel comfortable. The important thing is just to **get started**. Once you do, I predict your enthusiasm and moneymaking ideas will grow like a snowball rolling downhill.

Crafting a Success Plan

By now, you see the advantage of putting your plans in writing. A computer makes writing easier, but if you don't have a computer, a notebook will do. Instead of a spiral-bound pad, try a loose-leaf notebook that allows you to set up categories and add and remove pages. Give your notebook an exciting title that reflects your secret dreams and hopes for the future. After it's begun, reread it often to remind yourself of where you want to go and how you plan to get there. Following are some suggested categories to start with. Add others as they come to mind, and jot down your thoughts about each of them:

- My Dreams and Goals (immediate and long-term)
- Moneytalk (your reasons for working, your income goals, an estimate of how much money you'll need to get started and where you'll get this start-up money)
- Time (number of hours you plan to work each week, where you will find them and how you plan to fit everything into your daily schedule)
- Business Brainstorming (business names you like, ideas for products you might make, where you will set up a business management corner in your home, what office supplies and

equipment you'll need to manage your moneymaking endeavor, how family and friends might help you achieve your goal, etc.)

■ Production Plan (supplies and materials needed, supply sources you need to locate, how you or others will produce goods for sale, what outside help you might need)

■ Marketing Plan (how and where you plan to sell everything you make)

■ Start-up Plan (follow the specific steps given in this chapter)

If you are not doing it already, I suggest you grab a highlighter pen and start marking any part of this book that rings a bell in your mind or gives you a great idea (providing, of course, that the book you're reading hasn't been borrowed from the library). If it has, I believe you will want your own copy for future reference.

Tip

As you read, jot notes in the margin the minute you get a good idea because ideas don't keep. If ideas aren't captured the minute we get them, they may be lost forever, like dreams briefly recalled in the morning. Or, as someone once said, "To err is human; to forget, routine."

After you've finished this book and have set up your notebook, go back and pick up on the highlighted portions and transfer your "idea notes" to the appropriate pages of your notebook. Periodically, when you feel you're ready for a change or a new challenge, reread this book and your entire notebook. As time passes, your vision will change and things you cannot relate to now will have new meaning. It's like rereading the Bible or seeing a great classic film once again. Because of how we change with each passing year, the way we respond either at the age of forty or sixty will be totally different from the way we responded at the age of twenty. Leafing through your notebook will also motivate you and help plant ideas and goals more firmly in your subconscious mind. Make a promise to yourself to follow your dream, and don't let others discourage you.

People who don't have dreams and goals of their own are often quick to put down other people's ideas. Cindi, a beginning dollmaker, told me that as a child she had only two dreams: to create living dolls (a family) and t o be Madame Alexander. "It was as I began to get older," she wrote, "that adults taught me to think more 'sensibly.' Now, at forty, I've realized something important: my dreams were the reality and others' dreams for me were fantasy."

Karen, a teddy bear maker, told me that when her craft business wasn't going the way she wanted it to, she began to lose interest in it. "I finally figured out what the problem was," she said. "I was listening to what others said I should do instead of listening to myself."

What these letter-writers didn't realize at the time was that in telling me about their dreams, they were putting their goals in writing and strengthening their beliefs in the process. When they believed their goals were possible, magical things began to happen.

A Time Management Exercise

One of your goals might be to find more time for crafting and selling. "Time is what we want the most and what we use the worst," someone has said. Anyone who is currently in the dreaming-about-a-business stage needs to take a good look at how their time is presently being spent (or wasted). Before we can capture time that is slipping through our fin-

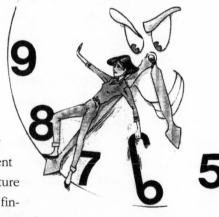

gers, we need to study how we're spending it.

Every day for a month, keep track of how you spend your waking hours. Before long you'll be able to identify time-wasting patterns you can

Time Management Tips

- Be firm. Don't let family and friends steal your time. Set specific times for family activities or visits with friends.
- Make lists of things to do, putting the most important things at the top. Don't fret because you can never get to the bottom of your list; just start anew each day and keep putting the most important things on top.
- In trying to manage all the information you collect, forget about filing things alphabetically or even by subject category. Instead, file everything in terms of how you plan to use it in the future. (Examples: New product ideas, marketing tips, business resources, Web site design ideas, etc.)
- Reorganize or rearrange your workspace to avoid wasted movements. Group certain jobs that require similar physical movements, tools, supplies or a particular mindset because every unnecessary movement you can eliminate will save time and speed production.
- To avoid interruptions while you're working, turn on the answering machine or let your voice mail take calls until you're ready to respond to them. Ease your stress by not taking business calls after 5 o'clock. (You may be working around the clock to fill orders, but that's no reason to answer calls before or after normal business hours.)

change. You may be surprised to learn how much time you spend reading the paper over a cup of coffee, chatting with neighbors, visiting with friends on the phone, running errands, watching television, surfing the Internet, working around the house, doing community projects and so on.

We all have extra time. The challenge is simply to find it. Generally, this means we must stop doing one thing to make time for another, or at least rearrange our time so we have special blocks of time for other activities, such as developing a profitable little business at home

"Set Goals, Make Gains"

To stay excited about your business, try setting new goals every six months, and also do a complete re-evaluation of your business at year's end. Catherine Lee Schmid, owner of Blue River Pottery Studio Gallery, Inc., offers a good example. After eleven years of operating a studio in her home, doing retail shows and wholesaling to galleries, Catherine opened her own gallery in July 2001. (She says having a retail gallery allows her to test-market new designs and colors and get immediate feedback.)

Catherine credits part of her success to the fact that she has always been goal-oriented. "I make a list of new goals every six months," she says, "and I'm happy if I can accomplish the top three on any given list. When I study my lists of goals at year's end, I'm always energized because I can see that I've accomplished a lot, survived the season, and have ideas for many new products and new goals to achieve."

At year's end, Catherine does two other things to advance her business. While reorganizing her office and studio, she also analyzes her supply sources. "I have to keep everything really clean, and must also inventory everything I have every six months (finished products in one area; glazes; and work ready to be glazed), so I know what supplies to buy. I always have a minimum supply of finished product in four different styles to accommodate the needs of my established customer base. I am always looking for new supplies, and I need to keep an eye on which suppliers I want to drop or continue ordering from. My main concerns are quality of product and consistency (which is hard to find in my business)."

Years before she started her Glass Things business, Marj Bates wrote herself an annual letter listing a dozen goals she wanted to achieve in the coming year. "I still do that," she says, "but now my goals include both personal and business goals. Lately, I've begun to move 'the dollar thing' of business to focus more on running my business on the same spiritual level as I run my life. I used to work myself to death, but I'm slowing down now, weeding out the old, and taking time to nurture myself. Curiously, my business has blossomed even more as a result."

Setting New Goals

Do you want to be a carefree crafter, a hobby seller, or a real crafts business owner? Do you have ambitions of success, money or fame? Many people fail to achieve their goals because the goals have not been clearly expressed. Instead of speaking in vague terms about having "a really successful home shop" or "a craft business that is profitable," establish a specific money goal, an annual dollar amount that would make you feel your business is a success.

The trick to achieving any goal is to first picture it in your mind, so put all your goals in writing and reread them periodically to reinforce your mental success pictures. You're halfway to achieving a goal when you believe it's possible. "You are everything you choose to be. You are as unlimited as the endless universe," says Shad Helmstetter in his motivational book, *What to Say When You Talk to Yourself.* Look in the mirror each morning and repeat this message until you believe it!

In setting goals and writing your plan, include your own definitions for "profitable" and "success." To many, these words have little connection with money. "Profitable" might mean experience, acquired knowledge, valuable personal contacts or a new understanding of your capabilities or limitations. "Success" can mean being in control of your own life, making new friends or discovering a new world of possibilities. To one middle-aged woman in North Dakota, success was expressed simply and poignantly like this: "I want to make my own way so I won't have to depend on someone else."

A reader once told me that her greatest ambition was to become rich and famous for her art. Another said she wanted "to create something all her own that she could sell for hundreds of dollars at an art show." While such goals are possible, they are not realistic financial goals for beginners. It is always wise to temper dreams of riches with thoughts of reality, lest you become discouraged when big profits aren't realized. It's also better to seek recognition than fame. In expressing this ambition, a beginning crafter said, "I want to be recognized as a professional craftsperson and designer, to be able to make a living as a craftsperson." This is a worthy and achievable goal.

Craft Networking

Do you know how "craft networking" got started? Back in 1981, these words were unknown in the crafts community. Until a friend uttered them the day we were discussing a talk I was to give for the Society of Craft Designers, I had never thought of them as a pair. They carried quite a punch because I suddenly realized this was what I had been doing for years.

After presenting my craft networking speech, I turned it into a special report and slowly began to educate the crafts community to the idea of networking as a way to get ahead in crafts business at home. I explained that one of the greatest satisfactions from craft networking is the emotional reinforcement you gain. We all need networks of friends to survive and, as one of my readers put it, "It's nice to know there is someone out there you can turn to for moral support." Through networking, individual confidence builds and grows, and through communication with one another, we learn that our problems are not unique. How reassuring it is to know that the same things that have happened to us have happened to others.

Generally, I find women to be better networkers than men. Maybe this is because women have always networked under the guise of *kaffee-klatsching*, chatting at the beauty parlor or lunching with friends. In earlier years, quilting bees and threshing events drew women together, enabling them to be more helpful and supportive of one another. While many craftspeople are networking today, others remain secretive about their craft ideas and marketing outlets. Some fear that a sharing of confidential information or "trade secrets" will hurt their business or chances for future sales, but this is unlikely to happen. My homebased business has never been hurt or held back because I shared hard-to-get information with a business friend or even a competitor. I have always operated in the belief that we have only what we give away, and everything we give comes back double. What goes for love and friendship also goes for information and ideas. As someone once said, "We make a living by what we get, and we make a life by what we give."

Inspired by one of my articles, a dollmaker wrote to tell me that she had started networking and asking questions. "The price of all those long-distance phone calls was worth it," she said. "I was amazed at how generous other craftswomen were with their help, advice, praise and encouragement."

If you're dreaming about starting a crafts business, or interested in expanding one already begun, networking with people who share your interests and ambitions may be the single most important thing you can do now and throughout the life of your crafts business. Now, with e-mail and the Internet, this is incredibly easy to do. There is an old saying that "knowledge is power," so the more you have, the greater your chances for success in any new endeavor. Too few craftspeople take advantage of their networking opportunities, however. The excuse I've heard most often for not joining an organization or subscribing to periodicals that will connect them to other craftspeople is, "Oh I'm much too busy producing crafts . . . or designing them . . . or selling them . . . to read periodicals or join an organization."

Starting your own supportive local network is as easy as inviting a few craft friends to lunch and arranging to meet regularly in the future to discuss mutual problems or concerns. To expand the size of any support group, set up a meeting at the library or other public building and ask your newspaper to announce it. You may be surprised by the turnout, especially in rural areas where crafters may feel particularly isolated.

Barbara's Success Story

The most important thing I've learned from my many years of self-employment—and the most encouraging thing I can tell you now—is that one thing always leads to another. Perhaps my story will give you added encouragement to pursue your secret dream.

When I developed a passionate interest in arts and crafts in the mid-60s, I never imagined that my crafts hobby would lead me to a full-time homebased writing and publishing business. I often think back to the day when three little words changed my life and put me on an exciting new road of discovery.

On graduating from high school, I went to work as a secretary in

Motivated to Succeed

Nothing motivates one to success like a genuine need for money. When doctors told Joyce, a self-taught artist and designer, that her husband had multiple sclerosis, she found the motivation she needed to become the family breadwinner. With a husband in a wheelchair and three small children depending on her, she stopped marketing her wood products at craft shows and launched a home party business featuring her custom-designed furniture and folk art. She got free information and assistance from the U.S. Small Business Administration (SBA), which also gave her a small business loan to get started. Before long, Joyce was employing up to fifty people during peak production periods, and more than a hundred women across the country were hosting home parties featuring her products.

Chicago. Five years later I met and married Harry Brabec, my knight in shining armor. I kept working for the first five years of marriage, after which time Harry suggested I stay home and just be Mrs. Brabec for a while. "But I'd be bored to tears with nothing to do all day," I said, and he said, "Get a hobby." Those three little words changed not only my life, but his. *I discovered crafts.*

First there was my "Glitter All Over the Place" period, which Harry put an immediate end to the first time he found glitter in his soup.

Then came my "Ceramic Chips in the Shag Rug" era, which ruined more than one of my husband's sly barefoot runs to the refrigerator after I'd gone to bed. The jig was up each time he stepped on a sliver and yelped with pain. Harry often said that entering the living room in the days when I was cutting mosaic tiles was like walking into a war zone since he never knew when a flying chip would hit him in the eye.

I dabbled in oil painting for a while, but that didn't last long. In a one-bedroom apartment, the smell of turpentine at dinnertime was too much even for me to bear. Harry was relieved when I switched to acrylics but alarmed when I told him I'd found a supplier who had dozens of unfinished basswood items I could paint and sell. By now, we were living in a two-bedroom apartment, and one bedroom had been turned into a crafts studio for me. I was getting serious about selling, and before long, I had diversified into driftwood plaques by the dozen. I discovered a whole new world of possibilities the day I bought a book titled *You, Too, Can Whittle and Carve.*

I recall the evening I retired to one corner of the living room with my how-to book, a small piece of balsa wood and my new X-Acto knife. "What are you doing?" Harry asked. "Carving a donkey's head," I replied. We hadn't been married long at that point, so he naturally found this amusing. (Until that moment, the only thing I'd ever carved was a Thanksgiving turkey, yet I had not the slightest doubt I could do what I said I was going to do.) A couple of hours later when I astonished my husband with a finished carving, I was off and running on another road of discovery. For many evenings thereafter, Harry would sit in the living room to read and I'd join him with my whittling. Just to let him now I loved him, every so often I'd zonk him on the nose with a flying wood chip.

When we purchased our first house, the extra space spurred my creativity. My purchase of a Moto Tool to speed my woodcarving soon led to my "Sawdust in the Basement" period. The fine sawdust from this tool seemed to drift throughout the house, which annoyed Harry because he likes both a clean house and workshop area. It was about this time in my life that I started shirking my homemaking duties. I was much too busy making crafts to clean house, you see, and when I started my present business in 1981, things only got worse.

In addition to putting up with my craft antics and loss of interest in housework, Harry also found his patience sorely tried every time we went somewhere because I'd insist on visiting that "cute little craft shop down the street." Of course, I was trying to figure out what was selling, and for how much, and could I sell my stuff there, too.

Does any of this sound familiar?

For the next three years, I created a variety of products that I offered for sale through several local shops and fairs. I'm so grateful now that some of my best one-of-a-kind music boxes, sculpture and carvings never sold because I have enjoyed owning and looking at these pieces all these years. I now realize that if they had been sold, I never would have replaced them.

Why Dreams Are Delayed

In just four sentences, one of my readers perfectly described the roadblock so many women encounter when they consider a small business at home. "I delayed my business first of all because my children were small and needed all the love, attention and help I could give them," writes Diane in Illinois. "Second, I lacked knowledge about my favorite craft and the business world in general. Third, as a young, struggling family, our finances were limited. Fourth, doing something scary—like starting my own business—also made me wait so long before taking the plunge."

But there is still another stumbling block, and it's bigger than all the rest, Diane said. "In all the excuses I have mentioned, I have found one thing in common of which I was totally unaware: Time. I now realize that time managed me instead of me managing it. And now that I look back, I can see there was much I could have done if only I had managed my time better."

Diane's business is now a reality. She has learned more about time management, business basics and her favorite craft of needlepoint. Money is still a consideration, but she is no longer afraid to fail. Best of all, she has learned something special about her family. When she finally told her children and husband of her dreams and desires, she was stunned by the support and encouragement she got from them. "How I wish I had called upon them sooner," she said.

If you haven't done so already, take time now to have a talk with your family. Give them a chance to help you realize your special dream.

That is why I urge you never to sell a piece of artwork that means a great deal to you unless you are sure you can make a replacement item for yourself. Some crafts are made to be given away, some are made to be sold, and some should be made to keep. Money is a poor substitute for a beautiful item that speaks to your heart and can't be replaced once gone.

In 1971, after three years of selling my crafts, I stopped making things for sale when Harry suggested that what the world needed now was a crafts magazine that would help other crafters sell their work. Almost overnight, we found ourselves involved full time in the publication of a magazine we named *Artisan Crafts.* This quarterly survived five years before quietly dying during the 1975 recession. For a long time afterward, Harry joked that the magazine was a literary success and a financial flop. It's true this venture was not *financially* profitable, but in time it proved to be one of my most profitable life experiences.

If I had not had the courage to try something new and totally foreign to me (magazine publishing), I never would have met the person who referred me to the book publisher who asked me to write my first book. That book, *Creative Cash,* dramatically changed my life because it led me to start the full-time writing and publishing business I still operate from my home today. It was at this point that I launched a newsletter that led to my first speaking job, which led to the writing and publishing of other books and more speaking engagements in both the United States and Canada.

My crafts hobby dramatically changed my husband's life as well. Because of my involvement in crafts, he was drawn into the industry in the 1970s. Among other things, his work as crafts festival producer for Busch Gardens got us two six-week trips-of-a-lifetime traveling first-class through-out Europe on a company expense account.

In 1989, because of the popularity of another of my books, I was invited to Hollywood for a week-long appearance on ABC-TV's *Home Show.* Their home-business segment, titled "Homemade Money" after my best-selling book, prompted thousands of people to rush to bookstores to purchase a copy. This led to other television appearances.

By telling you this, I hope to illustrate how one thing always leads to another and why it's so important to *just get moving!* Since I first began to develop my artistic and creative talents, I've never had a boring day, and I owe it all to my husband for uttering those three little words ("get a hobby") in 1965. None of the creative-thinking people who have contributed to this book have boring days either, and in every chapter you'll find their encouraging words and solid how-to advice to help you get going on your art or crafts business idea. "Just remember," says soapmaker Cheri Marsh, "not to be so in love with any part of your business that you can't change directions if things aren't working. And don't associate with negative people. There are

Pursuing Your Dream

Marj Bates offers a wonderful example of the importance of persistence in pursuing a dream, and faith in one's abilities. Even as a little girl, she had an interest in art and took a variety of art classes. In college, while taking metalsmithing classes, she also discovered the magic of making glass beads and knew that was going to be her passion.

Prior to becoming a professional glass beadmaker, however, Marj earned a living as a long-haul trucker, and she began her business on a nickel-and-dime budget while working three part-time jobs. "When I began my business in 1995, it was a struggle financially to buy one glass rod," she says. "I started with one minor bench burner torch and very little in the way of tools and glass. But now, only a few years later, I have a fully equipped studio in the ocean front home my business made possible. I manage my own Web site and also teach workshops on a regular basis."

Marj says her greatest lessons and tools are (1) networking, sharing and giving back; (2) remaining teachable and open minded; and (3) being tenacious. "Several years ago, I began to repeat the words, 'Don't quit before the miracle,' over and over again, many times with tears streaming down my face. And those words have gotten me through several tough phases in life. I never had a big break, but I've had a lot of neat stepping stones and I and my business have consistently grown as I've continued to hammer metals and melt glass. It's a very satisfying life."

those who will spend all their energy explaining why you can't (or shouldn't) try to do something, and that is a contagious attitude. Such people also tend to be envious of successful people and may attempt to undermine you."

"My philosophy," says weaver, writer and teacher Bobbie Irwin, "is that when you're doing what you're supposed to be doing with your life—selling or whatever—the rewards will come and the opportunities will open up for you. It doesn't mean it will always be easy, but you will have more successes than failures."

It's Okay to Be Scared

Selling is a natural step in looking for a response to your creative efforts, but the desire to sell is usually accompanied by feelings of fear. So the first hurdle you will have to overcome is likely to be lack of self-confidence. Perhaps you can identify with Holly in Massachusetts, who told me she had always wanted a craft business. "For a long tine I lacked the confidence to take the first big step," she said. "I finally checked out the items being sold in country stores and compared them with what I could accomplish. I'm still in the early stages, but it was your words of encouragement about getting started and taking risks that tipped the scales in favor of trying. I hope to someday reach the point where my work is a significant supplement to our income and that it always remains exciting."

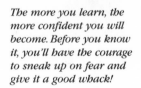

The more you learn, the more confident you will become. Before you know it, you'll have the courage to sneak up on fear and give it a good whack!

We are always most comfortable when we're operating within our personal "comfort zone," doing things we know how to do, in places we've already been, around people we know. I like what quilt designer and author Jean Ray Laury once said on this topic: "If you are being pulled out of your comfort zone, out of your area of competence, you are being challenged. Anything that challenges tends to push us to the extremes of our abilities . . . and that is when we discover things about ourselves."

Lacking experience, I was scared the first time I tried to sell my crafts at a show. And I was scared when I began to publish a magazine because I wasn't a writer then, and I knew nothing about the publishing industry. (As an ex-secretary, my greatest business skill was typing 120 words a minute.)

It took me more than a week to write one article for the premier issue, but after a while I got the hang of stringing words together. When a publisher asked me to write my first book, I confidently replied, "Sure," and then began to worry about making a fool of myself. Even after five years of producing a magazine, I knew nothing about the *craft* of writing. I quickly realized this was something I would have to learn the hard way.

Remember, they don't call it "learning the hard way" for nothing. Fear is part of the package, and all people—including long-established and successful business people—tend to tremble in their boots whenever they are challenged to do something they've never done before. So this book begins with the idea that it's okay to be scared, and you can take comfort in the fact that the more you learn about the unknown territory you're entering, the less fearful you will be.

Chapter Three

Getting Serious About Business

The first step to building a profitable crafts enterprise at home is to think of it as a business, not a hobby. It doesn't matter whether your annual income goal is $500 or $50,000 a year—what's important is that you treat your new endeavor as a real business.

"**C**an a person really make enough money in the crafts business to support a family?" a crafter asks. "If so, how? Everyone I talk to simply does it for extra money."

It's natural for beginning sellers to consider money from crafts as "pin money" or hobby income hardly worth mentioning, let alone reporting to the Internal Revenue Service. In time, however, the dollars begin to multiply with something left over after expenses. At the point when this money becomes regular supplemental income, it takes on new significance. Although many creative people could go on to build a business that would generate enough money to support themselves or a family, most back off at this point and settle for extra income. As I explained in Chapter Two, the reasons for this are many, but often they boil down to being afraid of the unknown.

There is nothing wrong in selling crafts for fun and extra money. Everything in this book is designed to help you do exactly that. An involvement in art or crafts is a life-enriching experience and today, when job security has become a thing of the past, even an extra thousand dollars a year from a hobby activity can make a big difference to an individual or a family. *But so many people settle for making just a little money when, with extra effort and a change of attitude, they could earn a lot more.* If you want to sell mostly for the fun of it, that's fine. But if you really need supplemental income or want to turn your art or craft into a full-time homebased business, this chapter contains the nitty-gritty information you need to get started on the right foot.

While it's true that a well-managed homebased crafts business can become a wonderful little money machine that regularly contributes much-needed income, this money isn't going to pour from heaven. You're going to have to *work* to earn it, and the amount of money you can expect to make from your crafts activity will be directly related to

1. The kind of products you are selling and the quality of materials being used
2. The quality of your designs and how well your products are crafted
3. Whether there is a need in the marketplace for the type of products you make
4. How much competition you have
5. How well your prices are matched to your targeted buying audience
6. How professionally your products are packaged and presented for sale
7. How efficiently you manage the business details of your moneymaking activity
8. How diligently you work to improve your marketing strategies
9. How willing you are to keep trying to improve everything you do
10. Your attitude about what you are doing

Most of today's successful crafters began as hobbyists who knew how to do one thing exceptionally well, and they achieved financial success because they paid attention to the ten points above. Whether your financial goals are large or small, you will find yourself way ahead of the competition if you begin your new crafts endeavor as a real business and not just a moneymaking hobby. Once you believe you are really "in business" and not just fooling around, your whole attitude will change and your opportunities for profit will begin to multiply.

Tip

The more professional you become in your approach to selling, the more money you are likely to earn. The more you earn, the more serious you will become about your small business endeavor.

Ten Craft Business Start-Up Steps

Because this is a crafts marketing book and not a home-business guide, my discussion of business must be limited to a brief discussion of what I believe to be the ten most important things you should do when starting a small crafts business at home. If you are already selling your crafts and have neglected to take care of some of the legal and financial matters discussed below, take care of them now. It is never too late to do things right.

For detailed information on all of the following topics and dozens of others related to starting and managing a crafts business at home, see my *Crafts Business Answer Book and Resource Guide.*

STEP 1: Find out about Zoning Regulations, Licenses and Permits

Zoning. Call your city hall or the library for a copy of your community's zoning regulations. Find out what zone you're in and read the section that pertains to home occupations. Depending on where you live, and when your community last updated its zoning laws, you may or may not have a zoning problem. Generally, artists, craftspeople, writers, designers, and mail order businesses have few worries about zoning laws because such businesses cause no noise, customer traffic or parking problems. In fact, unless a neighbor complains, zoning officials have no way of knowing what people are doing in the privacy of their homes. If someone does complain, and you are investigated by zoning officials, you may be asked to cease your home-business activities. Although there have been exceptions, people are rarely fined for a zoning violation unless they persist in the operation of a business after they have been warned to stop.

Note: If you rent or live in a condominium, your lease or title papers may specifically restrict any kind of business, thus the operation of one could invalidate your tenant's or homeowner's insurance policy.

If zoning conditions in your community are not favorable, be particularly careful about attracting attention to yourself through publicity in your local paper, and avoid customer traffic to your home shop or studio. This kind of activity in a quiet residential neighborhood is likely to trigger complaints and an investigation by zoning officials.

Licenses, Permits and Zoning Issues. When you start to sell arts and crafts, you automatically become a "homebased business owner" in the eyes of city officials, although you may think of yourself as only a hobbyist. In their zeal to collect additional tax money, many communities are now requiring all homebased businesses to get special licenses or permits. Check with your city or county clerk to see if you need any kind of permit or license to do whatever it is that you want to do at home; i.e., make items for sale elsewhere, teach on a private basis, or sell products in your home through home parties, open houses or boutiques. Zoning laws naturally prohibit home shops in residential areas, but in some cities today, even private open house sales and annual holiday boutiques are being outlawed because products being sold are new. (For years, zoning officials considered such temporary sales in the same light as garage sales. Now some have decided to separate these events in terns of whether merchandise for sale is new or used.)

STEP 2: Acquaint Yourself with IRS Regulations

You may sell what you make and call it "extra money," but the IRS will call it "profit or loss from business" and expect you to report all your income from crafts, along with related expenses, on a Schedule C (Form 1040).

The IRS says you are in business if you (1) are sincerely trying to make a profit, (2) are making regular business transactions, and (3) have made a profit at least three years out of five. If you make sales, but do not meet the above criteria, your business will be ruled a "hobby," but this income must still be reported on Schedule C if it is $400 or more a year. With both types of business, you deduct expenses against the income, but in the case of a hobby business you may deduct expenses only up to the amount of hobby income. Discuss this with your tax advisor.

Many crafters sell at fairs, take cash only, and do not report their earnings to the IRS. You can usually spot such people at a crafts fair because they are the ones who ask for cash instead of checks or credit cards, and they never charge sales tax on purchases. I hope you will not be one of these people,  because the risk isn't worth it. This practice can only lead to worries about getting caught, and it does nothing to help a small crafts business grow. There are severe penalties for intentional tax evasion or falsification of tax returns.

Actually, there are many personal and financial advantages to declaring your extra crafts income to the IRS. Besides having peace of mind as a legal taxpayer, you may find that your small business profits will give you extra power when applying for a loan or a new credit card. Currently, home-business owners are also entitled to many special home-related tax deductions not enjoyed by the average taxpayer, and taxes can be completely avoided on a portion of net profits through such strategies as hiring one's spouse or children or placing funds in an Individual Retirement Account (IRA) or other retirement fund.

Note: This book assumes that the legal form of business most readers will be using is a Sole Proprietorship. If you wish to form as a Sub-Chapter S, C Corporation, Partnership or Limited Liability Company, it would be wise to consult an attorney or other professional for information on the tax consequences of each of these legal forms of business.

STEP 3: Register the Name of Your Crafts Business with Local Officials

When you operate under any name other than your own, you are using a fictitious or assumed business or trade name that must be registered with local authorities. Thus, if you are Mary Smith, and you call your crafts endeavor Knotty But Nice, you would be using an assumed name. On legal documents and at your bank, it would read, "Mary Smith, dba Knotty But Nice." (The "dba" means "doing business as.")

The registration procedure may vary from state to state, but you will probably have to complete a form given to you by the county clerk and pay a small registration fee. In most states, you must also place a legal ad in a general-circulation newspaper in the county and run it three times (The appropriate ad copy will be provided to you on request either by the county clerk or the newspaper.) After the ad has run, you will receive a certificate that will be forwarded to the county clerk, who will file it with your registration form. This will make your business completely legitimate. (If you don't want your neighbors to know you're running a business at home—perhaps because you're violating local zoning laws—the newspaper ad can be run in any nearby town or city in your county.)

Optional: To give your business name wider protection and prevent any corporate entity from using it, register it with your state. Call the office of your

Picking a Good Business Name

The name you give to your crafts business says a lot about who you are and what you do. More important, your business name, coupled with the kind of printed materials you use, or the Web site you may develop, gives prospective customers an immediate impression that will ultimately affect their buying decision.

If a name sounds more like a hobby than a business, buyers may be dubious about the quality of products offered or be unwilling to pay the price you need to make a profit. For example, consider the different mental pictures you form when you compare "Kathy's Krafts" to "Katherine's Keepsakes." The latter name not only sounds more professional but suggests a higher-priced line of products.

Many crafters use their first name as a part of their business name, such as "Candy's Country Baskets" or "Lou's Stained Glass Art." Other sellers cleverly incorporate their first or last names into a business name appropriate to what they do. Trish Bloom chose "Once in a Bloomoon Creations" for her name and then designed a nifty logo with blue moon faces in the four o's in "Bloomoon." (See an illustration of her card in Chapter Fourteen.) Cleverness is always to be congratulated, but be careful to pick a business name that accurately describes your business and will not become obsolete when you expand your product line.

Common phrases often inspire great business names that customers are unlikely to forget. For example, designer Ellen Goldberg turned the phrase "whether or not" into "Leather or Knot," a perfect name for her line of "art to wear" accessories. And do you remember that old movie with Natalie Wood and Robert Wagner titled *Splendor in the Grass*? It inspired Lorraine Kallman to name her folk art and decorative painting business "Splendor in the Crafts." Later, at a crafts fair, Lorraine discovered a business named "Splendor in the Glass," suggesting that other craftspeople have also played around with the words in this old movie title. "Creative minds are all on the same plane," observes one crafts seller. "Sooner or later different minds are bound to have the same ideas."

secretary of state to obtain the necessary form. Expect to pay a small registration fee. National protection for a business name and logo may be obtained with a trademark. Information on how to do this will be found in booklets available from the Patent & Trademark Office. (See Step 7.)

Tip

If you have not registered your business name to date, *do so now.* Since the form you will complete does not ask when you started your business, the county clerk will assume you're just starting and there should be no problem. *Don't ignore this small legal detail.* If you fail to protect your crafts business name through local registration, anyone who wants to steal if from you can do so simply by filing the form you failed to file with the county clerk.

STEP 4: Call Your Telephone Company

Many crafters print their home telephone number on their craft business card not realizing this may be a violation of local telephone regulations. Generally, a personal phone number may not legally be advertised on your business card, letterhead, promotional printed materials, in advertisements, or on a business Web site. If you use your telephone only to make outgoing calls and not to directly solicit business, you may be able to operate indefinitely without the expense of a separate business line. But you're certainly going to need a second line or broadband line so you can be on the Internet without tying up your home phone number.

If you plan to invite business by phone, or are trying to build relationships with wholesale buyers, you'll probably have to bite the bullet and install a separate line with voice mail for business and perhaps a toll-free number as well. Because so many people now work at home, telephone companies offer many affordable second-line options you need to investigate. One commonly used by crafters is the addition of a second number to one's home phone that has a different ring to it.

STEP 5: Open a Checking Account for Your Business

The IRS frowns on taxpayers who try to operate a business out of their personal checkbook because this is not a clear separation of personal and business income and expenses. Call all the financial institutions in your area to get comparative costs of a small business checking account. Ask about charges for checks deposited, deposits made, bounced-check charges, cost of checks, etc. If you have a mail order business, pay particular attention to what a bank will charge to process out-of-state checks. To avoid these high fees when I had a mail order business, I ran all my checks through an account in a savings bank (formerly called a savings and loan association). Although I no longer have a mail order business, I retain that account because there are no service fees, and the balance draws interest besides. The only problem with using a savings bank for your business account is that such financial institutions do not offer business line-of-credit loans or merchant account services, so take this into consideration when opening a new business checking account.

There are different types of business checking accounts, so emphasize that you want to begin with the least expensive account available. (One big difference is the amount you will be charged for printed checks.) If you feel you cannot afford a standard business account, and don't plan to write many business checks, open a separate personal checking account in your name. Don't put your business name on the checks, however, (only your name) or your bank may insist that you open a standard business account instead. By depositing all your business income to this account and paying all your business expenses from it, you will be creating the necessary separation of personal and business income and expenses the IRS requires.

When talking to the various financial institutions in your area, also get comparative prices for a safe deposit box. I think of my business safe deposit box as another form of insurance because it contains valuable and irreplaceable business papers, computer software and backup tapes, copyrights, master sets of published material, a photographic record of insured property and much more.

STEP 6: Obtain a Retailer's Occupation Tax Registration Number

Many crafters believe that if they sell "just for the fun of it," they are not considered to be in business and thus do not need to be concerned with the collection of sales tax. This is not true. It doesn't matter to your state's Department of Revenue whether you are "in business" in the eyes of the Internal Revenue Service or not. All this agency is concerned with is *whether you are selling directly to consumers on the retail level.* If so, you must collect sales tax and file regular reports with the state. Hobby sellers are not exempt from this law, regardless of how few sales they make.

With few exceptions, all states have sales taxes, and in most states there are county and city taxes as well. If you make anything for sale, or if you buy goods for resale, you are required to register your crafts business (even a hobby business) with the Department of Revenue (Sales Tax Division) in your state. (Depending on where you live, the place you must call to obtain this number may have a different name. The easiest way to find it is to look under "Government" in your telephone book, and look for a listing that comes closest to "Revenue.")

Registration is a simple and painless procedure. You complete a form to receive a special document from the state that will bear a tax exemption number that is sometimes called a "Retailer's Occupation Tax Registration Number" or, more generally, a "resale tax number." The registration fee varies from state to state ($5 to $25), with some states requiring a bond or deposit of up to $150. This tax number will enable you to buy materials at wholesale prices without paying sales tax. Once you have a tax number, you must start to collect sales tax on everything you sell to consumers, sending the appropriate reports and payments to the state. (It is illegal to collect sales tax and retain it as income.)

If your state has no sales tax, you will still need a reseller's permit or tax exemption certificate to buy supplies and materials at wholesale prices from manufacturers, wholesalers, or distributors. (You cannot, however, run down to the corner crafts store, buy a few dollars worth of supplies and avoid sales tax.)

Note: You do not have to collect sales tax when you sell crafts through a consignment shop, craft mall or rent-a-space store. It is a shop's responsibility to collect this tax and forward it to the state. Craft wholesalers do not need to collect sales tax on their sales to shops and stores, but they are required to obtain for their own files the resale tax number of any retail shop or store with whom they do business. As for sales made on the Internet, they are taxable like all other sales to consumers

STEP 7: Learn About Federal Regulations Applicable to Your Business

There are several laws and regulations that have significance for artists and craftspeople. Generally, they relate to consumer safety, trade practices, the labeling of certain products and the protection of intellectual property. An explanation of all of these laws and regulations is beyond the scope of this book, but they have been discussed at length in my *Crafts Business Answer Book*. Readers can also do their own research simply by contacting the various organizations mentioned below and requesting all their free literature. (See the Resource Chapter for mailing addresses, phone numbers and Web site URLs.)

■ The Consumer Product Safety Commission offers information on safety standards for toys and other products designed for children. All sellers must be doubly careful about the materials used for children's products because lawsuits in this area are common. Problems can be avoided simply by following this agency's guidelines.

■ The Bureau of Consumer Protection offers information on labels or tags required by law for items made of wool or textiles (including garments, quilts, stuffed toys, knitting, rugs, yarn, piece goods, etc.).

41

- The Federal Trade Commission (FTC) offers information on trade practices and labeling rules, and all crafters need to be aware of these rules. In addition to labels required by the Bureau of Consumer Protection, the FTC requires a label for wool and textile products when imported materials are used. It also requires a permanently affixed "care label" on all textile wearing apparel and household furnishings. Mail order sellers also need to be aware of the FTC's truth-in-advertising laws and the 30-day mail order rule.

- The Copyright Office offers information on how to register and protect your original designs, patterns, books and other intellectual property. Request all free publications, particularly those on how to file a copyright claim, protect your rights under current copyright law, and investigate the copyright status of a work. Note that there is no need to hire an attorney to get something copyrighted. This is easy for the average individual to do.

- Patent and Trademark Office. Few crafters will have a serious interest in patenting anything because of the very high costs of obtaining a patent today, but many may want to protect their originally designed business logos, company name, or new product names with a trademark. Obtain this information now so you'll have it when you need it.

STEP 8: Set up a Good Record-Keeping System

People who lack business experience often worry needlessly about keeping records and tax information. I have no great love for the Internal Revenue Service, but one nice thing about the IRS is that it does not require any special kind of bookkeeping system for businesses. It simply requires one to keep accurate records on all money that comes in and goes out.

You may decide to do your bookkeeping on a computer using software designed for this purpose, or you can do it by hand using a simple journal and ledger book from an office supply store. (Check out the *Dome Simplified Monthly* record-keeping book.) As you begin to sell, you will quickly learn what kind of records you need to keep to monitor sales and

42

Samples of care labels from Widby Fabric Labels, Knoxville, Tennessee.

figure profits. Devise any system that feels comfortable to you and gives you the necessary figures for your annual Schedule C form. Your book-keeping will automatically improve as you learn more about business and the kind of information you want to record for your own use. If you keep accurate records during the year, it will be easy at year's end to work with a tax advisor or accountant to prepare your annual tax return.

For help in setting up a professional bookkeeping system, see the book *Small Time Operator* in the Resource Chapter.

STEP 9: Make Sure You're Properly Insured

Homeowner's or Renter's Policy. You may have quite a bit of money invested in tools, equipment, raw materials and finished hand-crafts, so be sure to tell your insurance agent that you are running a business at home. Anything you use to generate income would be exempt from coverage on a personal policy. To protect such items, you can add a special rider (very inexpensive) to your homeowner's or renter's policy to cover business equipment, supplies, inventory, goods made for sale but not yet shipped, etc. Or, check out the special home-business policies now being offered by various insurance companies.

Some art and craft organizations also offer insurance programs to their members. For example, the American Craft Council offers a studio policy that protects against loss of both unfinished and finished works, at home or away, including craft fairs, malls and rent-a-space shops. To find other organizations with insurance programs, check your library for a national directory of associations and organizations.

Computer Insurance. If you use a home computer in your business, do not insure your computer system on the same business rider that protects your office or workshop. Such coverage is usually limited to fire or theft, and losses may be calculated on a depreciated basis instead of replacement cost. The best coverage will be obtained from a company that specializes in computer insurance and offers broad, all-risk coverage on a replacement cost basis. One such company is Safeware, The Insurance Agency, Inc., in Columbus, Ohio. Check computer magazines for ads from other companies.

Personal Liability Insurance. The average homeowner's policy includes some personal liability insurance but does not cover business activities on the premises. Be sure to find out how much personal liability insurance you have. This is especially important if customers regularly come into your home to buy crafts. (Why people are on your property may determine the amount of liability coverage your policy provides.) Discuss this matter with your insurance agent and ask if an umbrella policy might extend your personal liability coverage on homebased business activities. A million dollars' worth of coverage may cost less than a hundred dollars a year.

Car Insurance. Be sure to tell your insurance agent if you occasionally use your car for business purposes. Make sure you have coverage for an accident that might occur when you are driving to or from a crafts fair or delivering merchandise to buyers. Also, if you plan to let an employee drive your personal vehicle, ask your insurance agent about "nonownership contingent liability protection," which would protect you in the event that your employee has an accident while driving your car. Where insurance is concerned, the more questions you ask, the safer you'll be.

44

Product Liability Insurance. Few craft sellers purchase product liability insurance because their products are considered relatively safe. Much depends on what is being offered for sale and whether the average buyer could conceivably suffer any kind of injury from such a product. If you eventually move into wholesaling, however, you may one day discover that some buyers will not purchase your merchandise unless you carry product liability insurance. The cost of a policy varies from one area to another but is generally based on one's annual gross sales, the number of products sold, and the possible risks associated with each of them. Few craftspeople can afford to buy liability insurance on their own, but group policies are available to members of some crafts and home-business organizations, such as the American Craft Council, Home Business Institute, Inc., and National Craft Association (see Resource Chapter). Such policies generally offer a million dollars of both personal and product liability insurance coverage.

Step 10: Decide Which Printed Materials You Need to Do an Effective Promotional and Selling Job

This topic is so important that I've given it a separate chapter of its own. (In Chapter Fourteen, you will find tips on the specific printed materials you can use to increase sales, improve your professional image and get higher prices for everything you sell.)

You may have noticed that "call a lawyer" is not on my list of the ten most important things to do. Contrary to popular belief, there is no need to consult a lawyer when starting a homebased business as a sole proprietorship. Sure, a lawyer will be happy to charge you a big fee for answering a lot of small business questions, but you can get the same information and more from any of the small business books I've recommended in the Resource Chapter.

You would be wise, however, to consult a lawyer if you are forming a partnership or corporation, entering into a long-term agreement, making a licensing or franchise arrangement, buying property, negotiating or enforcing any kind of contract or trying to stop someone's infringement of your registered trademark or copyright. You do not need a lawyer, however, to file a copyright form.

Handy Checklist of
Telephone Calls to Make

❑ **City or county hall.** Ask for information about:
- Zoning regulations in your area
- How to register your crafts business name
- Licenses or permits needed for homebased business

❑ **Local IRS office.** Ask for these free tax booklets:
- Publication #334, "Tax Guide for Small Business"
- Publication #587, "Business Use of Your Home"

❑ **Local telephone company.** Ask about the cost of a second line for business and any special services offered to people who work at home.

❑ **Local financial institutions.** Get information on the cost of a business checking account and safe deposit box

❑ **Your State's Department of Revenue, Sales Tax Division.** Ask what you need to do to get a sales tax number or tax exemption certificate.

❑ **The insurance agent who handles your homeowner's or renter's policy.** Check on adding an inexpensive rider to your policy that will cover all the supplies and materials in your homebased office, crafts studio or workshop. Also ask about "umbrella policies" that offer extra liability coverage.

❑ **Your auto insurance agent.** Explain that you will occasionally use your vehicle for business.

❑ **Your secretary of state, state capital.** Ask for information on how to register your business name on the state level.

❑ **The U.S. Small Business Administration (SBA).** Call 1-800-827-5722 to reach the SBA's "Small Business Answer Desk" and access a variety of prerecorded messages. A wealth of free information and publications are available to you on request.

Chapter Four

Developing Your Product Line

The real secret to selling more of what you make is to make more of what people want to buy.

This chapter offers perspective on what buyers want in a hand-made product and what you can do to make your products more appealing to them. You'll find guidelines on how to do market research and develop a successful product line, and how to begin designing your own original creations. You'll also find many ideas for specific products you might make for sale, as well as categories of products that have proven popular with buyers through the years. For even more ideas on how to develop a great product line, I encourage you to read *Make It Profitable,* a companion to this book also published by M. Evans and Company. It includes two lengthy chapters on product design, packaging, and production methods and strategies used by nearly a hundred professional crafters in my network.

47

Doing Market Research

Before entering the crafts marketplace, and as long as you remain in it, you need to do market research to find out what other artists and crafters are selling. Think of this as interesting detective work. Visit craft fairs, craft malls, handcraft shops and gift shops that carry handmade items. Pay particular attention to prices, sizes, and the kinds of raw materials used in products. Observe how the price increases on items that use better materials. Watch how colors change each year, reflecting hot new trends. When you see the same colors or shades of color everywhere you look, that suggests a color trend for that particular year. If you try to sell flashy colors in a year when earth tones are hot, your sales may suffer.

As you do your Sherlock Holmes bit, ask yourself how your crafts compare to what's available locally, regionally or nationally. If you plan to make and sell what everyone else is trying to sell, it will be hard to compete. However, if you can come up with even a few unusual items, and will make an effort to find the right marketing outlet for them, you may find yourself smiling all the way to the bank.

How can you tell if something will be a hit or not? Is there a way to get a feel for what people are looking for? One of the best ways to do this is to take your products to a craft fair. Then you watch the response that people give you, their facial expressions, their comments or the way they talk to the friends they are with. This is all part of market research.

To know what people are going to buy is always difficult, but one of the best ways is to ask yourself what you want to buy—what you are interested in. You're a consumer (and probably a crafts buyer, too), and you have the same needs and interests as many of your prospective buyers. Another way to tell if certain items are popular is to check craft malls and shops in your community. Don't hesitate to talk to shop owners or managers to see what they think is hot in the shop at that time. You also need to read periodicals in your field and subscribe to free craft e-zines to find out what others are selling.

Brainstorming for Product Ideas

People like handcrafts because (1) they don't look like commercial items; (2) they are likely to be made of uncommon materials and (3) they are unique in one way or another. The most successful artists and craftspeople make products that appeal to a small but accessible group of people and many say they get their design inspiration from things in their everyday life. Sometimes the best way to stir up your creative juices is to pull back a bit, put on your thinking cap and take a sharp look around. Here are three things to do when brainstorming for new product ideas:

O Consider products that will help people fill leisure hours, such as games, puzzles or humorous playthings for adults. Patterns or kits for toys, dolls, teddy bears and other things people enjoy making for themselves or as gifts are always in demand. Due to time constraints, however, many people prefer leisure projects that are "quick and easy."

O Try thinking backwards. Think first about the problems, special needs or personal desires people have that you might be able to solve with a particular product. Then think how you're going to market it by imagining typical buyers in terms of the publications they read, the organizations they belong to and places where they are likely to gather.

O Ask yourself what you can do with all the odds and ends of supplies you have left over after you've made your regular line of products. Lay them all out together and see if the combination of materials, colors, textures, etc. will suggest new product ideas. Consider doing small versions of larger products for dollhouse or miniatures collectors . . . novelty or souvenir items . . . or a promotional item or freebie you could give to children as a device for drawing adults in to your craft booth.

And then there's the Internet. What a terrific market research tool this has become! Here you can study the product lines of thousands of sellers, compare their prices, check out the colors they're using on certain products, and much more. Of course, there is no way to tell if the products being displayed on crafter Web sites are actually selling or not, but just learning what your competition is *trying* to sell will be an education in itself.

Before beginning her online soapmaking business, The SoapMeister, Cheri Marsh researched products online that were likely to be competition. "I decided early on that I would not market locally," she says. "Hobby soapers are a dime a dozen and so are their products. I decided to go for sixty million potential customers, rather than twenty thousand local customers. I also decided to market a premier product to people who understand quality and don't mind paying for it. That eliminated about 80 percent of my competition. In time, my phenomenal customer service eliminated another big chunk of the competition."

Several Things to Consider

A mistake commonly made by beginners is to produce items in several craft mediums that are not related to one another. For maximum success, you need to diversify and have a variety of products in different sizes and price ranges, but don't offer a hodgepodge of crafts made from many different kinds of materials. Specialize in one or two major craft areas and be creative by combining popular craft materials that aren't normally used together, such as stitchery with ceramics or sewn items with wood. What's important here is that you give buyers the impression that you've "got it all together" and are not just a hobbyist who can't decide what to sell.

It's always better to focus on a particular craft area—not necessarily one craft, but a group of crafts that fall into a family or are compatible with one another. Beginning crafters typically go to market with a little of this and a little of that because they have many craft interests, but professional sellers quickly learn the importance of specialization. By building on their particular talents and art or craft skills, they develop one or more product lines that complement one another.

While it's important to focus on an art or craft you love and do well, you must also consider the marketplace. What you love to make is not necessarily going to be what people want to buy, so you must do some market research before you begin to develop your product line. Many crafters do the same art or craft, of course, but they have each developed their own style, and that makes them stand out in the crowd.

In the first edition of this book, tole painter Barbara Dunn shared her "formula" for the perfect product. I've lost touch with Barbara, but her advice remains timeless. She said crafters ought to try to produce high-quality work that falls into one of these three categories: (1) so cute it can't be resisted, (2) functional with fair price (giving buyers further reason to buy), and (3) original and totally different from anything they've seen (keeping the market new). Here are other things you need to consider in the development of a successful product line:

- **Think in categories.** In developing a line of products, learn to think in general product categories such as home decor, toys, clothing, gifts for men, collectibles, dolls, Christmas ornaments, bath items, etc. Or, concentrate on one or two crafts and create separate product lines within those categories.

- **Listen to your customers.** Often the best and most profitable product ideas will come from your own customers. Marj Bates added drawer pulls to her line of lampwork glass beads and jewelry only after an open house client expressed interest in buying the ones Marj had designed for her own cupboards. "I never dreamed to sell them," she says. "I just wanted a splash of color in my kitchen." After adding knobs to her line, Marj kept rolling with the idea by adding Make-a-Knob kits to her growing product line.

- **Stay up on colors currently popular.** If your product's colors are not "in tune with the times," they may not sell well. Newsletters and magazines for professional crafters generally report on color trends each year, but you can get a good idea of what's hot simply by spending a day in a shopping center and browsing clothing racks. You can also research current color trends on the Internet (see "Color Marketing Organization" in the Resource Chapter.)

■ *Study your profit potential.* Do some careful figuring to determine the profit potential of each new product you're developing. List all raw materials costs, packaging, printing and postage (if it's an item you plan to sell by mail). Consider how much of your (or someone else's) labor will be involved. Set a retail price appealing to buyers and profitable to you, then double it to see if you'll be able to wholesale it. Finally, consider the market for your product to make sure you can produce the volume that may be necessary to satisfy it. (Helpful guidelines for hiring outside help for your growing business are in *The Crafts Business Answer Book,* my encyclopedic reference guide for crafters.)

■ *Have more than one supply source.* Always locate more than one supplier for any raw materials used in products for sale so you'll never get stuck if one supplier goes out of business or stops making a particular item or material. If you are not qualified to buy supplies at wholesale, stock up on supplies when they go on sale and also look for ways to lower the costs of your products at retail by comparing raw materials prices from a number of suppliers. Buying in a larger quantity may get you a discount while buying from a supplier closer to you may lower shipping costs.

■ *Name your products.* A name gives a product personality, which in turn increases its salability. In developing new products, give both your product lines and individual products names of their own. Use humor whenever possible or appropriate and be sure to create hang tags for everything you make. (See Chapter Fourteen for hang tag design and content tips.)

■ *Check legal issues.* Thinking about offering limited editions of a new product? Many states now have laws that impose strict disclosure and warranty requirements on sellers who offer limited editions of art or craftwork that include certificates. Before doing this, check with an attorney who can answer your questions and help you draft certificate forms that will comply with your state's laws. (Also see *The Crafts Business Answer Book* for detailed information about all the local, state and federal laws applicable to a crafts business.) If you are developing products for children, be careful to comply with consumer safety laws. A wealth of consumer product information is available from the Consumer Product Safety Commission's toll-free hotline and several publications related to toys and children's products are offered. (See Resource Chapter.)

■ **Protect your creativity with copyrights.** Fill out the appropriate copyright form and register valuable designs, patterns or other written or drawn material with the Copyright Office. (Photographs of finished handcrafts can be submitted with a copyright form instead of the actual craft items.) Request free booklets and registration forms from the Copyright Office by phone or online (see Resource Chapter). (For a detailed yet plain English discussion of copyrights as they are applicable to craftspeople or designers, see *The Crafts Business Answer Book.*)

Products That Always Sell Well

Below, I've identified seven main categories of products that seem to sell consistently in both good and bad economic times. Make a list of the individual craft items you've thought about selling and see if they fit into one or more of the following categories:

1. Functional items people can use in their daily lives

2. Gift items that answer specific needs

3. Decorative accessories and furnishings

4. Collectibles and other nostalgic items

5. Garments, jewelry and other fashion accessories

6. Custom-designed products

7. Leisure interests

Not every product that falls into one of these categories is going to sell, of course. One reason is that consumers do not merely buy things—they buy products (and services) that offer **benefits.** Thus, the more benefits you can include in a product, the easier it will be to sell. To identify the benefits of your products, consider that:

▼ *Buyers appreciate and will always be interested in pur-chasing functional items they can use in their daily lives,* but when money is tight, such items may have to offer something more than practicality. If a useful product also offers a timesaving or organizational benefit, makes a dreary job more fun, elicits feelings of nostalgia, or merely makes one smile, it has a greater chance.

▼ *Even when there is little money for luxuries, people need gift items,* and they will buy crafts that solve specific gift-giving needs. The Christmas season is always a big bonanza for crafters, but don't overlook all the other times during the year when people need special gifts for such occasions as birthdays, anniversaries, a job promotion, graduation, housewarming, baby shower, Valentine's Day, Easter, Thanksgiving, Mother's Day, Father's Day, and so on. When such products can also be personalized in some way, their value increases.

▼ *People buy decorative crafts and accessories because such products satisfy particular decorating needs* or an individual's desire to own something beautiful. Some people derive great satisfaction from buying something special for themselves when they don't have money for larger purchases. Many years ago when the country was in recession, my husband and I were sad because we didn't have enough money to buy a house or a new car. So, when we could least afford it, we rewarded ourselves with our first piece of expensive artwork. Benefit? It did wonders for our morale.

▼ *Craft items that always seem to find a market are those that appeal to collectors,* a group of buyers who are less concerned with price than the average consumer. They tend to buy on impulse whenever they find something that strikes a nostalgic chord or satisfies a longing of the heart. And make no mistake about it, *these are marketable benefits.* You may already produce collectible items that can be easily marketed to such collectors as animal lovers, sporting enthusiasts, musicians, circus fans, carousel buffs, people who love dolls, teddy bears, miniatures, stained glass, woodcarvings, toys

Customized Signs

Looking for new product ideas? Think *signs!* Whenever you can zero in on buyers' special interests or make them laugh or remember something nostalgic, you'll find signs to be a good profit maker. They can be made in all sizes, shapes, colors and materials, but decorative painters seem to have the most fun with them.

Suzanne Lloyd started out to make some signs just to cover her booth rental fees, but they turned out to be so profitable that she just kept painting them. Some of her signs capitalize on the popular gambling trend, such as "Mom's missing, dial 1-800 Couchatta" (a hotel that has gambling); or, "Gone to the Casino, be back someday." Depending on what customers want, she changes the names from Mom to Dad, Grandma or Grandpa. "I paint not only words," she says, "but also add a picture to each sign, using copyright free pictures from Dover's Pictorial Archive books."

Since Suzanne's business name is The Stuffed Cat, she also sells cat signs with verses such as "Cat hair sticks to everything but the cat." Her best-selling item, however, is a "Welcome to My Porch" sign, which she paints on weathered wood or fenceboard whenever she can find it.

Decorative painter Susan Young has been doing signs for fifteen years—all kinds and sizes and many to do with cats. "A lot are clichés but people still love them," she says. "Now selling her work out of her own shop, The Peach Kitty Studio, Susan says she gets a lot of requests for "over the door" signs—approximately 4 inches x 24–36 inches long to hang over a doorway or over the mantel (basically a long strip of good quality pine, with or without routed edges for accent trim). "Some months ago a repeat customer came in and wanted two signs for Christmas gifts," Susan recalls, "only she wanted one of them customized with a picture of a Basset Hound flanking each side of the family name. 'Have you ever painted Basset Hounds?' she asked me. I said: 'No, but I will now!'"

The secret to success here is always to be ready to cater to the customer's whims. Give them what they want, and they'll happily part with their dollars!

Gifts for Babies

If you don't already have products for babies, maybe you should consider adding some. Try to think beyond crocheted or knitted items, which rarely can be sold for prices that justify the time spent in creating them. Think instead of the novelty items suitable for baby showers, custom-made items that can be personalized with a child's name and higher-priced decorative items for a nursery or child's room.

One mother I met at a conference told me how she had used her art talents to design "fantasy rooms" envisioned by new mothers—painting the walls with scenes from fairy tales. She lived in an affluent neighborhood and could charge a pretty penny for this service. It wasn't long before she had all the work she wanted.

. . . the list goes on and on.

▼ ***Everyone needs clothing,*** even when money is tight. Sellers who offer handmade garments, designer jewelry and related accessories need to emphasize how their products will make people *feel.* Remember that people naturally want to feel more attractive, and they enjoy wearing clothing and accessories that make them stand out in a crowd *(the benefit).* Even people who work at home may buy designer jeans, humorous sweatshirts and handmade sandals to get the benefit of sheer comfort and the satisfaction of looking good in their private environment.

▼ ***When you offer custom-design services, you are offering buyers a very special benefit:*** a product made especially for them and one that is truly unique. Products can be customized by giving buyers a choice of colors, sizes, styles, designs or personalization with initials or a name. Never hesitate to charge extra for custom-design services because they simply can't be found in any store, and the kind of person who wants such items for personal use or gifts is not likely to haggle about price.

▼ ***If you can offer a product that will help people fill their*** *leisure hours, you will have no trouble selling it.* Many craft professionals successfully sell handcrafted musical instruments, games, puzzles, and humorous playthings for adults. Patterns or kits for toys, dolls, teddy bears and other things that people enjoy making for themselves or as gifts will always be good sellers. Anyone who does stitchery is always looking for yet another new needlepoint canvas or cross-stitch chart. (For more information on this topic, see "Other Ways to Profit from Your Creativity" in Chapter Fifteen.)

Bread-and-Butter Items

Bread-and-butter items—also called "widgets" by some craftspeople today (see many examples in my *Make It Profitable* book)—are those products in your line that you can always count on to sell . . . your "hot sellers" that yield a great profit for the amount of time they take to make, or the cost of supplies and materials used. Although bread-and-butter items are usually low-priced, some crafters manage to create higher-priced items that become guaranteed sellers. Often, it is the extra profit from these popular sellers that makes it possible for an artist or crafter to spend time on the more creative but less profitable items they love to make for sale.

"Over time I have proven to myself that I must have items that sell for $3 and $5," says Rochelle Beach, who has developed a line of "Cinna-minnie" dolls made from her own secret cinnamon clay mixture. Her dolls sell for $8 to $15 dollars, but her best sellers are small items that do not take long to make and cost only pennies in terms of time and materials. "These products appeal to those who just want something small and simple, such as two cinnamon-scented hearts hanging from a wire. For example, my double-heart dangler that sells for $3 costs only 40 cents to make. We would all like to sell our higher priced items," Rochelle muses, "but the truth of the matter is that when times are hard, people need low-cost gift items under $10."

Sherrill Lewis's bread-and-butter item is a product she calls her three-beads-on-a-headpin earrings. "They are quick to make by putting three to five attractive beads on a headpin wire, making a loop, and attaching a finding," she says. "Once the beads are chosen, a pair takes about two minutes to make, and I can sell them for $5 to $15, depending on the bead or semiprecious stone used, and whether the findings are sterling or not. With a 300–500 percent markup, these products are very profitable, and I think of them as my 'rent-payers.'"

One secret to getting a higher price for a bread-and-butter item is to offer a product that appeals to an affluent niche market. Although Jacqui Collins-Parker now sells her lampworked glass bead products only on eBay and through her own Web site, she sold a variety of bead products at craft fairs before getting on the Internet. In those days, her best sellers included small turtles, hearts, or frogs on plain, black satin cord with a simple overhand knot closure. "These sold for $5–$8 at shows," she says, "while glass bead pins sold for $10–$15. Most of the beads used on these items took no more than ten or fifteen minutes to make, so these were very profitable items for me at the time."

To illustrate how things change as one progresses in business, look how Jacqui's product line and market have changed, and how her profits have increased as a result. Today, she produces a different, higher-priced line of lampworked bead products, and her bread-and-butter items are single beads priced at $15 each. "These sell well to my niche market of mainly jewelers who are looking for beads to incorporate into their designs," she says. "Of course I encourage this by giving them usage ideas in my listing description. Often these jewelers also sell  their completed items on eBay, and in most cases have given me a plug as the artist of the bead."

The custom-designed products in a crafter's line often become their literal bread and butter because here, price is rarely of concern to customers. Decorative painter Susan Young, who sells her work in her own retail shop (see Chapter Eight), enjoys catering to the whims of her customers. Her "Birdhouse Mailbox" is one example. "My investment in materials for each mailbox birdhouse runs $10–15," she says, "and I sell them for $45 to $85. I attach a wood platform to the top of the handpainted mailbox (which requires a saw to cut curves in the platform so it fits the regulation mailbox), and then I attach a wood birdhouse to the platform, painting it to look like the client's home, or whatever design they may request."

Something else that's working for Susan and many other crafters is painting on items customers or clients already have in their possession (a great way to cut the cost of materials). Susan will paint any object a customer brings her, with any kind of artwork or design they may want on it. "I have no up-front cash layout for the items," she says. "I simply charge for the complexity of the design and the time it takes, plus a couple bucks to replenish my paints. Gallon jars painted on one or both sides net me $13 to $25 and chairs, end tables, jelly cabinets or porch benches bring in $65 to $200, depending on size, detail, and my time."

Find a Niche and Fill It

A market niche is a place where product and buyer fit like a hand in a glove. There are large market niches, small market niches, and niches within niches. (See nearby "Niche Market Checklist" to identify general niche markets for your products.) As you plan your product line, keep asking yourself who's likely to be most interested in each product. It's always difficult to sell something to a mass market, so anytime you can narrow your market by targeting a specific niche, your sales are likely to improve.

For example, Christine Zipps suddenly found a niche market when she decided to specialize in the preservation of wedding bouquets using the natural technique of flower drying. "It was not until I saw my technique becoming so well honed that I was convinced I had a true niche in this market," she says. "I am only one of two in the Denver area using this natural technique. Most of them freeze-dry bouquets, which is a far inferior method in terms of getting fresh-looking results."

Christine reaches the bridal market in a variety of ways. In addition to the usual word-of-mouth advertising from satisfied customers, ads in a local wedding guide and occasional bridal shows, she gets new customer leads from direct mailings to florists and bridal consultants. As a member of two organizations in her field, she also gets new business through networking.

Artist Leslie Miller Bertram, who for years has specialized in painting horses, found a new niche market for her work when she saw that people's interest in nautical themes had surged. "I am blessed to live on the waterfront," she says, "so I have taken advantage of my skills to capture much of the history and day-to-day activity of a coastal lifestyle in a new line of paintings."

Don't overlook tourists as a niche market for your products. If you live in a tourist area, try to come up with new product ideas that fit the following categories of products generally purchased by tourists (in addition to antiques and crafts in general): Postcards and booklets about local attractions, T-shirts and other clothing with a name or picture of a location or attraction, local food products, items that can be added to a collection and mementos (novelty items) of location or attraction.

Remember that product benefits can be not only practical, but humorous or nostalgic as well. Here are some other examples of niche markets crafters have reported to me:

- Mother-and-daughter team Liz and Maryn targeted pet owners with a sense of humor for their line of amusing cat and dog costumes that include devil horns and capes, Santa hats, and angel wings.
- Sharon found a terrific niche market for her hand-painted, Christmas-ornament eggs when she began to paint Santa Claus in his sled flying over the skyline of particular cities, such as Chicago, San Francisco, and New York.
- Judy from South Dakota and Marie from Missouri each found a niche when they began to offer gift baskets that featured special products made in their own state, thus catering to buyers who were proud to live in those states or yearned to return.
- After Jerry invented a pet-grooming comb for dogs and cats, he found two special niche markets: people who keep angora rabbits, and spinners who need to comb locks before spinning.
- Faye found a new market when she began to do "Grandma" and "Grandpa" sweatshirts embroidered with the names of peoples' grandchildren.
- Joy, who raises sheep and sells wool, found a large niche audience of buyers who appreciate wool products. After identifying this niche, she went on to develop a line of over a hundred sheep-related products she could sell by mail.
- Susan, who sells teddy bears and other toys made from recycled

Profits from Mother Nature

Many beautiful items can be made from raw materials that cost you nothing. Rocks, driftwood, flowers and seashells immediately come to mind. I recall two women who established a successful crafts partnership built on Mother Nature's bounty that kept a dozen people working part time in their homes. They manufactured a varied line of character doll ornaments with heads hand-carved from the burrs of teasel plants, a weed that grows plentifully along West Virginia's country roads. One secret to their sales success was locating specialty stores that appreciate Appalachian crafts, and they found them in such unlikely places as California. Working through a sales rep, they also found an international market for their products in several far-eastern countries.

fur coats and other products, caters to ecologically minded people.

- Roz targeted brides as her niche market when she began to do beadwork on wedding gowns and veils.
- Katie found an interesting niche market for her hand-painted saws when she realized that many widows wanted paintings on saws their husbands had used all their lives.
- Shirley targeted the handicapped elderly as her niche market when she began to manufacture knit garments that closed with Velcro and snaps.
- Sidney's niche market is huge: women who stitch items as gifts. She will create a custom-designed needlework chart from a photo of a house, car, boat, or business logo. (Other designers offer similar services doing pet pictures or people portraits.)
- Myra found a sizable "military niche" for her needlework charts of ship emblems and "patches" of all divisions of the U.S. Military service.
- Judith tapped the "lefties market" for her T-shirt line when she began to add quotes on them about left-handedness.
- Norma glazes photos onto ceramic plates, cups and picture

frames. She found all kinds of niche markets by focusing on items that make great gifts for such people as graduates, nurses, new moms, grandparents and newlyweds or anniversary couples.

Niche Market Checklist

Consumer Markets

❏ **Women**

Homemakers

Brides-to-be

New moms

Grandmothers

❏ **Men**

Sports enthusiasts (baseball, golf, hunting, boating, etc.)

Grandfathers

Fellows who need gifts for wife or secretary

❏ **Business professionals/men and women**

Doctors, lawyers, accountants, teachers, office workers, nurses, home-business owners, etc. (Literally hundreds of categories here)

❏ **Farmers or farm families**

(with special interest in horses, sheep, pigs, cows, steam engines, special crops, etc.)

❏ **People who live in a specific city, state or region**

❏ **Disabled elderly**

❏ **Ecologically minded consumers**

❏ **Craft enthusiasts**

(List all the individual crafts and look for niche interests within each craft category)

❏ **Collectors and nostalgia buffs**

(Hundreds of categories here—circus, carousel, trains, dolls, music boxes, toys, miniatures, etc.)

❏ **Pet lovers**

(Identify specific pet groups)

Wholesale Markets

❏ **Gift shops**

Handcraft shops

Commercial gift shops (general)

Gift shops in tourist areas or hospitals

Christian gift shops

Shops featuring collectibles and novelties

Year-round Christmas shops

❏ **Mail-order catalog houses**

Profits from Recycled Items

Cathy Colley has developed a good-selling and very profitable line of recycled products that she calls her "Recyclements line." It includes handpainted jars, bottles and light bulb ornaments. "The glassware comes to me for fee," she says. "My friends all save their burned out light bulbs and the jars they were going to throw away. I then hand paint them and resell them in the cooperative I belong to, as well as on my Web site. Since the cost of materials is so minimal (paints and varnishes), my profit point is high. Sometimes I can hardly believe people are buying these silly things! The best part is that they are incredibly fun to make. All the doodling I did as a school-kid in the margins of my notebooks is now paying off!"

John L. Dilbeck is an artist and metalsmith who makes unique steel roses out of old car body panels. "I like the idea of recycling old metal parts into a new product," he says. "It can take nearly 8,000 hammer blows to texture the petals for one large rose—and, yes, I did count it one time! I think it's worth the extra effort to pro-  duce a superior representation of one of nature's most treasured beauties, and to produce another hand-forged, one-of-a-kind, signed and numbered representation of "The Rose that Never Wilts.™" John sells his roses on his Web site for $100 to $500 each.

General consumer gift catalogs
Special-interest consumer catalogs (books, tools, supplies, kits, kitchenware, jewelry, etc.)
Special-interest craft and hobby catalogs.
❑ **Specialty shops, stores or departments in stores**
Cookware, Baby, Sewing, Toys & Dolls, Christmas, Sports, Woodenware, etc.

Using Commercial Patterns and Designs

Some crafters tend to "lift" designs used by others. This is both impolite and unethical, not to mention illegal when a crafter has protected an original design by copyright (which most professional crafters are now doing). Since you could be sued for wrongly using someone else's pattern or design, it's important to learn a little about copyrights and the copyright law.

All commercial patterns are protected by copyright and sold to consumers with the understanding that they are to be used *for personal use only.* The fact that you have purchased a pattern or design does not give you a right to sell products made from that pattern or design, any more than your purchase of a piece of artwork gives you the right to recreate it for sale in some other form, such as notepaper or calendars. Only the original creator has such rights. You have simply purchased the physical property for private use.

In spite of this "legality," crafters have been using commercial patterns and designs for years to make products for sale at craft fairs. When sales are limited to this market, problems are not likely to occur. Legal problems may arise, however, if such patterns are used to make finished items offered for sale in consignment shops, rent-a-space gift shops and other retail outlets. Although I am not qualified to give legal advice on copyright law, I have made a thorough study of this topic and have checked with a copyright attorney to verify the accuracy of the information that follows. It will help you avoid legal problems when using commercial patterns and designs to make products for sale.

Projects in Craft Magazines

Generally, it is okay to make products for sale from patterns and designs found in craft and needlework magazines, *provided such publications own the copyrights to those designs and authorize readers to use them for profit.* Most craft magazines have a policy of allowing their readers to make projects for resale, but the rule is *you must make the entire project your-*

Dry It and Sell It

Two things that rarely fail to find a market are miniature food items and dried gift products such as herbal mixes, flower arrangements or applehead dolls. Think about a special crop you might grow to diversify your farm income, but don't think miniature only. Also consider products you might grow for sale as supplies to crafters, such as corn husks for dolls and related items, wheat for wheat weavings or dried items for making wreaths, pictures, flower arrangements or potpourris.

self and be the only one who profits from it. That means you may not set up an assembly line, have someone else do part of the work, or sell your finished items through any outlet that takes a commission on sales.

The big question is whether the magazine or the designer owns the copyright. Some designers sell their how-to projects on an all-rights basis, while others sell only "first rights" (meaning they have retained the exclusive right to sell finished products or kits made from their own patterns or designs). If you learn that a copyright is owned by a designer, you could write to him or her in care of the magazine, requesting permission to make and sell the item. Some designers may give permission to make a limited number of items for sale at the retail level, and most would be receptive to the idea of being paid a royalty on a product that might reach a large wholesale market.

Quilting and Sewing Patterns

Contemporary quilt designers will find eager buyers among people who appreciate fine art, and they may be able to copyright their original creations. Many buyers, however, prefer to buy quilts made from traditional patterns they recognize. Because the old quilt patterns are not protected by copyrights, they can be freely used for commercial purposes.

Patterns that you buy in your local fabric store can be used to make custom-made clothing and other items for individual buyers, but you cannot wholesale a line of products from such patterns. In some cases, it is legally dangerous even to sell a few products at a crafts fair or home boutique. For example, the fact that you can buy a pattern to make a Raggedy Ann doll does not mean you can legally make that product for sale. Crafters are walking on dangerous ground whenever they offer for sale any product that bears a reproduction of famous characters such as Snoopy, the Sesame Street gang or the cartoon characters of Warner Brothers and the Walt Disney Company.

Famous Copyrighted Characters

While browsing a sidewalk craft fair in my town, I noticed that several crafters were selling originally designed clothing made from fabric with Walt Disney characters on it. Trying to be helpful, I explained to one seller that unless she had a licensing arrangement with Disney, she was violating their copyright and could get into trouble. She didn't take kindly to my advice, saying, "Everyone else is selling things with Disney characters on them, so why shouldn't I?"

The fact that everybody is doing something doesn't make it right, and in this case, it was not only illegal but financially dangerous for the crafters in question. (This problem was compounded by the fact that a quantity of fabric with Disney characters on it had accidentally slipped into retail sewing stores that year. Disney later recalled this fabric and reportedly sued some retailers for selling Disney-related merchandise without a license.) Because the Walt Disney Company is aggressive in protecting its rights, you should never, *ever* sell a product with one of their designs on it.

Changing Patterns for Your Own Use

I'll bet some of you are thinking you don't have anything to worry about because when you use a pattern, you always make changes to it. Unfortunately, changing a pattern does not entitle you to claim the revised pattern as our own. You can't just lift something here, add it to something there, change this and rearrange that.

Reevaluate Your Product Line

After you've been selling for a while, take time to reevaluate your product line and consider new buyer groups you might target. Do you have an interesting variety of things in different sizes, shapes, colors and designs? What could you do to spice up your line? Could you change certain products in your line to make them appeal to different people, for example:

▶ Men instead of women (or vice versa)
▶ Boys instead of girls
▶ Corporate buyers instead of consumers
▶ College students instead of younger children
▶ Sportswomen instead of sportsmen
▶ Career women instead of homemakers

Imagine this scenario: A consumer has purchased a pattern to get ideas for items she can make to sell at retail. She decides she can improve the pattern by making changes here and there. In time she comes up with what she actually believes is an "original pattern," and she justifies the originality of this pattern by the fact that her finished item does not look *exactly* like the one that inspired her design. But if it only looks "similar," that would be sufficient grounds for a lawsuit, provided the copyright holder wanted to go that far. (Generally, if you're found to be innocently infringing on someone else's copyright, you'll get a polite but stern letter from the designer's attorney telling you to cease selling that item at once.)

If your "similar creation" is sold in finished form at the retail level only (fairs, holiday boutiques, bazaars, or by mail), chances are good that no one will ever notice (or care) that, technically, you've violated the copyright law and a designer's rights. But let's take this a step further. What if our imaginary consumer now decides to print her "original pattern" for sale to other crafters. Whoops! Now she's really asking for trouble. You see, if any *portion* of her pattern is identical to the pattern she originally bought, or if she has merely rearranged the order of the printed instructions or changed a few words here and there, she has violated the original designer's copyright.

Never assume that such copyright infringement will go unnoticed by the original designer. The crafts community has an excellent word-of-mouth network and today, with e-mail, mailing lists, bulletin boards, and chat rooms, news like this can spread in a flash. Moreover, designers commonly purchase copies of all patterns for items similar to those they've designed just to be sure no one is profiting from their copyrighted work. They lay the patterns out side by side to determine if their patterns have "inspired" copies. If so, they will be quick to put an end to the matter with a letter from an attorney. If pattern sales do not cease, the copyright infringer may be forced to refund all money customers send in the future or give all profits to the original creator.

The Designer's Viewpoint

Most designers realize that craft consumers are using their patterns to make a few items for sale in local fairs, boutiques, and shops. While they rarely encourage this practice, most do nothing to curtail it unless an individual abuses this privilege. What concerns them are individuals who try to build a business around their copyrighted patterns and designs. It is at this point that "commercialization" raises its ugly head and begins to threaten the profits of the original designer or publisher.

For example, let's say that a designer sells an original doll pattern to a magazine on first-rights basis. This means the magazine can publish the how-to pattern once for the benefit of its readers with the idea that they will probably make one or two for their personal use, as gifts, or maybe for sale at a local fair.

Now imagine that the designer sees a market for her doll in kit form, or a major manufacturer wants to buy the rights to produce *en masse,* offering royalties on each sale. If craft consumers across the country are selling finished versions of her original design in the same marketplace, this will obviously hurt her potential for profit. At this point, a professional designer may be forced to take legal action. I recall the story of one doll designer who sold her patterns by mail for years. Then a woman used one of her patterns to create a variation of the doll, claiming it as her own. When the original designer learned that a rip-off of her doll had been offered to a manufacturer for mass production, she had to sue the craftsperson to protect her copyright.

To reiterate, some people believe it's okay to take bits and pieces from several copyrighted patterns, a head here, a leg and arm there, facial features from another source. But this does not constitute "originality," and since the original designers of any feature that has been copied can come after the infringer, the possibilities for a legal confrontation have only been multiplied.

Developing Your Own Designs

As one who has spent her life encouraging creative people, I don't like to break bubbles by discouraging hobby crafters where the use of commercial patterns is concerned. But I do want to keep my readers out of trouble, and the only way to do that is to share what I've learned about legal matters such as this.

I'm all for hobby crafters selling their wares for extra income, but there is a big difference between running a little hobby business and a real crafts business. While hobby sellers commonly use the patterns of others to make products for sale, craft professionals who are trying to build a profitable business know the importance of selling originally designed products. If you truly cannot create your own original products for sale, then you must accept the fact that you will be limited both in the kind and number of products you can sell, where you can sell them, and how much you can get for them.

If you don't like to be held back, however, I urge you to follow the lead of thousands of other crafters who once thought they couldn't create original products either, but learned to do so. I believe you, too, can come up with your own original ideas if you put your mind to it. This is a topic I can only touch on in this book, but I've discussed it at considerable length in *Make It Profitable*. This book contains hundreds of ideas on how professional crafters brainstorm for new product ideas, design for a niche market, redesign existing products and develop successful "widgets," a word craftspeople have now claimed and applied to their bread-and-butter items—products they can always count on to sell.

I think I just heard someone moan, "But I'm not an artist! I can't even draw a straight line." True, you may not be an artist, but we all have a God-given natural streak of creativity and artistry. Some people design by making sketches. Others design by feel and intuition, trying first one idea or technique, then another. My most creative ideas generally come in the form of a "brilliant brainstorm" when I'm in the middle of a project. This creative design process can be speeded up simply by getting in the habit of constantly feeding your mind with fresh images and ideas. Then you'll have a reservoir from which to draw when you want to express a new level of creativity.

I've always believed that creativity is merely the discovery of something that's been there all along. The trouble with most people is that they begin with a negative attitude, dismissing the possibility that they may really have creative abilities. Instead, why don't you look in the mirror and say to yourself, "I've got a lot of undiscovered talent somewhere, and I intend to find it!"

Randall Barr's story offers an example of how the creative process works. The year I met Randall, he sold nearly 6,000 of his "Time Flies" Birdhouse Clocks, and he would have sold 10,000 if he could have figured out how to make that many. Although Randall is now retired from manufacturing and selling, he continues to craft for his own enjoyment while also designing prototypes for products that can be licensed. After an illness forced Randall to stop manufacturing and selling his products, he licensed the rights to his Birdhouse Clocks to another manufacturer, but eventually got them back when the licensing arrangement proved to be unsatisfactory. "Licensing holds many pitfalls for the inexperienced crafter," he told me, "but it's a nice way to earn extra income if you can connect

© 1995 by Randall Barr

Add Greeting Cards to Your Product Line

Now that so many creative people have computers, scanners and graphic art software, they're beginning to produce their own greeting cards and note cards for sale, printing them on an inkjet or color laser printer. For designs, many artists work from photographs of their work, while others use pen-and-ink drawings of their products (such as Cathryn Peters, Chapter Eleven). Crafts that are particularly suitable for card designs include teddy bears, dolls, toys, needlework and reproductions of drawings or paintings.

Rebekah Rowe sells soft sculptures that hang on the wall, from magic wands to stars, moons and hearts. To create her card designs, she simply scans her flat sculptures to get reproductions as good or better than a photograph. (The illustration at right of a card measuring 5½ x 8½ inches does not convey the beautiful colors in Rebekah's cards, but does show the detail possible from a scan of the actual product.) After making desired adjustments (color hue, size, cropping, etc.), Rebekah transfers the image to a template she created in WordPerfect so she can add any desired text. Using HP greeting card paper and her HP DeskJet printer, she prints as many cards as are needed to fill orders. The material cost in each card is about 65 cents, and they wholesale for $1.25 each.

A little bit of magic never hurts....

"My profits are good," says Rebekah, "and once the originals have been scanned in, barely any labor is involved. I now have about 30 card designs and a growing number of 8 x 10 inch glossy posters. I wholesale my line to shops and stores across the country, most of them found through research on the Internet."

with the right manufacturer."

How does Randall get his clever product ideas? "Most of them come to me either when I'm just going to sleep or just waking up," he says. "I kind of program myself to be aware of ideas, and the Birdhouse Clock was just one of those 'Ah-ha!' ideas we all get from time to time. After having bypass surgery, I had to get out of the oil business, but I still needed something to do. As I was programming my subconscious mind to the idea that I needed to come up with something more unusual than this, my younger daughter came home one weekend with a handmade gift for her mother. It was a little birdhouse she had made with a mushroom bird on it. I had never seen a mushroom bird before, but after finding a supply source for the item, I remembered George Washington Carver and how he had asked God what he could do with a peanut. So I asked what I could do with a mushroom bird, and Birdhouse Clocks were the answer."

This is a perfect example of how creativity and serendipity work hand in hand (with a little help from the Divine Creator), a topic I've discussed at greater length in Chapter Fifteen.

Chapter Five

Pricing Problems and Solutions

"Price" is the figure something sells for. "Value" is what that item is worth to the buyer. Quite often the two have nothing to do with one another.

Do successful sellers use formulas to set prices on their products and services, or do they just charge what they think people will pay? Yes, to both questions. Smart craftspeople do use pricing formulas, but they also weigh their formulated prices against the marketplace itself, and either raise or lower them according to their instinct about what the market will bear. Formulas are fun, but they are often impractical. Here is a simple one you can play around with:

Materials + Labor + Overhead + Profit = Wholesale price × 2 = Retail

Although pricing formulas appear in all the craft business books, few crafters use them with success, so let's put formulas aside and explore common pricing problems and solutions that have worked for others. To give you an idea of how insecure others are on this topic, consider the following questions posed in one of my pricing workshops for members of a professional arts and crafts organization (most of whom had been selling at arts and crafts fairs for years):

- How do you get the price you are worth?
- Why do I feel guilty asking the price I think I'm worth?
- How do we convince a customer that the price of our items is fair?
- Why do we always feel that we need to underprice our items in order for them to sell?
- Is it best to price your items at even or uneven figures?
- How do you figure overhead costs?
- Does pricing too low make your product appear inferior?
- Should I charge more than I am now getting for a product that is absolutely unique? I sell out nearly every show.
- How can I sell at wholesale when I have trouble getting people to pay my retail price?
- How do you set a price and stick with it? If someone says "Oh, I can't afford that," I feel sorry for them and lower my price. Then I'm mad because I lose.
- Once I have established a price, is it okay to change it, depending on where my show will be?

In working with this group of professional crafters, I conducted a little experiment. I asked everyone to write two figures on a slip of paper: What they thought their time was worth an hour, and what they figured they were actually getting per hour for the time they were putting into their art or craft. Here is how 107 individuals responded to that question. (The slash mark between crafts indicates different craftspeople):

My Time is Worth:	I'm Actually Getting:
$1	$8 (wood items)
$4	$4 (painting and needlework)
$4.50	$1.50 (paper products)
$5	$7.50 (fabric); $3.50 (fabrics and needlework/soapmaking); $2.50 (woodcrafts); $2 (quilting and stitchery/floral and wood/wire trees); $1.50 (knitting/eggcraft); $1 (tole painting)
$5.50	$1.75 (folk art)
$6	$4 (ceramics); $3.50 (weaving/wood and fabric crafts); $3 (mixed media); $2 (fabric); $1 (mixed media)
$6.50	$10.75 (tole painting)
$7	$4 (wood and fiber); $3 (cloth dolls/fabrics); $2 (woodworking/woodturnings)
$8	$4 (sewing); $3 (pottery); $2 (fiber artist/dried flowers)
$9	$4 (wooden furniture, toys); $1.20 (fiber)
$10	$10 (stoneware pottery/paper/fabric lampshades); $8 (stained glass); $7 (cut and pierced and fabric lampshades); $6 (bread dough art/hand-painted crocks/glass/wood and decorative painting /wreaths/dried flowers/dried arrangements/fabric sculpture); $5 (wood crafts/ceramics/folk art and basketry/ floral work, fibercrafts/baskets/weaving/wood products/stained glass/wood and decorative painting/silk flowers and lap quilts/soft sculpture toys/floral design/metals/wood cuts and folk painting/tole painting/stained glass); $4 (quilting); $3 (mixed media/stained glass/dried florals/wood/lace); $2.50 (cloth dolls/silver jewelry); $2 (pine cones/painting/cross stitch/needlework); $1 (fabric); $.50 (cross stitch in handmade frames)
$12	$6 (wood items); $5 (wood and folk art painting); $4 (baskets); $1 (pierced lampshades)
$13	$5 (baskets)
$14	$5 (fabric crafts)
$15	$10 (fiber arts); $9 (wood and fabric); $7.50 (decorative painting); $7 (wheat weaving); $6 (fibercrafts/clothing); $5.50 (Victorian painted wood); $5 (woodcarving/macrame and wreaths/woodcrafts); $1 (dried flowers)
$18	$10 (porcelain repair); $4 (teacher)
$20	$10 (fiber/dried flowers/goldsmith/lampshades); $7 (wood signs); $5 (needlework/oil painting/basketry/fabric sculpture)
$25	$12 (silhouette pictures); $10 (doll design patterns); $2 (photographer)

As you can see, the greatest area of response was in the $10 per hour category, and within this category, most crafters reported earning just $5 per hour. Only in a couple of instances did people report earning more per hour than they actually thought they were worth. Notice the different values craftspeople working in the same medium place on the worth of their time and what they are actually receiving per hour. For example, people working in wood reported receiving as little as $2.50 and as much as $10 per hour. Notice that only a dozen people out of 107 (11 percent) thought they were worth $20 an hour, but *none* of them were making this much. In fact, on average, these 107 crafters thought their time was worth $10.87 an hour, but on average they were making $2.82 an hour.

Rather than discourage you with such figures, I'm hoping to shock some of you awake, to make you realize that your prices and craft profits are never going to climb higher until you learn to take pricing seriously. First, you need to study the marketplace to see what's selling and what you might offer that no one else is selling. Then you need to "psych out" your buyers.

The Psychology of Pricing

Have you ever noticed that people with limited funds will often pay more for a product or service than they originally intended, simply because they need to buy a little confidence or prestige along with their purchase? Paying more for something gives some people a feeling of importance or something to brag about to friends.

When you realize that people will also pay a great deal more for certain things nostalgic, whimsical or collectible, you will have discovered yet another important pricing secret related to human nature. People do not buy products or services per se, they buy *benefits*. And that is exactly what you provide each time you satisfy a buyer's secret urge or inner longing. You also provide benefits when you save buyers time, money or aggravation, solve some difficult gift-giving problems, allay certain fears or add to their general peace of mind.

Knowledge about pricing comes with time, experience and confidence in your own worth as a producer of quality handcrafted merchandise. As a cre-

Selling in Hard Economic Times

In a survey of Barbara's magazine column readers during one economic recession, crafters reported that craft fair shoppers seemed most interested in practical items that could be given as gifts. In trying to meet consumer needs, 83 percent of survey respondents said they had priced most of their wares under $25, and items under $10 had sold best. In stark contrast, the rest of those surveyed said they had successfully sold items priced from $25 to $200. Many commented that the recession hadn't affected their sales to any degree. In fact, several reported an increase in sales in one of the toughest economic years many crafters have ever known.

This proves once again that it is not always necessary to lower prices in hard times, because there will always be some buyers with extra money to spend. The real secret to sales success is, and always will be, having products consumers want or need. Price is rarely the most important reason for lack of sales. More often than not, the fault lies with the product itself and the fact that people just don't need or want it.

ative person who appreciates handmade things, it may be hard for you to accept that most buyers do not care how long it takes you to make something or how much it costs to make. Their only concern is whether your price matches their pocketbook and their estimation of the worth of your product.

If your prices are on the high side, buyers will naturally weigh their desire for your craftwork against the money they have to spend. Some of them will mentally compare your beautiful creations to the price of machine-made imitations and walk away feeling that your prices are unrealistic. On the other hand, if your prices are too low for the high-quality work you are offering, some people may feel you do not place a high enough value on your work, so they do not care to own it.

Because you are dealing with human nature when you sell handcrafts, it helps to develop an invisible shell to protect yourself from less appreciative people.

Keep in mind that other consumers and wholesale buyers are currently spending millions of dollars each year at fine craft shows across the country, proving that many people do appreciate the value of handcrafts and are willing to pay a good price to obtain them. Your constant challenge as a crafts seller will be to find these buyers.

Underpricing Crafts

After giving a series of crafts marketing workshops in Michigan at the height of the 1982 recession, I realized that the biggest problem of beginning sellers is not just pricing but underpricing of their products. Many people I spoke with in Michigan felt their handcrafted products could not sell at higher prices, yet most had never *tried* to sell them at a higher price. They were instead basing their "pricing logic" on their own limited knowledge of what the local market would bear, and they had no conception of what tourists or buyers in larger cities might pay.

If the rest of the country was then in a recession, Michigan was in a depression, according to the home economists I talked with. Yet, in Midland, Michigan, a craft shop owner told me that price was not the object when items were well made and in keeping with what buyers wanted to buy at that time. And a craftswoman who was then selling lifesize cloth sculptures at $350–$400 told me, "The economy has had no adverse effect on my sales. If anything, the recession has helped sales because people need something to make them laugh, and my sculptures do just that."

In the years since I did those workshops in Michigan, recessions have come and gone and crafters are still underpricing their work. From a survey of thirty professional craftspeople who attended one of my all-day seminars in Missouri in the mid-1990s, I learned that

- 38% were earning less than $5 per hour, with two reporting 20 to 30 cents per hour
- 44% (nearly half) said they figured they were earning between $5 and $10 per hour
- 1% reported between $12 and $15 per hour
- 17% between $20 and $50 per hour

In gross dollars annually,

57% were earning under $5,000

28% were earning between $6,000 and $20,000

2% were earning $21,000 to $50,000

13% were earning more than $50,000 (with one business reporting nearly $500,000 a year)

As a hobby seller, you may be content to take what you can get from local residents, but if you are striving to be more successful and you can't sell something at a profit in your area, *go somewhere else.* Enter craft fairs of a higher caliber outside your usual market area. Sell through craft malls or rent-a-space shops in more affluent areas, explore your options on the Internet, or test an ad in a consumer magazine that showcases American handcrafts (see Chapter Thirteen). Also consider creating a few products you can wholesale and present to buyers in other cities. As one bright craftswoman pointed out in one of my workshops, "I don't see a brick wall around our town."

Why You Shouldn't Lower Prices at a Fair

Some crafters say they negotiate prices at craft fairs or lower them toward the end of the day, but this is an unprofitable strategy used mostly by hobby sellers. If lack of sales convinces you that your prices are too high, change them before trying to sell at another fair, but don't mark them down at day's end just to get rid of your crafts.

"I have been going to craft fairs for four years now," says a crafter from El Paso. "In my opinion no crafter should lower prices at the end of the day at a fair. Customers do watch everything that goes on. If customers notice you lowering prices at the end of the day, they will wait to see how low the prices will go, and they may even ask you to lower your prices more. Also, customers may come to you and ask you to lower your prices in the morning because they have something else to do, and because they recall that you lowered your prices at the last fair. What would you tell

Price Endings: Even or Uneven?

If you pay close attention to price tags on all kinds of merchandise, you will begin to notice that each industry uses a certain pricing structure. Books, for example, have prices that end in 95¢ or 99¢. Fine art is always priced in even dollars and no cents. Gift shops seem to like merchandise that ends in 50¢. Some people think $9.98 sounds less expensive than $10, but to me it sounds like the price you expect to pay for something in a discount store. For that reason, I do not recommend using prices that end in 98¢ or 99¢. There are no hard and fast rules, but I think you also should avoid using the following prices, which I have rarely seen used by professional sellers:

$8, $9, $11, $13, $14, $17, $18, $19, $28, $29, $31 and so on.

Using a price that ends with 25¢ seems foolish to me since a quarter means nothing to most people. In moving up to 50¢, the most popular prices for crafts seem to be $2.50, $3.50, $7.50 and $12.50. Instead of using $5.50, however, I suggest you move the price up to $6; instead of using $8.50 or $9.50, go to $10; instead of $13.50 or $14.50, go up to $15 and so on. My logic has always been that if I were willing to pay $4.50 for something, I would just as easily pay $5. In transferring this logic to buyers, I believe that anyone who is willing to pay $16.50 will probably pay $20 without question. If they're willing to pay $32.75, they will pay $35, and so on. Remember that people often buy crafts because their heart has dictated the purchase, so they are not likely to quibble over a quarter or a couple of dollars.

such a customer when new customers are listening?

"You always have the few who try to get you to lower your prices by belittling your craftsmanship. You can have a fair on one side of town and crafts you felt would sell, don't. Then across town you attend another fair and everything sells. What has worked for me is not to lower prices but to pack up my crafts and say I did well and will do better at the next fair because people's tastes are different everywhere I go."

Anticipate questions you're likely to get from customers and be ready with answers. I like the strategy used by Bruce Baker, a veteran of hundreds of crafts shows. He has a collection of stock phrases he uses at fairs, which he calls his "Don't Go Away Mad (Just Go Away)" comments. For example, if someone whines, "$75 for *that?*" he just smiles and says, "They're not for everyone." Or if someone is quibbling about the price of everything, he might say, "Does this look like a garage sale to you?" or, "I'd love to be able to sell it for that, but I can't. If you check around, I think you'll find my prices quite competitive."

The important thing, Baker emphasizes, is to always deliver your don't-go-away-mad messages in a good-natured manner. "Aggressiveness is harmful; assertiveness gains respect."

The next time your fellow crafters start lowering prices at the end of a day, refuse to lower yours on the grounds that your beautiful creations are worth as much at the end of the day as they were at the beginning. If you hold fast and refuse to mark down your prices—and tell customers why—I believe you will make as many sales as anyone. And you will certainly stand out in the crowd! If someone really likes your work, they will buy it at full price and respect you for not lowering your standards.

The Value of Your Time

One of the most important elements in any pricing formula is value of one's time. Many factors come into play when you try to figure out the value of your tine, including your age, previous salaried job experience, where you live, your need for money and so on. If you are selling with the thought of eventually making crafts a part-time profession, you will naturally want to receive as much per hour as possible. But if you are retired or involved in crafts strictly for pleasure, your entire outlook on selling will be different. You may be selling only to get rid of all the things you're making that you no longer have room to keep. When I began to craft, I used to joke that my mother's home was decorated in "Early Barbara." Once all my family and friends had received

Don't Carry "Quality" Too Far

A crafter named Judi once complained that people didn't appreciate the Christmas ornaments she made, each of which took up to fifteen hours to make. "I mold my ornaments myself with a combination of plaster and stone, painstakingly paint the tiniest details on them, then give them three or four coats of clear varnish," she wrote. "Yet I have found that people are unwilling to pay more than a few dollars for them. I would rather give them away than sell them for such a low price."

Judi said her husband suggested she put less detail in her work, change to a cheaper plaster mix and give the ornaments only one coat of varnish, but Judi felt she shouldn't do this. "I take pride in what I make and I can't bring myself to peddle something I have no pride in," she said.

Although such an attitude about quality in crafts is admirable, it is also impractical from a marketing standpoint. You can't put fifteen hours into an object as ordinary as a Christmas ornament and expect the average person to pay you for your time in making it. Like so many others before her, Judi soon learned that she had to make a decision: Did she want to be "an artist," or did she want to be a professional crafter? "Artists" tend to make what they want to make, not what people want to buy. One-of-a-kind creations are their specialty, and they are always hard to sell at a profit.

"Professional crafters," on the other hand, create for the marketplace, making multiples of each of several items in a line. Sure, it's boring to make the same items over and over again, often in assembly-line fashion, but if making money is the object, then this is what you must do. In the end, all creative people who offer their wares to the public have to decide whether their ultimate goal is

my crafts as gifts, I felt I either had to start selling or stop producing.

I once knew an amazing woman who began a successful crafts career at the age of seventy. She said, "I figure my time does not have much market value at this point in my life, and labor costs definitely do not enter into the picture. For one who has been familiar with time and cost studies in my business years, I'm ashamed to admit to such unbusinesslike methods of pricing, but I'm sure about one thing: the people who buy my work appreciate handwork and pay my asking price without question. I'm sure if I figured materials and labor accurately, the prices would have to be much higher, and I wouldn't sell as much as I do."

Older crafters often underprice their art or craftwork for the above reason, but others who do place a high enough value on their time almost always forget to include overhead expenses and the profit factor in the pricing formula I presented earlier. Many people believe that the best way to set prices on crafts is simply to double, triple or even take ten times the cost of materials, but there is a big flaw in that theory and it has to do with the time it takes you to produce an item.

If something costs you $2 in materials, and you can make 6 of them in an hour and get $4 each, that would yield a gross profit of $12 for an hour of your time. But if each item takes an hour to make and costs you $2 in materials, a doubling of the cost of materials would yield a pitiful profit of just $2 for your labor. As you can see, time is everything.

Let's really dig into this problem. Let's say you're producing a product that takes three hours to make. You've been selling it at $25, subtracting the cost of your materials (let's estimate them at $5) then dividing $20 by three hours and feeling pretty good about making $6.66 per hour on your craftwork. But that is not the right way to figure it.

Let's look at what happens when you get businesslike and take into account your overhead expenses (let's estimate them at $5), and factor in some profit (10 percent of the selling price). And while we're at it, let's look at what a difference it would make in your year-end profits if you raised the selling price another $10:

$25.00	Selling Price	$35.00
− 5.00	Cost of Materials	− 5.00
− 5.00	Overhead	− 5.00
− 2.50	Profit	− 3.50
$12.50	(divided by 3 hours)	$21.50
$ 4.17 *per hour*		$ 7.17 *per hour*

Certificates of Authenticity

Do you create one-of-a-kind pieces that sell on the high side? Artist Leslie Miller Bertram, who does a lot of custom-design work, says it's often difficult to justify her prices to new clients. "Until they begin to work with me, they do not understand the amount of time, talent and vision that goes into creating their one-of-a-kind treasures, so I spend a lot of time educating my customers and ensuring their trust in me."

One way Leslie does this is by issuing a "Certificate of Authenticity" for each piece she creates. It describes the piece itself and the materials used to create it. If the image contains subjects of local or historic significance, she includes this information, as well. Using her computer, she prints the certificate on decorative stock, includes a full-color photo of the finished painting, and encloses a separate page with artist information (biography and contact information). The certificate is enclosed in its own presentation folder and delivered in an envelope. Much care is taken to keep all materials archival.

"Commission work can be very time consuming and mentally draining," says Leslie, "but when I find someone I want to continue working with on a custom-order basis, I sometimes include a gift or discount certificate with delivery of their paid-in-full order. My 'thank-yous' have included notecard sets, a small handpainted ornament, or a small print related to the client's favorite genre or theme. My customers find these items a pleasant surprise, and I often get new orders from them as well as new customers from their word-of-mouth advertising."

When you sell something for $25, you end up with a net figure of $12.50 or 50 percent of the retail selling price. But when you increase the price by $10, you end up with a net figure of $21.50, or 61 percent of the retail selling price. That's because your materials and overhead costs remained the same. It's rather like the difference you pay when you buy only a small amount of printing. The printer has to get all his overhead costs and expenses out of that first run, so if you order only 500 copies of something, you end up paying all those costs. If you order 1,000 copies, however, the second 500 copies might cost only half what you paid for the first 500 copies.

Isn't it interesting how a $10 increase in the retail price of a product almost doubles the hourly wage? You might want to try this pricing exercise with each individual item in your line to find out which ones are the most profitable.

If your financial goal is merely to earn extra income, an hourly wage of $7 per hour would amount to a tidy sum at the end of the year, as you can see from the figures below. However, if your goal is to build a full-time homebased business that might eventually support your family, you should aim for an hourly wage of $25 to $30 per hour, minimum. About the only ways to make this kind of money are to produce high-priced products, get into wholesaling or sell a product or service that does not entail so much labor. (See Chapter Fifteen for other ways to profit from art or craft skills besides making finished products for sale.)

To estimate how much money you might be able to make in a year, first figure out how many hours you might be able to spend producing crafts. Then multiply that number by your hourly rate. In the above example, if you could produce crafts 20 hours a week 50 weeks a year, that would be 1,000 hours of production time. If it took you an average of three hours to make each product in your line, you could produce only about 333 units a year. If, however, you could design a product that would sell for the same price and could be made in an hour or less, the number of units you could make would jump to nearly a 1,000 per year. Here is a visual illustration of what I've just said:

A product that takes three hours to make:

◆ On the $25 product, a profit of $2.50 per item × 333 items made in a year = $832.50 plus 1,000 hours × $4.33 per hour for labor = $4,330, for a total of $5,162.50 per year.

◆ On the $35 product, a profit of $3.50 per item × 333 items made in a year = $1,165.50 plus 1,000 hours × $7.17 per hour for labor = $7,170, for a total of $8,335.50 per year (or $3,173 more).

Now look what happens if you triple your production by making a product in only one hour instead of three:

- On the $25 product, a profit of $2.50 per item × 999 items made in a year = $2,497.50 plus 1,000 hours × $13.00 per hour for labor = $13,000, for a total of $15,497.50 per year.
- On the $35 product, a profit of $3.50 per item × 999 items made in a year = $3,496.50 plus 1,000 hours × $21.50 per hour for labor = $21,500 for a total of $24,996.50 per year (or $9,499 more).

If you're making lots of crafts but aren't making lots of money, maybe it's time to analyze every product in your line, pull out the unprofitable items, create some new products, and bring your prices up to the point where you are truly making a profit from all the hours you are putting into your endeavor.

As you can see, pricing a product at $35 instead of $25 makes a huge difference in year-end profits even when it takes three hours to make a product. By tripling the number of items produced in a year, however, the figures shoot up to an impressive level. (See "Production Strategies" elsewhere in this chapter for ideas on how to increase the number of items you make each year.)

Paring Costs to the Bone

The easiest way to increase profits is to lower costs. For years, a common complaint of craft sellers was that they couldn't obtain supplies at wholesale because the policy of the manufacturers and distributors in this industry was to sell only to storefront businesses. Now, however, the HIA acknowledges that craft designers and "converters of craft materials for the gift market" comprise a legitimate market. Although professional crafters are now invited to attend HIA trade shows, the companies who exhibit here may or may not have high minimum orders of $200 or more.

When trying to buy supplies by mail, a professional approach will make it easier for suppliers to sell to you. The quickest way to ensure that your letter to a manufacturer or wholesaler ends up in the wastebasket is to write it by hand on paper torn from a yellow tablet, steno pad, or notepaper with butterflies all over it. To get wholesale prices, you have to look like you're really in business. Even when you request a wholesale catalog on business stationery, some companies won't send a catalog until you complete their Dealer Information form. The policy of most manufacturers and wholesalers is to sell only to companies with a valid sales tax number, exemption certificate or vendor's license.

Tip

If you can't meet the minimum quantity requirements of some manufacturers, ask for the names of distributors and dealers near you. Local dealers may give you a 20 percent discount on supplies ordered in quantity if you present yourself as a legitimate business owner. (Regular orders from you might help a small retailer order in greater quantities for lower prices and increased profits.) Don't approach a shop owner as an ordinary customer, however. Phone first for an appointment, one business person to another.

In addition to shopping for bulk supplies and new wholesale sources, many crafters report they have added craft products to their line that incorporate natural or found items, such as wild roses, grasses and weeds, old jewelry, wood scraps and recycled materials (as previously discussed in Chapter Four). Many crafters also browse resale shops in search of usable lace, buttons, old fur coats and garments containing fine material. Trish Bloom, who makes a variety of beaded items, reclaims beads from old necklaces and other beaded items found at thrift stores, garage sales and flea markets. "I see the same things over and over at craft stores," she says, "but in old necklaces I find unusual beads that are no longer being made, and the selection is never ending."

Sell it at Double the Price

If you can't sell something at a certain price, try reverse psychology. Don't lower the price, raise it! Yes, you may lose some customers, but your higher price will automatically attract a totally new audience of buyers.

Once there was a woman who started a teddy bear repair service. When she eventually decided to do something else, she thought she had an excellent strategy for killing her bear business: she would simply double her prices to discourage customers. To her amazement, business increased. As one customer explained, "I was reluctant to bring my antique teddy to you before because your prices seemed suspiciously low. Now I'm confident you can be trusted to do the job."

After reading this story in one of the author's magazine articles, artist Grady Harper reported on his experience:

"One of my full-sheet paintings just never would sell even though it seemed to be the main attraction in my exhibit at all of the shows. After reading your pricing article, I decided to follow your suggestion about doubling prices instead of lowering them. I increased the price of my painting from $325 to $750 and it was purchased after being on display only a few hours."

When to Raise Prices

Most sellers automatically lower prices when things won't sell, but they rarely stop to think that the problem may be that prices are too low to begin with. Buyers have preconceived notions about what things should sell for. Something priced too low, when compared to items of similar quality offered by others, may make them suspicious. If you are thinking about dropping a product you like to make because it just isn't profitable, try offering it to a new audience at double the original price and see what happens.

Many crafters report that products priced at $10 continue to sell best. There seems to be something magical about the figure of $10 that has appealed to buyers through the years. Even in a weak economy, it remains a price that seems affordable to most of us. I am concerned, however, that so many crafters seem to think that, because times are hard, products must be priced at $10 or less, even as low as $2 or $3. If you can make a profit on a three-dollar item, that's fine, but lowering prices on something that should sell for $10 or more is rarely the solution to sluggish sales. As stated earlier in this book, the real secret in selling more of what you make is *to make more of what people want to buy.* There will always be people with money to spend. The serious crafts seller will make every effort to find such buyers, employing new selling strategies while also improving the quality of his or her product line.

While today's buyers are more price conscious than ever, they still want top quality and they're willing to pay for it when a product gives them something they want or need. It's time to raise your prices when your production, selling or overhead costs increase, when you notice that others are selling similar products at a higher cost, and particularly when you can't keep up with the demand for a certain product.

I believe you should always raise the price of your "hot sellers." As a test, try adding one or two dollars to the price of one of your best sellers the next time you do a show. If it still sells quickly, increase the price a bit more at the next show, and keep on increasing it as long as the item sells at a rate that is satisfactory to you. (You may be astonished to learn just how much you have underpriced some of your items, and how much more you could get for them.)

Is Wholesaling in Your Future?

If you produce high-quality work, sooner or later a shop owner is going to stop by your booth and ask for your wholesale price list, so you might as well prepare for this eventuality. And now you come to the hardest part of my pricing lesson: If you don't set your prices high enough to begin with, you'll never be able to offer a shop a 50 percent discount, which is standard and absolutely necessary if a shop owner is going to realize a sufficient profit to stay in business.

In checking the retail price lists of craft sellers in small towns, I've often advised them to leave their price list alone, except to change its heading from "retail" to "wholesale." Yes, it's true, many crafters could double their present retail prices if they simply changed their marketing outlets and began to sell to established shops in larger cities.

If you do decide to wholesale, you'll have to stop messing around with your prices. Develop a line and price each product high enough to yield a profit *when offered at wholesale prices.* If you want to sell that product at the retail level, you must offer it at the same price that retailers are selling it for. Nothing upsets a shop owner more than discovering that a craftsperson is wholesaling an item at the same price they're selling it to consumers at a fair. Craft sellers are self-defeating if they decide to become wholesalers and then go to a fair and sell at less than retail prices. They are then underselling their dealers. Only by maintaining your retail prices at all times can you hope to realize the profit that is rightfully yours, and only by operating in a professional manner can you hope to maintain good business relations with your shop customers.

The temptation to lower this price is great, especially when you think the shop has set a too-high price on an item to begin with and you would be happy with less. But as soon as you lower a price, shop owners may begin to get comments like these from customers: "I saw this same item at a local fair for only $15. Why should I buy it here for $25?" If this happens, the shop will stop buying from you.

One solution to this problem is to have two different lines: one that you sell exclusively to shops at wholesale, and another that you sell only at craft fairs, boutiques, craft malls and so on. If two separate lines aren't possible, consider changing your materials. For example, use pine for the line of lower-priced wooden items you can sell with success at craft fairs, and produce the same designs in walnut or other fine woods for items sold through shops. Or use one kind of fabric or fur for soft sculpture items sold at a fair, and a more luxurious fabric or fur for items sold to shops. If you make a product in two sizes, consider offering the smaller, lower-priced items at fairs, and sell larger items of the same design exclusively to shops.

90

Getting a Grip on Expenses

All businesses deal with three sets of expense figures: production costs, selling expenses, and overhead. Production costs include all the raw materials that go into your products, while selling expenses include such things as show fees, display costs, photography, packaging materials, samples, sales commissions, and website development/maintenance costs. Overhead expenses include telephone, fax and computer expenses, monthly Internet and Web-hosting costs, equipment purchases, maintenance and depreciation, office supplies, stationery, postage and postal fees, bank charges, legal and professional expenses, travel and auto expenses, subscriptions, memberships and conference fees, advertising, bank fees and cost of accepting credit card charges, employee or independent contractor expense, and "home office expenses" (a percentage of your rent or mortgage expense, taxes, insurance and utilities).

For simplicity's sake, most crafters include selling costs in with their regular overhead figures. Once you know what your average overhead is each year, you can use this figure and divide by the number of hours you work each year to arrive at an hourly overhead figure. For example, if your overhead is $3,000 and you work $1,000 hours a year, your hourly overhead would be $3. You could either add this to your hourly labor wage or apply it proportionally to each of your products on a percentage basis. Thus, if you can make three of something in an hour, and you've calculated your hourly overhead to be $3, you would then add $1 to the price of each item you make to cover your overhead. Or, if it takes two hours to make a product, you would add $6 to the product's cost

Production Strategies

Of course, wholesaling requires a different mindset, more aggressive marketing strategies and different production techniques. You don't have to become a factory, making hundreds of the same item, but you do need to think in terms of producing dozens of the same item. To satisfy strong creative urges, some professionals produce one-of-a-kind pieces for sale at fairs and shows while wholesaling a commercial line to shops. Perhaps this idea would work for you, too.

If you alone plan to produce everything you sell, you'll have to get your workshop or studio organized for maximum efficiency. Set up an assembly-line operation that will enable you to work on twelve or more items at a time. You may not derive as much personal satisfaction from working in this way, but I guarantee you'll produce a lot more in the same amount of time. Further streamline your production methods by eliminating some of the time-consuming detail work that may please you but has little effect on the salability of an item. Also look for technological solutions to special production problems you may have. For example, could a design be silk-screened instead of hand painted? Could cutting be done by laser instead of saw? Could you cut hours of labor by buying a component part instead of making it yourself? Order a collection of craft supply catalogs to see how many pre-cut and presewn parts are available.

Tip

Many craft sellers have solved their production problems by hiring homeworkers to do some of the routine production work—cutting, painting, sewing, gluing, packaging, affixing labels, tags, etc. To avoid problems related to the hiring of independent contractors, consider farming out piecework to sheltered workshops that hire disabled workers.

Count the Hours

Before you automatically say no to the idea of moving from retailing to wholesaling, tally all the hours you normally spend on show correspondence, packing for a show, traveling to a show, unloading, manning your booth, repacking after the show, loading the car, traveling home and unpacking again. Whew! That's a lot of time and work, isn't it? Now imagine how nice it would be if you never had to leave home to sell and could spend all these hours just producing crafts for sale. With all this extra time, you could probably quadruple your production, and if you could turn your retail price list into a wholesale list as I explained above, you could also quadruple your annual income. Think about it.

For more detailed information on how to successfully move into wholesaling, see my lengthy chapter on this topic in *Creative Cash*. And for detailed information on production methods and strategies used by professional craftspeople, see *Make It Profitable.*

Pricing Tips

Knowledge about pricing increases with time and experience, but it is always a challenge, even for professionals who have been selling for years. In addition to the many pricing tips found throughout this chapter (which I hope you've highlighted), here are some additional things to remember:

- To appeal to the largest audience possible, offer an assortment of items priced in a broad range. Also consider offering a quantity price for customers who buy several items of a kind. If you have some old, lower-priced items you'd like to get rid of, consider offering one as a freebie with the purchase of a higher-priced new item. (Everyone likes to think they are getting more than they're paying for.)

- It's easier to set prices if you know what "the going prices" are for items similar to yours, so start a pricing reference file or scrapbook. Check newsstand magazines that showcase American handcrafts, clipping ads for products similar to yours. Add descriptive listings from mail order gift catalogs. Record what others are charging for your type of crafts at fairs, malls and gift shops.

- If you can't get the price you need on a particular product, don't stop making it, just look for a new market for it. The same item offered at different fairs or shops across the country might sell at a much higher price, depending on the economy of the area, the sophistication of buyers and the way the product is presented to them.

- Remember that people have preconceived notions of what a product should cost. Some will automatically pay more for something if they feel they are buying "art" instead of "craft." Example: A handcrafted object affixed to a plaque might be perceived as "craft" while the same object in a shadow box behind glass might be considered "art."

- The names you give to your products will have everything to do with the prices you can command for them. A "handmade patchwork vest" is likely to appeal to the type of buyer who might pay from $25 to $45 for the item at a crafts fair or small shop. But if you were to create a line of unique vest designs bearing a fancy name and designer label, you might be able to sell them in exclusive outlets for ten times that amount.

- The type and quality of the materials you use in your work may also determine your market and the prices you can charge. When you elect to work with ordinary or common materials, buyers may expect your prices to be common as well. When you use luxurious or exotic materials, however, you automatically attract more affluent buyers.

- The easiest way to get higher prices for any product is to lower the cost of materials. To find new suppliers, check *The Thomas Register of American Manufacturers* in your library. This multivolume directory lists products by category as well as trade and brand names. Manufacturers who won't sell to you direct will be happy to refer you to distributors who will. Also check out the wholesale supply source directories published by the National Craft Association. (See Resource Chapter.)

- Never apologize for your pricing. This only opens the door to dickering. And never discount your prices at the end of the day at a crafts fair. Your work is as valuable at 5 P.M. as it was at 9 A.M.

Pricing by the Inch

One of the most difficult things to sell at a profit is needlework. One professional needlepoint artist told me she charges by the square inch. "This is one case where that famous rule of thumb (three times the material price) cannot be applied," she says. "I scale my prices to stitches per inch, the finer the stitch, the higher the price. I give the stitch count with it (e.g., 1 square inch of 12-mesh canvas is 144 stitches = price). I began with a figure of 60 cents per inch and gradually increased it as time went on."

- There will come a time when it's necessary to raise prices not merely because they are justified by increased costs, but simply as a matter of principle. If you do something better than someone else, don't be afraid to say so, and charge accordingly.
- Stay alert. At fairs, study the reactions of people as they look at your work. Do these reactions make you feel your crafts are priced too low, too high, or just about right? Although your feelings here are an excellent guideline in pricing, you should exhibit in two or three shows before making drastic changes in your prices.
- When selling the same products at craft fairs and shops, establish firm retail prices for every item you sell and do not discount them for any reason. When profits from one sales outlet are greater than another, consider them "gravy."
- In setting prices for products to be sold by mail, carefully calculate shipping and handling charges. Pass actual shipping charges along to your customers while building handling charges into your retail prices. (Handling charges include packaging materials, labels, sealing tape and labor—yours or that of an employee.)
- The only way to know if you're making a profit on your work is to keep records on what each item in your line costs to make. Also set up a notebook with sales information. Every year, carefully monitor your inventory records and review sales to learn

which items are selling best. Weed out poor sellers, replacing them with new items.

- Never feel guilty about taking a larger profit on something you have produced easily and quickly, because this may allow you to make another item for sale that gives you great pleasure, yet yields little or no profit. Your customer will never know how long it took you to make one item versus another.

One way to get higher prices to to have high-quality printed materials. Different sellers use different sized cards and tags to relay messages that make their product seem more valuable to customers. Artist cards, like the one shown at right, are used by many. The card at right, shown in reduced size, measures 35/8 × 81/2 inches. Here, basketmaker Cathryn Peters talks about her "quaint studio" and mentions her credentials as a wicker restoration specialist who offers heirloom basket repair services and handmade deer antler baskets.

Below is a card used by soapmakers Tammy Hodson and Shirley Harrison. Many crafters use simple hang tags that include their business name and address, price, product care instructions, etc. (see Chapter Fourteen), but informative tags like this one may increase sales by educating prospective buyers to the benefits of a particular product. Here, customers are assured that they are getting a high-quality product when they buy from Mother and Daughter LLC. The card emphasizes that all colorants used in the company's handmade soap are FDA approved, highlights the personal benefits of bathing with "a finely crafted bar of soap," and adds a touch of humor at the end by reminding people not to forget to wash behind their ears.

Cathryn Peters

THE WICKER WOMAN
531 Main Street   PO Box 61
Zumbro Falls, MN 55991
507/753-2006

Victorian era charm flourishes at THE WICKER WOMAN. Window boxes, lace curtains and antique wicker greet each visitor to this quaint studio. Owner Cathryn Peters is a self-taught wicker restoration specialist. She has woven her magic on time-worn cane and wicker furniture since 1975.

Peters is committed to perpetuating the nearly lost art of chair caning and wicker restoration through teaching, demonstrating, lecturing and writing.

With meticulous attention to detail she restores a variety of wicker furniture to its original condition. She preserves the integrity of each piece by duplicating the fine craftsmanship and quality materials used in manufacturing these exquisite pieces.

Whether you have an heirloom that needs repair or purchase a restored piece from Cathryn, you are assured of a quality product. Also offered for sale are cane and basket supplies and handmade deer antler baskets by Cathryn.

Catch a glimpse of the past in her quaint Zumbro Falls studio. Watch as she weaves – to preserve American wicker history.

Mother and Daughter lc.,
Glycerine Soaps
"A Matter of the Heart"

Extra Creamy
approx 4 1/2 oz.

4887 W. Mt. View Cir
Highland, Utah/Phone/Fax 801

What's so Great About Mother and Daughter Glycerine Soap?

Soaps made by Mother and Daughter start with a soap base that includes 100% vegetable oils. Unlike store bought soaps that can be full of harsh detergents and additives, Mother and Daughter uses only high quality essential oils, fragrance oils and natural fragrance oils. All of our colorants are FDA approved. We also 'superfat' many of our bars with special emollients such as jojoba oil, cocoa butter and shea butter. This makes for a rich bar that rinses away clean.

But soap isn't just about getting clean. It is about awakening your senses. The smell of the soap, the color and design, the feel of the rich lather on the skin.

All of these things enrich our spirit and sense of well-being.

A long relaxing bath with a finely crafted bar of soap can go a long way toward relieving the pressures and stress of a busy day. Where else can you get that kind of pampering for just the cost of a bar of soap?

So, spend some quality time with your soap. It will be good clean fun! And be sure to take good care of your soaps by letting them thoroughly air dry between uses.

Oh...and don't forget to wash behind your ears!

We use only the best ingredients available, but should irritation occur, discontinue use.

Chapter Six

Fun and Profit at Fairs and Shows

The crafts fair scene has changed a great deal in the past decade, but for many sellers, this remains the most popular and profitable method of selling art and handcrafts.

No one knows for sure how many art and craft fairs are presented annually, but most states present hundreds of craft fairs and festivals every year. The crafts fair scene has changed considerably in the past five years, however, due to the proliferation of imports and other commercial products now being introduced into many shows (see next section). Because of this, you will have to learn to be discerning about which events you enter and ask a lot of questions before plunking down your entry fee for an event. (See "Questions You Should Ask a Show Promoter" later in this chapter.)

As a serious craft fair seller, you will need to subscribe to some show periodicals (print) or find information on the Web about shows in your area. Depending on the publisher, show information may be regional or national in scope. Listings include the name and date of each upcoming event and who to contact for entry information. Some publishers also include expected attendance or sales figures from previous shows. (All the major show listing publishers now have Web sites, and you'll find links to them in the Resource Chapter.)

In speaking to Marsha Reed, publisher of *CraftMaster News*, she confirmed the flood of crafters now moving to the Web. In 1999, when Marsha began to include e-mail and Web site addresses on her show listing and subscription forms, about 30 percent of her subscribers and 70 percent of all show promoters were sending this information. By the end of 2001, 90 percent of Marsha's subscribers, and most of the show promoters as well, were working electronically.

How the Crafts Fair Scene Has Changed

In talking with Bill Ronay, a publisher of arts-and-crafts-show guides for several southern states, I learned that the number of quality events in each state he monitors has gradually dropped over the past five years, and the quality of the shows has also changed.

"Being in this business for nearly a quarter century, we have now entered into the 'next generation' of crafters," says Bill. "There are not only fewer shows, but many events are now suffering from the attitude of the 'buy-sell crafter,' and the quality of the industry, overall, is suffering."

Buy-sell crafters are those who buy cheap imports or other commercial items for resale at craft shows, sometimes adding little handmade touches, but often just reselling them in their original state. While there is nothing wrong in buying products for resale, the problem comes when such products are mixed into a show that is advertised as being populated with artists and craftspeople who are selling products they have made themselves. In this case, it is always the serious artist or craftsperson who suffers.

In one large show in Georgia, which draws tens of thousands of visitors over a period of four days, Bill was asked to comb the show to help spot the proliferation of buy-sell items. What he found was disturbing. "This particular show has been generous in the past in its tolerance of such activities, but now the craft dollar is being sliced thinner," he says. "A trend has been to supplement the 'handmade by the exhibitor' to 'handmade by anyone' and even wholesale purchase and delivery of 'well, it looks like it might be handmade.' Of the 250+ exhibits we reviewed, about ten percent were in this category to major extent, but most every exhibitor in this show had some form of item that was not totally made by them."

"The shows do seem to be changing," adds Marsha Reed. "We hear all the time how vendors are upset that there are not enough quality handcraft shows around any more. They get mad at the promoters and say they should know the difference. This is true, but there is so much buy-sell merchandise now that it's hard for even the best promoters to identify all of it. It is frustrating when they say they will only take product made by the vendor themselves and yet they don't ask for some form of proof the vendor actually makes the product. It used to be that some of the bigger shows required videos and such to prove they made their own product. Today even those shows have slacked off. For perspective, I think we have to look around and see how much is out there in the regular stores today verses several years ago. You didn't use to find handcrafts in stores unless they were a very unique store. Today we find them in the department stores, drugstores, the home improvement stores, on the Internet, on home shopping clubs and just about everywhere else. I have even seen handcrafts in grocery stores."

Reports from many craft fair sellers confirm that the buy-sell problem is evident at craft shows nationwide, as well as in craft malls (see Chapter Nine), so plan accordingly. The trickle-down effect of so many imported "handmade" items being available in every retail outlet in the country—and particularly now at craft fairs, malls and shops that used to sell 100 percent American crafts—is that the whole industry is much smaller than it was a decade ago. There are fewer shows because there are fewer people interested in sponsoring or promoting them, and there are now fewer shoppers as well because the Internet is changing the way people buy.

"Many show promoters have just gone on to do other things now," says Marsha. "I've noticed that many of the smaller shows have ceased to exist. It seems that cities have put so many regulations on the small show promoters that it is no longer fun to have these shows because there's such a pile of paperwork to do now. Many cities also require craft sellers to have a special license, and if they are selling any food, they have to go through inspections with the health department and get the special permits required. It used to be really fun and relaxing to go to the old home boutiques, see all the new items, visit with friends and buy some home baked goodies to take back home and give as gifts to friends, but those days are pretty much gone. Show promoters/presenters either move to bigger facilities that usually already have the permits and licenses required, or they just don't have the shows. We don't even see as many church shows or parks and recreation shows as we used to see." (See nearby sidebar for more craft show insight from Marsha.)

There are still some great craft shows in this country, but it will take effort to find them. As you become more professional in your approach to selling, you'll automatically become more selective about which shows you do. Quilt designer/maker Joan Bleakly, who exhibits in shows with her husband, a weaver, explains why they have reduced the number of shows they do. "We're limiting ourselves to the long standing quality shows patronized by people looking for the high-priced, handcrafted items," she says, "and we have seen our sales rise as a result. We no longer make items that would generally be found at an arts and crafts event, and limit ourselves to products that take considerable time, but also can command a much higher price."

In summary, today's craft sellers must assume that the industry has changed completely over the past decade and it will never again be the "good old days" where every show and shop across the country featured only American handcrafted merchandise. Imports are here to stay, and complaining about the way things are isn't going to do much good. "Rather than complaining about the success of someone who's selling products you don't appreciate, just try to make a living the best way you can," advises production artisan Susan Gearing, who has been selling crafts for twenty-five years. "Competition is what makes this country great. We don't live in a controlled economic system where people are guaranteed a living or freedom from competitive market influences, so deal with it. That's simply how it is."

The Advantages of craft Fair Selling

A good craft fair offers many opportunities to see, to touch, to learn, and to be entertained. Crafters who sell at shows go not just to sell but also to meet other creative people. They enjoy exchanging information and ideas and observing new techniques. Sometimes a craft fair becomes a pleasant vacation away from one's studio or workshop.

Even when sales at a fair are poor, there are benefits from this kind of selling that can't be obtained in any other way. Nowhere else can you get the kind of customer feedback to your work that you get at a craft fair. After exhibiting in a show, you will be completely exhausted, but you will also be exhilarated, and you will probably find yourself making plans for the next event on the way home. Yes, if you do one show, you will want to do another! That's because craft fairs are infectious by nature, and the kind of fever they carry is the kind you'll be happy to catch. Pleasures aside, there are several real advantages to craft fair selling. Here you can

- Test your prices
- Get consumer reaction to various products
- Learn which designs, colors or products are most appealing to buyers
- Do market research by visiting the booths of other sellers
- Expose your work to retailers who might want to buy from you at wholesale
- Take custom orders for higher-priced items you wouldn't want to make in quantity
- Meet new craftspeople and exchange information, ideas and techniques
- Lose some of your shyness
- Gain confidence and experience in selling

What to Know Before You Go

Here are several questions you should answer before entering a show. In parentheses after each group of questions, you will find a reference to where these questions are discussed in this or other chapters:

- Am I meeting all the tax and legal requirements involved in crafts fair selling? Do I need any kind of license? Are the rules different for me if I'm just a hobbyist and not really in business? (See Chapter Three.)
- What kind of show is it? Indoors, outdoors, juried, non-juried, country, contemporary, themed? How does my work compare to other work likely to be in the show? (See "Different Types of Shows" in this chapter.)
- If the show is juried, what will I have to do to be accepted into the show? (See "Show Promoters and Juried Shows" in this chapter.)
- How important is my craft booth to making sales, and what should I know before I create my display? (See "Designing Your Display" in this chapter.)
- Can I increase sales by demonstrating my art or craft during the show? And how can I get past my fear of facing the public to sell? (See Chapter Seven.)
- What kind of sales and attendance figures are available from previous shows, and how can I use these figures to estimate the amount of merchandise I should take to a show? (See Chapter Seven.)

Different Types of Shows

There are so many different kinds and types of art and craft shows, fairs and festivals that it's almost impossible to describe them. There are little shows and big shows, indoor shows and outdoor shows, juried shows and non-juried shows. Some shows feature contemporary art or crafts, some

Business Advice for Craft Show Sellers
from Marsha Reed, Publisher, Craftmaster News

"The crafting business is no longer a 'Mom & Pop' business. Profits are still there for the few who know how to market and have unique items, or can demonstrate at the shows, but the sales definitely aren't what they used to be. To be a successful crafts fair seller now, you need more than talent—you need some business sense.

"To get into many of the shows today, you must know how to fill out the applications correctly and even have the right kind of photographs of both your product and booth to show the promoters. When you get into the shows you must then learn how to keep a positive attitude (no matter what), and work hard at your business. You can't just sit back in your booth and expect to make sales. You have to learn how to talk to your customers, learn how to build a profitable mailing list, keep up on display skills, and stay up on changing market conditions. The thing that often breaks many vendors is their failure to make changes to their product line as times and consumer buying habits change.

"If you want to make it in today's market you must also take a few classes, read some books, and attend some seminars. I didn't get my education for business by going to school, but rather from business seminars and meetings. I joined many networking groups and several Chambers of Commerce. Through the chambers, I was able to get a good business education for free (with the exception of my chamber dues, of course). From speakers at chamber meetings, I have not only learned how to be a better networker, but have also gained skill in advertising, speaking, publicity, public relations, sales techniques, marketing, accounting and more.

"As a crafts publisher, I see crafters come and go all the time. Many do well; others don't. Some will be gone for several years and then reappear all of a sudden. Some just get burned out with the business because they want to do the creative end but not the business end. Others simply go on to other things. Then, as life changes for them, they eventually come back to their creativity because, once crafting is in one's blood, it's there to stay."

have only traditional or country items while others may sell only one kind of art or craft, such as miniatures, dolls and woodcarvings.

Some shows are costumed events with a special theme, such as Early American, Victorian, Ethnic, Renaissance, Pioneer or Native American. Others are themed around holidays such as Easter, Thanksgiving or Christmas, or are tied to a local community event such as a flower show, music festival or food fair.

Outdoor shows and fairs may be held in a park or parking lot, on the sidewalk in front of a shopping center, in a town square, at the county fair grounds or other open country area. Indoor shows are usually held in a school, church or civic center, in an individual's home, or in a shopping mall or exposition center.

Some shows are open to the public while others are juried (see below). Any widely publicized craft fair will attract an interesting variety of exhibitors, including hobbycrafters who are trying to break into the field or get additional selling experience, part-time sellers who have other jobs and count on craft fairs for extra income, and craft professionals who rely on such shows for a living.

Some shows are sponsored by a local art or craft organization, chamber of commerce or other civic group. Most of the professional juried arts and crafts shows, however, are produced by a couple of hundred show promoters who do this for a living.

Street Fairs and Church Bazaars

Such events generally attract beginning sellers and consumers who are looking for low-priced merchandise. Entry fees may be as low as $20. While such events can be great fun and are good for getting your feet wet as a seller, they are often unprofitable.

Serious sellers eventually find they need to stop doing small fairs and concentrate only on larger ones, preferably those that are juried events (see below). "It takes just as much time to set up, build inventory, and sell at a tiny show as it does a big one," says a crafter who has been selling at fairs for two years. "And the big ones mean so much more in terms of exposure and volume-dollar sales."

One crafter who began by selling at church bazaars later reported to me that her sales shot up eight times when she exhibited in a show that drew 8,000 visitors. "I learned I was simply exhibiting in the wrong kind of shows," she said.

Juried Art & Craft Shows

In a juried event, hopeful exhibitors must submit slides or photos of their work to prove it is of a type and quality desired for a particular event. In addition to a show's entry fee, there is often an extra, nonrefundable jurying charge. Nationwide, it seems that entry fees for small shows run between $50 and $125. More prestigious shows that attract thousands of people, however, may charge $300 to $500 per day or more.

Shows that are juried tend to have a loyal following of buyers because such shows have gained a reputation for high-quality art and crafts. This is particularly true of the annual craft festivals sponsored by art and craft organizations and associations throughout the country in which only members are allowed to exhibit and sell. Other juried shows, including those presented in shopping malls, convention centers and county fairgrounds, are open to sellers nationwide. Because of their high quality and buyer following they often have more applicants than exhibit booths or spaces. Many of these shows have between 200 and 700 exhibitors and attract 30,000 to 50,000 people.

Tip

"Be selective about the shows in which you will participate," says a professional basketmaker. "Look for a juried show with strict quality guidelines, and inquire as to how many of your type of craft will be participating. I prefer to be the only one who is doing baskets unless the look is entirely different."

Present Your Own Crafts Show

Jarmila, in Canada, learned how profitable it could be to present her own craft shows when she began to rent a community hall five times a year in April, May, October, November and December. The hall held seventeen tables, six of which she kept for herself. Unlike boutique presenters who often take a percentage of each seller's sales, Jarmila simply rented tables to other sellers whose products complemented her own. "If you do not charge an admission fee, make sure your crafter rental fee is sufficient to cover the rental of the hall, printing costs of promotional flyers and classified ads in community newspapers," she says. "Also make sure that each exhibitor collects and pays his or her own sales tax."

Mall Shows

Professional artists and craftspeople have mixed feelings about mall shows (juried events held in shopping malls nationwide). Being indoors is a great advantage over an outdoors show, but mall shows are not without problems. For example, if you try to do one of these shows alone, there is the problem of leaving your site unguarded as you bring in your merchandise. Although security is always promised, theft is not uncommom after the exhibit is closed for the day. Make sure your products are appropriate for this retail environment. Otherwise, after you get set up to sell, a nearby retailer may complain that your wares are causing them to lose sales. (Those who sell clothing and jewelry may not be accepted in mall shows for this reason.)

Before entering a mall show, ask how the show will be advertised. Some show promoters do this job while others leave it to the shopping mall. If advertising is poor, most of the people who come to the mall during the show will be there for some other purpose. They may see the craft exhibits as an interesting attraction to their shopping day, but any purchases they make are likely to be made on impulse, and only if they can be charged.

Tip

If a mall is loaded with people, it may be difficult for some to see your exhibit. One seller suggests stringing a banner across the top of your display that clearly tells people what you are selling. Another suggests displaying some objects on a tall stand or bookshelf so they can be seen above people's heads.

Renaissance Fairs

These outdoor events offer consumers a mixed package of food, entertainment and crafts exhibits or demonstrations. To sell here, you will need to design a special and very sturdy booth in the medieval theme. This could cost up to $2,000, says crafts business author James Dillehay. "Since you rent the space for most of the weeks of the show, you become a lessee or tenant," he says. "Management also takes a percentage of your sales. Sales can be slower than other kinds of craft shows because the renaissance fair is often an entertainment event first, and a place to buy crafts second."

Consumer Attractions

Be wary of shows that use artists and craftspeople as a drawing card for other events such as antique shows, concerts, outdoor picnics, horse races or carnival-type attractions. As one veteran craft fair seller told me, "We soon learned that the big celebration with the beer tent and carnival rides was not conducive to good sales."

A note about county fairs: While this is not a place to sell handmade items, putting work in a county fair exhibit is how many hobbycrafters get started selling. Thousands of people may see their work and the crafter and his or her family will take special pride in any ribbons that may be awarded. Often this experience gives the timid seller enough courage to enter that first crafts fair.

Flea Markets

Flea markets—sometimes called swap meets—enjoyed a great revival in America in the 1990s. Every product imaginable is now being sold through such markets. Presented in both indoor and outdoor settings, the quality of such markets can range from terrible to terrific. Entry fees may range from $20 per day to several hundred dollars a month. Flea markets are popular because they offer bargain prices and a chance to barter, a fact that makes them one of the least profitable markets for the average crafts seller. But there are exceptions, says Susan Ratliff, author of *How to Be a Weekend Entrepreneur.* She told me about one event in her area that draws over 45,000 tourists each weekend. "Of the 4,000 vendors who sell at this market, about one-fifth are crafters. I consistently see people who are selling items such as wooden coyotes, cactus mug holders, handpainted T-shirts and other tourist-type novelty items."

Show Promoters and Juried Shows

Let's say you want to enter a juried show. You send away for the application and, as you begin to complete it, you wonder if you're going to be accepted or rejected. Remember this: As a seller, the most important thing is not just that your work be up to standards required for a particular show, but that the show itself meets your requirements. Being juried out of a show doesn't necessarily mean your work is not good, only that it is not appropriate for sale at this particular show. Try another one.

Your Photographic Presentation

If a show promoter rejects you for reasons you don't understand, the problem may not be with your craft, but with the way you are presenting it to the show promoter, explains Marsha Reed, publisher of *Craftmaster News*, a California show calendar. "Many promoters are getting very picky, but the thing they look at the most is what your display may look like. When you send in photos of your work to be previewed for the shows, you should be as professional as possible. Do not put too many pieces together in one photo. Show promoters want to see the details in individual items. If you are not good at taking pictures of your product you may wish to hire a photographer to do the job for you. It will pay off in the long run."

Where to find an affordable photographer? Marsha suggests calling the photography department of local colleges. "By going to the colleges you get students who charge a fraction of what they will charge after graduation. Many will work for free, just for the experience or to make a great portfolio for themselves. The colleges will send their best student because the school's reputation is riding on that student."

What Show Promoters Want

According to one show promoter, the ideal exhibitor is "a special person who wears an optimistic smile despite torrential rains, sweltering heat, or buyers aimlessly roaming aisles searching for 'nothing in particular.'" Here are some things you can do to find favor with show promoters:

- Complete the show application neatly and professionally. Follow directions, sending exactly what the promoter asks for—nothing more, nothing less.
- Offer unique, quality crafts. Don't try to sneak in imported or commercial items.
- Be cooperative with show management and other exhibitors and attentive to your customers.
- Don't leave a show early. This is a mark of unprofessionalism that will irritate the show promoter (who will never hire you again) and hurt your fellow crafters.

I would add another: Don't bring small children to a show with you, then let them run around creating problems for other exhibitors. Like shop owners, craftsellers are *retailers,* and shop owners don't bring their children to work with them.

109

Questions You Should Ask A Show Promoter

"Promoters and car salesmen have much in common," says one artisan. "They want to sell you something and they will tell you anything to make the sale."

"Never let your 'desperation instinct' take over when trying to decide whether or not to do a show," cautions Bill Ronay. He recalls a couple of disastrous shows he once did on the Virginia Beach Boardwalk ("people don't carry much money in their bikinis") and a horse-racing festival ("we ended up in the parking lot a half mile from the track"). "Make every attempt to avoid falling prey to other people's greed," he emphasizes. "Be suspicious of any show promoter who comes on strong because he or she may simply be trying to fill up a show at the last minute due to cancellations."

"It's always a red flag if a promoter approaches you at a show," says Amy Detwiler, editor of *Sunshine Artist,* "because professional promoters don't tend to approach craftspeople. Craftspeople seek them out because they've heard good things about their shows." Here are some questions you should ask when considering any new show:

- What is your definition of "handcrafted?"
- Do you allow vendors to sell merchandise they have not made themselves?
- Is anything else being sold at this show besides art or crafts?
- What other shows have you done (type and location)?
- How long has this particular show been held?
- How many vendors return each year?
- Do you think my products are a good fit for your show?
- How many exhibitors are now signed?
- How many exhibitors are there in my art/craft category?
- How and where is the show being advertised?
- What is the expected audience? (If a first year show, ask how the figure was derived.)

Fairs That Charge Admission

Some crafters feel it is a mistake for fairs to charge admission. "This hurts the crafters," one complains. "The only ones making any money are the ones running the craft fair. A family of four that has to pay $12 or more to get in may not have money to buy crafts."

Other crafters think that some show promoters charge too high a price for their spaces. "Some of the finest crafters have given up the show circuit as a result," says a craftswoman in Vermont. "Crafters complain the show promoters don't advertise enough. Customers complain about the admission price because a show is really a place to sell, not a show."

The logic behind charging admission at a show is quite sound. In fact, it is the same as that used by mail order sellers who qualify their prospects by asking them to send a dollar for a brochure or catalog instead of giving it to them for free. Mail order sellers have learned that only those who are serious shoppers will send the dollar, while show promoters have learned that only serious shoppers will pay to get into an art or craft show. This qualification process automatically eliminates many curiosity seekers who never buy anything.

There will always be some promoters who are greedy, some who think they can "clean up" by sponsoring one high admission show in their area. Only the best show promoters survive, however, so in deciding whether to be in a show that charges admission, find out how many years the event has been held and how many exhibitors and shoppers have attended in past years. In many areas of the country, well-established shows that charge admission are the ones that attract the same serious shoppers year after year.

Designing Your Display

In designing a crafts display booth, you should strive to

1. Capture the attention of prospective buyers
2. Encourage them to stop, browse and get out without feeling trapped
3. Make it easy for you to sell to them

As you design your display, keep in mind how you're going to get everything packed into your vehicle, unloaded at the show, and back home again. Also consider who will help you with this work as well as cover base for you during the show when you need to take a break or have lunch. When the crowd gets heavy, you may need someone to help make sales, wrap purchases, watch for shoplifters or keep children's hands off fragile merchandise.

An eye-catching display will help you make sales, and it need not be expensive to be effective. For your first show, keep your display simple and portable. With each new selling experience, you'll automatically gain insight on refinements and improvements that can be made to grab buyers' attention and increase sales. "One's first display will never be the ultimate display because with growth many things change," confirms a seasoned show seller.

Barbara's "SPECIAL" Formula

Here's my "SPECIAL" formula for a good display. It should be:

S afe

P ortable

E ffective

C olorful

I maginative

A ppealing

L ively

Packing Tips

Moving all the individual items you plan to sell—without damaging them—can be a challenge in itself. One crafter uses baker's bread trays to move merchandise from show to show. These heavy cardboard trays (available through box outlets or paper supply houses) have handles and stack inside each other. Another seller uses banana boxes she gets from her grocer because they have hand slots for carrying and can be carried two or three at a time when lightly packed with smaller boxes of merchandise. Other wooden boxes or crates might do double duty for packing crafts and for display. Consider covering boxes with indoor or outdoor carpet. This will give a suitable background for display, and the carpet will serve as a shock absorber for crafts in transit.

Safe

Carefully critique your booth for customer safety. Will it stand up to the press of a crowd or a hard wind? What displays might fall over or break? Could your whole display topple, taking your neighbor's exhibit with it? You can save money by constructing your own display, but if you're not certain about its stability or balance, seek professional advice. If something should fall and injure a customer on another's property, the financial responsibility will be yours.

While on the topic of financial responsibility, I'll remind you to always ask show promoters what protection you will have against theft or damage to your crafts booth if it must be left overnight in a shopping mall or park. I recall one couple who told me they entered a large shopping mall show and lost everything when the mall caught fire one evening. They never thought it would happen to them, so they had no insurance for such a thing.

Damage to craft work sometimes comes in strange forms. A woman who exhibited corn dollies in a week-long outdoor festival lost hundreds of dollars of work one evening to squirrels who must have nibbled all night on items displayed on one table. Inclement weather can also cause loss. Any outdoor show is a calculated risk, so always be prepared for both wind and rain. Never leave work unprotected in a tent, because even new tents have been known to leak, and water can also seep in under the tent flap, ruining anything on the ground.

Portable

The ideal display will take little space in a vehicle, be easy to pack, transport, set up and dismantle. The average exhibit area is about ten feet square, but your display should be flexible in case you have to fit it into a smaller area. It should also be adaptable to changing conditions. (Example: How would you handle the challenge of tree roots, uphill slants, or pillars with electrical outlets?) "Prepare for surprises," advises one experienced seller.

Before trying to build your own booth, read craft magazines to spot ads from manufacturers who offer a variety of portable, modular, lightweight display booths and canopies, folding tables, collapsible carts and other quick-assembly display units. Tents and canopies generally feature snap-joint frames and they can be personalized with your business name and/or logo. An added advantage is the protection they offer from sun and rain. Before buying a canopy (expect to pay between $400 and $900), visit some craft fairs and talk to the exhibitors who use them to see how satisfied they are with the particular brand or model they're using. (Companies who make canopies, tents and other display items for craft fair sellers advertise in show listing periodicals and business magazines such as *The Crafts Report.*)

Tip

Be prepared to maintain and repair your exhibit and displays. Professional crafters advise that your crafts fair tool kit should include a wrench, hammer, pliers, nails, screwdriver, duct or masking tape, clamps and brackets, tie-down ropes or bungee cords, boards or woodblocks for leveling and backdrop weights. Setup/put-it-together items include thumb tacks, pins and twist ties, wire, tape gun, glue gun and fishing line (for invisible hangers).

Effective

Design your booth to keep customers exactly where you want them, whether it's in front of you, down the center of your booth or all around you.

An effective display will include merchandise that is displayed at several different eye levels (flat on a table, in containers, on one- or two-foot-high table props, portable riser displays, wall shelves or free-standing panels).

If you plan to hang artwork or other items on two sides of a wall unit, remember that you can see only one side at a time. Objects out of sight can easily be spirited away by mischievous children or light-fingered adults.

Remember that not everyone in a crowd will be honest. Display small, expensive pieces such as jewelry in a closed case. Or, instead of just laying jewelry on a piece of velvet or some other suitable background, make a fabric-covered A-frame display board that allows for tying items down, to be removed only when sold.

If you sell things that need to be touched or viewed close at hand, and customers do not have access to your work, you may be losing sales. In this case, you might consider an open display that allows customers entry, instead of trying to sell to them over a table or counter. Try to give this kind of display the illusion of a small shop, but never let the display itself overpower your work.

Colorful

To display vividly colored art or craft objects, place them against pale or neutral background colors. Give plainer pieces a background that emphasizes their shape or texture. When displaying individual pieces, also think *contrast*. For example, try glass against brick, straw with calico, fiber on wood, metal on acrylic, silver on velvet.

Carefully plan the use of color for table coverings, your costume and accent areas of your booth, being careful that the overall impression of your display does not compete with your products for prominence. Your exhibit will be enhanced by any special costume you can devise, preferably something that has your business name or logo monogrammed or painted on it (T-shirt, cap, apron, etc.). The consistency of your dress and display will make it easy for customers to remember you and describe your booth to friends.

"The public buys color—they are moved by it," says crafts business author James Dillehay. "Sure, you will always find a market for natural-colored work, but without the diversity of a wide and luxurious selection of color combinations, you can't compete with the vast array of products vying for your customers' dollars."

Imaginative

Emulate, but do not duplicate, the successful-looking craft displays you see at other shows. Add your own special touch to make your display different from everyone else's.

Look at your products with an objective eye to find a theme you can build on. Do you use ethnic designs? Practice a historic craft? Does your work fall into a particular period (Victorian, Early American, etc.) or is its style contemporary or country in nature? Can you build a theme around color? Shapes? Can you create an attractive vignette? (Ideas: dolls at a tea party, rocking horses inside a fence, soft sculpture animals in a woodland setting.)

Appealing

The foundation of your crafts display is just part of the challenge in making a good exhibit. Within the booth or display area, you will need a variety of appealing display props, organizers and attention-getters. Flea markets and antique shops will often yield delightful finds in the form of old hat racks, small trunks, shelf units, baskets, etc. Small items often need to be displayed in a bunch. Check your home for appropriate containers, from decorative

116

bowls and coffee mugs to baskets, flower pots and small crates and boxes. Nature items, from driftwood to hay bales, may greatly enhance displays of country products. Browse fairs and shops for more ideas. Note the texture and type of backgrounds behind certain products, the color combinations and the interesting accessory items used to hold or hang things. In stores, look at the kind of display cases and shelf arrangements used.

Do your products all look alike? If so, don't put everything out on display at once since many handcraft buyers like to think that what they are buying is unique, not mass produced. On the other hand, if you produce in quantity, yet make each item a little different in color or design, customers may appreciate seeing your whole selection so they can choose the one item that is just right for them. Experience is the best guide here.

Lively

Attract and appeal to buyers by teasing their senses with things in your exhibit area that move, sparkle, shine, make subtle sounds or release delightful scents. Make turntables revolve, let music boxes play, use mirrors to reflect, or move wind chimes or mobiles with the aid of a battery operated fan. Intermingle sachet packets with stitchery or sewn items, or hang spicy potpourri balls alongside Christmas ornaments. The idea is to prompt people to say or think, "Look!" "Listen!" or "What's that scent?"

Lighting is especially important to your display since the lighting in most indoor shows is terrible. Throw a spotlight on featured products or use lighted display cases for small items. Now owner of her own shop, decorative painter and designer Susan Young learned the importance of good lighting while selling at shows. "Whenever allowed by show management, I used one or two low-watt tasteful lamps that complemented my table covers and drew attention to certain items I was selling," she says. "The extra light really showed off detail work and literally drew customers into my booth."

To add a little activity to your booth, have a raffle box for a special prize or discount on a craft item that can be mailed to the winner after the show closes. This is a good way to capture names for your mailing list.

Display Props and Attention-Grabbers

Some craft fair sellers pick up commercial display units from local shop own-ers after a particular holiday season has passed. Christmas displays, in partic-ular, could be useful to many crafters. Such displays are usually thrown away after the season is over, so don't hesitate to ask for them or any other display cases in a store that you think would work for your products.

While you may wish to invest in some new display units (read ads in professional crafter magazines to find them), you can easily build a variety of inexpensive displays yourself. Here are some ideas to get you started:

- A-frame stands can be made by framing and hinging two sheets of quarter-inch plywood. Add stability with a chain at the bottom.
- Small modular units for special displays can be constructed from standard plumb-ing pipe and three-way elbow fixtures (see illustration A).
- Panels are adaptable to most any craft and are easily made in any size or shape from a pegboard, lattice or other lightweight materials. They are generally painted or covered with a textured fabric such as burlap. Craft items can be hung on decorative hooks, placed on shelves or tucked into hanging baskets.
- Cardboard or plastic boxes can be used first as containers to carry merchandise to a show, then as display props.
- A variety of decorative easel stands and holders are available from companies who supply gift shops. They are great for dis-playing decorative plates, pictures and many other items that need to be viewed in an upright position.

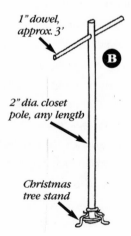

1" dowel, approx. 3'

2" dia. closet pole, any length

Christmas tree stand

- Poles are good for making floor or table stands to hang things on. Drill a one-inch hole near one end of a two-inch-diameter closet pole to any height desired, and stick a one-inch-by-three-foot dowel rod through the hole. Mount in a Christmas tree stand (see illustration B).
- Stepladders can be a good display prop for crafts that sit or hang, and they can be brightly painted or especially decorated to coordinate with a particular craft. For example, a rosemaler decorated two ladders, then placed shelves on the steps to provide an excellent display for the back of her large walk-in booth.
- Look for folding or specialty tables that allow for different configurations. Cover them imaginatively and completely to allow storage of merchandise underneath.

Tips on Protecting Displayed Items

Many shoppers carelessly handle items that can't take much handling before they break or become shopworn. In addition, people at fairs are often eating, drinking or smoking around a booth, further complicating exhibitors' problems. People who sell quilts and other fabric crafts are especially concerned about this problem. Here are some suggestions on how to handle it:

- A quilter has a sign in her booth that says, "Smoking is hazardous to my quilts!" She provides a sand-base ashtray in her booth and assertively tells people not to smoke or eat in it.
- A crocheter puts each of her items in a plastic bag, keeping just one sample of each item for touching and examining. Later, these samples are offered at reduced prices or discarded.
- When selling her quilts at shows, Denise Lipps always used this sign at right to discourage the handling of her work. A similar sign might also dissuade people

Food, Drinks, and Cigarettes make me NERVOUS because it takes 100 hours or more to make a QUILT!!

119

from handling soft sculpture, dolls and other fragile items.

• Another quilter displays one brightly colored open quilt in the back of her booth. On the center of her table is a portfolio of her designs, plus a couple of quilts in clear plastic bags. A note attached to each bag says, "Do not remove from package. Please see a salesperson for assistance." When showing a quilt, she takes it out in a way that many people can see it, but only one or two people at a time can touch it.

Chapter Seven

Learning How to Sell at Fairs

A Formula for Success: Quality Crafts + Affordable Prices + Attractive Booth + Friendly Attitude + Nice Personal Appearance + Effective Sales Strategies = Good Sales at a Fair

*W*hile selling does not come easy to most creative people, it should not be viewed as something scary. If you have a difficult time hawking your wares because you're shy, the good news is that you will become less and less shy the more people you meet face-to-face.

After her first experience at selling, a woman told me that while she was scared, she soon found that she enjoyed selling as much as crafting. "I also found that after selling many items, one negative response to my merchandise could very well have sent me home never to show my face or craft again. It was at this point that I had to learn not to take rejection as a personal affront."

If you plan to enter a few shows this year to earn a little extra money, remember that you will be completing with many others who are trying to earn a part- or full-time living from the sale of crafts. Although the competition from such professionals may be stiff, beginning sellers with nicely designed and beautifully crafted work can achieve good sales if they put a little time and money into the creation of a good display and learn some principles of selling.

Barbara's "SELL IT" Formula

This little SELL-IT formula will help you remember what to do when you're trying to learn how to sell:

S mile

E ntertain

L ook

L isten

I nterest

T alk

Smile

People are always drawn to friendly looking people, so when you notice someone who's looking your way, make eye contact with that person and *smile!* Don't bury your nose in a book when sales are slow. To look busy in your booth, Liz Murad suggests taking a notebook and mechanical pencil. "When it's a dog of a show, and you still want to look busy, scan through pages of your notebook and jot down reminder notes or ideas for new products," she says.

Do not sit in a chair and then get up as customers approach your booth because this gesture is threatening to some. "I have best results when I stand behind my display," says one seller. "If I must sit (as everyone needs to during a long day), I face the chair at an angle to the approach of my customers." Another option would be to sit on a high stool with a comfortable back on it. In this case, sitting from time to time would not be a problem because your eye level would still be close to that of the crowd.

Entertain

Many sales are lost by craft sellers who sit like lumps in their booths, arms folded across their chests in boredom. No sales? No wonder! It takes *action* to get sales! Successful salespeople in all fields *move*; they don't sit around waiting for money to fall into their laps.

Some fairs may not allow craft demonstrations, but for those that do, this can be a very good idea because many people go to craft fairs to be entertained. When you demonstrate your craft, you are automatically entertaining your audience, and if you can give people something no one else is giving them, they will give you not only their attention, but sales.

"Curiosity is a wonderful thing," says a needleworker. "I discovered I could increase my sales (115 percent at one show) by demonstrating. When people see a few other people gathered around a table, they want to stop and see what's going on. Even if they don't buy right then, they see my work and learn of the custom services I offer."

 TRY THIS: Think of some little "something" you could make from scraps to occasionally give to children as an attention-getting device. When you see bright-eyed children who seem entranced by something in you display, give them something to keep or just hold for a few minutes. Strike up a conversation with them, telling them how you made the object or something about the material it's made of, or some interesting thing about your craft's history.

Now you are being entertaining, and this will automatically attract the attention of nearby adults, bringing them into the conversation and nearer your displays as well. Once your prospective customers discover that you are as interesting as your work, you will automatically increase the odds of making a sale. (Yes, you are an *interesting* person or you wouldn't be involved in crafts to begin with!)

Look

Watch people as they approach your exhibit. Try to discover what interests them most. If they merely pause before passing by, pay attention to what they were looking at when they paused. Is something lacking in this area to draw them in? When people pause, and then stop, observe which objects they pick up to examine. During the show, take time to observe the exhibits of other sellers, paying particular attention to those that have the largest crowds. What seems to be attracting so many people, and how can you employ the same idea in your own booth?

 TRY THIS: Study the reactions of people as they look at your work. Do these reactions make you feel that your crafts are priced too low, too high, or just about right? Although your feelings here are an excellent guideline in pricing, you should exhibit in two or three shows before making drastic changes in your price.

Listen

Pay attention to the questions and comments people make while in or near your exhibit. Such remarks will provide clues on what you need to do to increase sales or correct a problem that may be deterring sales. Brace yourself for negative feedback from critical people who do not appreciate fine craft work. It's hard to take criticism, but you need to listen to your critics to get new ideas on how to improve your work or make it more salable. Just don't take it to heart.

Why Some People Don't Buy
(Comments Overheard by Sellers)

- "I think I'll shop around a bit . . . I'm looking for something unique."
- "There's too much of one particular theme in this show (country, calico, dried flowers, etc.)."
- "It's the same old stuff as last year—I want something new and different."

If you get really annoyed at someone, you might quote Zeuxis (400 B.C.). Once, when he was criticized for something he had done, he said (smugly, I'm sure), "Criticism comes easier than craftsmanship." Remember that the next time you hear a discouraging word, and smile to yourself. Your most appreciative buyer may be right on your critic's heels.

Interest

Appeal to your customers by offering products that are beautifully presented or packaged, ready for gift-giving. Irene Haddow has the right idea. She makes soft sculpture snowmen packaged in clear cellophane bags with snowflakes tied with raffia. "Then I add my hangtag, which can be used as a gift tag," she says. "This makes a nice ready-to-give gift item. So many times people comment on the nice presentation, not to mention the fact that I get so many customers as a result of their seeing someone going by with my snowmen in clear bags."

Also give your customers reasons to buy by working on their subconscious mind. People don't go to a crafts fair with a list of items they plan to buy; they go to browse and have fun. To sell more products, make a variety of small signs containing "Buy Me!" suggestions. Some signs might give ideas on how to use a product ("A great stocking stuffer!" or "Perfect for display outdoors"). Others could remind buyers of an impending gift obligation ("For Your Valentine," "For Someone Who Has Everything," or "The Perfect Mother's Day Gift!"). People who see such signs are likely to think, "Why, Grandma would love that," or "I forgot we need a teacher's gift," or "I never thought of something like that for Mom." Sometimes people who aren't as creative as you need a suggestion or a little nudge.

If you don't own a computer, ask a friend to print professional-looking signs for your display, and check out the variety of plastic sign holders available at office supply stores or in paper supply catalogs such as Paper Direct (see Resource Chapter). If you've had an article written about you, get it blown up to a larger size and mount it as an extra attention-getting display in your booth.

The way items are displayed can send messages to buyers that either encourage or discourage sales. For example, small stacks of fabric say "Thumb through—we're interesting," while the same items stacked too high may make buyers fear that the stack will collapse if touched. Representative samples of related items on a table suggest "There is more where these came from," while a table cluttered with too many unrelated items is the mark of an amateur seller. If your crafts can be handled without damage, encourage prospective buyers to pick them up. Sometimes the very feel of an object in the hand will prompt a purchase.

Tip

The desire to buy can be snuffed out in an instant by things totally unrelated to your work. For example, non-smokers may avoid the displays of exhibitors who smoke, while clothes-conscious individuals may be turned off by a seller's inappropriate dress or untidy appearance. Timid buyers may fear aggressive sellers, while gregarious people may resent exhibitors who appear aloof. You can't win them all, but you can strive for a happy medium that will appeal to most of your buying audience.

Talk It Up

Sales often begin with simple conversation, and you don't have to sell, just *talk*. (This will be easier to do if you remember that some buyers are prob-

What Sellers Hear Most Often from Browsers

"These are cute . . . how do you make them?"

"This is nicely done . . . but I won't pay that for it."

"Pretty . . . you do good work . . . could I have the pattern?"

"Beautiful . . . but I don't have the money."

"Lovely . . . but I really don't need it."

Crafters Lament: "If I only had a dime for every compliment I got!"

ably as shy as you are.) Also remember that many people shop at craft fairs so they can meet the people who are making the products being offered for sale. Talking to the artist is half the fun! "Be sure to greet every customer politely and briefly explain your line to see if they express interest," a folk artist advises. "I've had show attendees say that I was the only crafter who spoke to them when they walked a show."

"I like showing at art/fine craft shows because I believe there is nothing like the artist's presence and enthusiasm to entice people to look closer (and hopefully buy!)," says bead artist Sherrill Lewis. "This also gives me instant feedback on customers' reactions to price, color, design, and more."

When someone appears interested in a particular item in your display, volunteer some interesting information about the product's unusual materials, origin, name or usefulness. This will encourage bystanders to ask questions and give you the chance to share your enthusiasm and sell without really trying. Be prepared to handle all questions that may arise, from "Do you sell on consignment?" to "Can you make it in blue, instead of red?" and "How soon can you deliver twelve dozen?" (Just kidding!) You may, however, be approached by shop owners who will want to know if you sell at wholesale prices, so do be prepared to answer this question and know how long it would take you to deliver certain items in quantity.

Financial Tips

How will you accept and store money received from sales at a fair? Be sure to hide your cash box from view. Example: A seller who uses rustic apple crates to display her work turns one of the crates toward the back of the table with pen, paper, cards and other items hidden from customer's view.

Another crafter told me how she designed a special "money apron" with a secret zipped pocket to hold checks and large bills. This pocket was covered by a larger cobbler pocket. Smaller pockets were added to hold dollar bills and change. Here are some special tips on accepting payments from customers:

Accepting Cash. When customers pay cash, never put a large bill into your cash box until change has been given. Don't give people an opportunity to say, "But I gave you a twenty, not a ten." Prove the fact by showing them the original bill, still lying outside your money box. (Remember, there are con artists everywhere.)

Accepting Checks. If you take a check for merchandise, be sure to ask for identification and note the individual's driver's license number on the check. Also get a telephone number and address if it's not printed on the check.

Some retailers ask customers for a credit card number as a credit reference. But many consumers now refuse to do this because giving their credit card number to another individual leaves them open to fraud. And having this number does a crafts seller no good since a bounced check can't be covered by charging the same amount to a customer's credit card. Therefore, what you might want to do is simply ask to *see* a credit card for reference. Check the name, but don't copy the number.

Finally, don't cash checks for anyone, and don't let them write a check for an amount larger than the purchase, requiring you to give change. To protect the checks you do have, endorse them on the spot, "For deposit only."

Accepting Credit Cards. Although you might like to offer your customers the privilege of charging their purchases to a credit card, you may find it difficult to obtain merchant status from your bank. The situation is improving, but because many banks still consider homebased businesses to be risky, merchant status is often difficult to get. Curiously, the smaller your community, the easier it may be to get this service. If you're known in your community, have good credit history or a track record as a business owner, you may have no problems at all.

A better option, perhaps, would be to join a crafts or home-business association in order to get merchant status. Such organizations make special arrangements with banks that are favorably inclined toward home-based businesses, and sign-up costs and transaction rates are often better than anything you could get on your own. After a crafter e-mailed me saying she had been told it would cost her $750 to add credit card service to her Web site, I referred her to the National Craft Association (NCA), which offers its members an affordable credit card service. The next day, she told me she had joined NCA and her total cost for getting set up with merchant service was just $175. For more about your charge options as a Web site owner, see Chapter Twelve.

A lengthy discussion of this topic is beyond the scope of this book, but you'll find more information about the ins and outs of getting merchant status in *The Crafts Business Answer Book*. Many articles on this topic will also be found on small business sites on the Internet.

Selling Tips

Part of the secret in learning how to sell is understanding what makes the average person buy. For example, most people want comfort, ease, luxury and convenience. They may also like to buy things, even when they can't afford them. Appeal to these instincts, and let people know how your products can satisfy their needs and desires.

As a seller, it is your job to make your customers feel important. Although you may feel like the star at a crafts fair (having created all those beautiful things), it's the customer who counts. If your sales are good, figure that you're doing something right, and keep doing it. If they're not so good, look at your work more objectively, not as its creator, but as a prospective buyer.

Try to figure out what's wrong with it. Ask yourself if you would buy it at the prices marked. If not, why not? Then ask yourself if you are making what you want to make because it gives you pleasure to do so, or if you are producing crafts with buyers in mind. It is *their* needs, not yours, that must be satisfied if you are to succeed as a seller of handcrafts.

Always pay attention to what your competition is doing. Production artisan Susan Gearing emphasizes the importance of responding to the competition wherever it comes from and whatever the quality. "The customer votes on trends in the business with every sale, and it is up to us to discern the meaning of those votes and respond to them with products devised accordingly. This business is ever-changing, and that is what has kept me in it for so many years," she says.

"Many crafters are stuck in the 'old mode,'" says Marsha Reed, publisher of *Craftmaster News,* a show listing periodical for professional craftspeople on the West Coast. "They haven't learned the importance of being business like. The 'I-just-want-to-make-my-product-and-sell-it' routine doesn't work any longer. If you don't have the right products, the right signage, or a professional look, buyers don't pay attention. You need the right colors, too—most crafters lack a focal point in their booth. At a fair, you've got three seconds to get the customer's eye on a 10 × 10 booth. If there are 400 booths in a show, you've got to catch them immediately or they're gone."

Coping with Copycats

"A big problem the craft world faces is that there is so much duplication of designs," a basketmaker told me. "Any new idea is quickly copied by crafters and then offered for sale at lower prices. Before long you can see the same item at every other booth in every craft show around."

What's interesting about this statement is that I first heard it thirty years ago. Nothing has changed in this department, except that people have become more bold in their copying.

Every craft seller hates them: the people who saunter up to a booth, pull out a paper and pencil, and begin to copy the designs found on exhibited products—or worse, snap pictures.

Taking Custom Orders

"The crafters who bring home the most money are the ones with a diverse inventory," says a tole painter who makes "sure money" by accepting special orders. "That's money in my pocket and customers are getting something made especially for them," she says. "Many crafters think this is a bother and almost get insulted because a customer wants something a little bit different from what is already made, but shoppers are so individual. We need to listen to what they are saying."

If you decide to take a custom-design order, remember that some people will order something, then decide later they don't want it after you have spent several hours and many dollars in materials. That's why you need to either (1) ask for a down payment sufficient to cover your actual costs (to be kept if the customer later cancels) or (2) make sure your custom-designed item is something that can be sold to someone else.

One crafter told me that at the last show she did, there were signs around the building stating PLEASE NO PHOTOS OR SKETCHES, but people ignored them, and she had two people in her booth sketching her work.

Another crafter reported in a magazine article that she has had some very rude and inconsiderate people stand in her booth and draw right in front of her. "I made them mad when I asked them to leave my booth," she said, "but at least they left."

 TRY THIS: If you see someone with a camera taking pictures of you or your booth, ask for identification. Unless that person is with a newspaper or magazine, tell him or her to stop taking pictures at once. If your craft designs are copyrighted, emphasize that you have legal right to sue anyone who copies your designs.

The minute you put a good idea out there, the public will copy it. So the secret is to come up with new ideas every year because then you'll be ahead of the copycats. By the time they get around to copying you, you have new merchandise. Or, as one crafter puts it, "As soon as you have a new design or product, get it out there, saturate your market area all the while dreaming up something new or a new twist on the old."

What to Do When Things Aren't Selling

What should you do when you've created something you think is wonderful, but no one wants to buy it? The first thing to try is another marketing outlet because different buyers frequent different types of outlets. "If a product doesn't sell at a craft show, I take it to my gift shop in town where I have things on consignment," says Suzanne Lloyd, The Stuffed Cat. "I've learned that something that won't sell at a crafts fair one day may sell the next day at the shop, and vice versa. I've also taken things out of the shop that weren't selling and placed them in a show where they sold at once." Suzanne has another "secret marketing outlet" that works very well for her. She says she often sells more out of the trunk of her car than she does at a show. "I always take my new crafts with me because someone is always stopping me to ask what I'm doing now. All I have to do then is open the trunk of my car to make a sale!"

When a product isn't selling you have three other choices: Stop trying to sell it, change it, or make something else. Here are four ways you can change a product to make it more appealing to buyers:

1. Change your prices.

2. Change the materials being used.

3. Change your colors or designs.

4. Change the name or function of your product.

As explained in Chapter Five, the price you place on a product has a great deal to do with whether it will sell or not. Before you even think of lowering the price of a hard-to-sell product, try first to change it in some way to make buyers feel it is worth more to them.

The type and quality of materials you use in your work automatically determine your market and the prices you can charge for it. Some materials are ordinary or plain, while others are unusual or luxurious. When you elect to work with common materials, buyers may expect your prices to be common as well. When you use luxurious or exotic materials, however, you automatically attract more affluent buyers.

For example, you can either make teddy bears for children, using inexpensive washable furs from your local sewing store, or make designer bears for collectors, using expensive imported fur such as mohair. Whereas a teddy bear for kids might sell for $15 to $25, collectors will pay ten times this price for a one-of-a-kind bear. If you make furniture or wooden accessories, you can either use a common wood like pine and price it for the general public, or use uncommon or exotic woods that will appeal to buyers with bigger pocketbooks.

Even when you are using the right materials for a product, it may not sell if your colors or designs are wrong for the times. Stay aware of what's hot and what's not where colors are concerned, and strive always for more originality in your designs.

What you call your products has a great deal to do with whether they will sell or not, so try calling them something other than what most people might call them. For example, let's assume that you make wheat weavings. They might sell at higher prices if you were to present them as "Wheat Art Sculptures" or "Wheat Art Collectibles." That's because some people automatically expect to pay more for a product if they feel they are buying "art" instead of "craft." To further illustrate, a wheat weaving affixed to a plaque might be perceived as a "craft" while a wheat weaving in a shadow box behind glass might be considered "art." (And the extra benefit is that this product won't be soiled after it has hung on the wall for a couple of years.)

To change the function of a wheat weaving presently being sold as a plaque, consider placing it in a box with a recessed top so the arrangement is permanently preserved under glass. Such a box could be lined in leather or turned into a velvet-lined jewelry box. Now you've not only changed the function, but the name as well. And by adding a high-quality music mechanism that might add less than $10 to your materials cost, you could easily ask four times the price for this product because now the product has become a *handcrafted music box.*

Wheat weavings also make charming Christmas ornaments. The same people who aren't interested in another picture to hang on the wall may find it hard to resist buying another ornament for their tree. Or, think jewelry, always of interest to most women. Think pendants and earrings and designer pins, and remember that the quality of your metal findings will determine the price you can ask for jewelry. People will always pay more for gold-plated or sterling silver jewelry.

As you can see, price, material, color, design and a product's name and function will all work together where sales are concerned. Apply the above logic to your craftwork and see what happens.

Make Something Else

A reader in West Virginia who makes pine cone wreaths wonders why people aren't buying. "Many people tell me my work is the most beautiful, original and professional looking of its kind," she says. "Although it is priced below other work of inferior quality, people still won't buy. Why?"

Maybe it's because pine cone wreaths are too common in West Virginia, or maybe wreaths are considered a seasonal (Christmas) item by most buyers, or maybe buyers think they can do this craft themselves. It's hard to tell, but what is obvious is that this crafter is going to have to go outside her own area to sell with any success because she is meeting buyer resistance.

If it were me, I would first raise my prices to allow for wholesaling, then I'd make the effort to drive to the nearest large city to seek out high-quality shops that might place orders. I would begin to study available resources to find Appalachian or country shops in other areas of the country that cater to tourists. I'd also think about making up kits of materials and instructions for people who want to make wreaths themselves. Finally, I'd start thinking about other products I could make from pine cones, concentrating on products others aren't selling.

Sometimes the only logical solution to sluggish sales is to make something else. Consider the following letter I once received from a woman who crochets:

"I am not progressing in my moneymaking endeavors. I crochet and I have been trying for ten years to make it pay for itself, but at no time have I ever made a profit. I make the selling price three times the cost of materials, and I do not charge for my time, yet somebody is always sure to say an item is too expensive. A baby sacque and cap sells for about $20. Imagine what the true price would be if I tacked on the cost of the eight hours or more it took me to crochet it? To say I am beginning to get discouraged is putting it mildly. However, my natural optimism tells me there is a pot of gold at the end of the rainbow, so I keep plugging away."

I understand this crocheter's reluctance to give up her favorite craft, but if she wants to make money (and I don't mean just sell things, but make a *profit* from the hours put into them), she must begin to think in new directions. Profit rarely comes from making crocheted baby booties and other ordinary items because thousands of women know how to make them, and too many are selling them at giveaway prices at local fairs and bazaars. The serious crocheter interested in making money cannot compete in this kind of market, so the obvious thing to do is explore a different one by offering a different type of product.

For example, instead of using baby yarn to crochet common baby items, consider using fine thread to crochet small (three- to five-inch) pictures of dogs, cats, Victorian ladies or flowers as stand-alone designs that could be framed under glass. Now you're talking "contemporary art" that could sell for $25 or more. Consider jewelry, too. How about a miniature work of art that could be "framed" inside a pendant?

Whatever your craft, if you're not selling at a profit after a certain length of time, it may be that you're simply in a rut on the wrong road to sales success. Let this be your signal to stop and think about new roads you might explore. As any successful seller will tell you, changing directions in midstream is all part of the fun of selling what you make.

Tip

Instead of waiting for a pot of gold that may never appear, make some changes. As someone once said, you cannot expect different results if you keep doing the same thing. Creative ideas will come if you make an effort to stretch your imagination. To do this, pay attention to what others are doing. Read. Network. Experiment. Turn left instead of right. Ask "what if?" and "why not?" Dare to be different!

Reselling Earlier Buyers

A successful strategy used by many craft fair sellers is to send a postcard announcement of their next craft fair appearance or a new brochure to everyone who has ever purchased something at a fair. If you do the same shows each year, many of your customers might come back to see you if you send them a personal invitation. Sales at a fair will always increase in proportion to the number of years you have participated in that event. The better your customers know you, the more apt they are to buy from you. A mailing list will also be handy should you later decide to hold a home boutique, start classes, or start selling crafts through your own mail order catalog.

If you are building an e-mail database of all your customers, you can save money by sending e-mail announcements of your upcoming shows and the new products you'll be featuring at each. If you have a Web site, regular e-mail announcements are an absolute necessity if you want to encourage sales by mail.

Some craft fair sellers send a letter and a flyer to their buyer list with the suggestion that they place an order now for pickup at their next fair appearance. One seller told me how well this had worked for her: "Twice a year, I send everyone a list of all my upcoming shows—one for fall and winter, one for spring and summer. I give these customers a 10 percent discount when they come to my next show, and I've had 30 percent repeat sales so far. Once a year I also run a 20–30 percent-off sale on leftover fall and Christmas items after my last show on December 8."

Keeping Craft Show Records

It's important to make a written record of all sales. Try using a simple carbon interleaved sales slip book. For each item sold, write its name or code number, any information such as size or color that you wish to monitor, price and applicable sales tax. (Consider the use of removable price tags that bear the code number of items in your line—helpful for tallying sales by category at day's end.) Keep one copy of the sales slip and give the other to your customer. By keeping records of each product sale you make, you can learn which of your products sell best and which sizes, styles or colors are most popular. This information will enable you to plan for future shows.

How can you estimate the number of sales you will make at a show? It helps to know how many people are expected to attend. At one time, teddy bear designer Jan Bonner figured she made one sale for every 75 shoppers at a show, but as her prices increased, her percentage of sales decreased. "The more specialized your product, the more potential customers needed," she said. As competition from other bear sellers increased, Jan continued to raise her prices and eliminate smaller shows that were not targeted exclusively to teddy bear collectors. "If I'm going to enter a nontargeted craft show, I figure I need an expected audience of at least 25,000 for the show to be profitable. Even then, I would not expect to sell more than a hundred bears at such a weekend show."

That translates to a mere .004 percent, so when a crafter complained to me that she was making only one sale for every ten people who showed interest in her exhibit, she had no idea how well she was doing. Making one sale out of ten translates to a 10 percent sales response, which is unusual to say the least. Another beginner complained that she had "five lookers for every buyer," but that's a 20 percent buy response, which is *phenomenal*.

When I was selling my books by mail, if I could consistently sell a book to one out of every five people who asked for my brochure, I would have been delighted, not to mention rich. More often than not, I was lucky to get an order response of only 5 percent. Beginning crafters would be lucky to get a similar sales response at shows.

To learn how well (or poorly) you are doing at craft fairs, start recording the following information on each show you do:

- Name and date of show and where presented
- Number of sales you make at the show. (Individual items, not dollars).
- Total dollars generated at the show.
- Number of people who attend the event. (The figures you get from a show promoter are apt to be on the high side, but any estimate will be better than none.)
- Number of exhibitors.
- Other pertinent facts. (Professional craft sellers keep very detailed records about every show they enter because this information helps them decide whether it will be profitable to enter the same show again in the future. Note: such things as the weather, current economy, amount of advertising or publicity the show got and any other factors that you think affected your sales.)

How to Estimate Sales at a Show

Once you have some figures to work with, start a worksheet to record the figures you will get from the following four-step arithmetic process. I believe that your ability to keep and analyze craft fair sales records will have much to do with your success as a crafts fair seller. Few if any crafters keep the kind of records I am suggesting here, but this is the same kind of arithmetic that I and other mail order sellers use to calculate the profitability of a direct mailing. I may be wrong, but I believe you can do the same thing with fairs and shows.

I used to make several large direct mailings a year, usually mailing 2,500 to 5,000 mail pieces at a time. Prior to making a mailing, I could determine whether it was likely to be profitable or not because I had kept detailed response records of every mailing made in the past. By knowing the percentage of people who normally ordered, and the dollar amount of my average sale, I could closely estimate the number of orders I would get from each new mailing, as well as the total dollars the mailing was likely to generate. By comparing these figures to what it would cost me to print and mail each piece, I could then decide whether a particular mailing was likely to be profitable or not.

If you would like to try this idea, here are the figures you should record on your "Sales Analysis Worksheet" (see sample worksheet nearby).

1. After each show, tally your sales and divide the total dollars by the number of sales you've made. (Not the number of individual items sold but the number of customers who have made purchases.) This will give you the dollar amount of your average sale. Let's say you sell a variety of items priced from $5 to $50. The following examples illustrate how your average sales figure might change from show to show:

Craft event #1: $182 divided by 24 sales = average sale of $7.58

Craft event #2: $436 divided by 30 sales = average sale of $14.53

Craft event #3: $1,468 divided by 40 sales = average sale of $36.70

To find the size of your average sale for all three shows, total the three average sale figures ($58.81) and divide by three ($19.60). Thus, with a range of products priced between $5 and $50, it would be reasonable to expect that your average sale at any future show would be approximately $20.

2. After each show, divide the number of sales by the number of people in attendance to get a percentage figure of your average sales response. Examples:

Craft event #1: 24 sales divided by 2,500 shoppers = .010% sales response

Craft event #2: 30 sales divided by 10,000 shoppers = .003% sales response

Craft event #3: 40 sales divided by 25,000 shoppers = .002% sales response

To find the average, add all percentage figures (.015) and divide by three to get .005, which is less than half a percent. Adjust this *average sales response figure* as you continue to do shows. The more shows you record, the more reliable your figures and estimates will become.

3. To estimate the number of sales you might make at your next crafts show, multiply the expected number of shoppers by your latest average sales response figure.

Using the above average sales response figure of .005 percent and an estimated 7,500 shoppers expected, you would multiply 7,500 C .005 to get 38 sales (rounded off).

4. To estimate the number of dollars you might generate at your next crafts show, multiply the estimated number of sales times your average sales figure. Using the above figures, you would multiply your estimated 38 sales times your average sales figure of $19.60 to get a total of $745 in expected sales.

There is yet another figure (factor) that will affect the number of sales, and that is the number of exhibitors at a particular show. For example, if 5,000 people attend a show populated by 200 exhibitors, it's only logical to assume that each exhibitor will make more sales than they would if the show were to have 400 exhibitors. That's why you should also keep a record of the number of exhibitors at each show in which you appear. Even though all these figures will be mostly rough estimates (since you'll never know for sure how many people attend any given show), they are nonetheless valuable. After a while, a study of these figures will give you a reliable picture of what you can expect to sell at any given show, and this will help you figure out how much merchandise to take to each event.

Sales Analysis Worksheet

Name of Show	Event #1	Event #2	Event #3	Average
Date of Show	Dec. 14, '01	Jan. 23, '02	Apr. 10, '02	
Total Sales	$182.00	$436.00	$1,468.00	
Divided by Number of Sales	24	30	40	
Equals Average Sale	$7.58	$14.53	$36.70	$58.81 ÷ 3
Average of Several Shows				= $19.60
Number of Sales	24	30	40	
Divided by Number of People attending event	2,500	10,000	25,000	
Equals Sales Response Percentage (rounded)	.01%	.003%	.002%	.015 ÷ 3
Average of Several Shows				= .005%

Calculations

1. To get SIZE OF AVERAGE SALE, divide total sales by number of sales.
2. To get SALES RESPONSE PERCENTAGE, divide the number of sales by the number of people attending the event.
3. To estimate NUMBER OF SALES AT NEXT SHOW, multiply expected number of shoppers by your latest sales response figure.
4. To estimate NUMBER OF DOLLARS AT NEXT SHOW, multiply estimated number of sales times dollar amount of your average sale.

Evaluating the Profitability of Shows

Once you've done a round of art or craft fairs, you will probably plan to enter some of the same shows again the following year. To decide which shows were the most profitable, you will need to keep additional records. For each show, keep track of your booth fees and travel expenses so you can calculate an "expense percentage figure" for each.

For example, if your expenses for a nearby show were $150 for the entry

141

fee and $120 for gas, motel and meals, total expenses would be $270. Divide this figure by total sales for the show—let's say they were $2,872—to get an expense percentage figure of 9 percent. On another larger show several hundred miles away, your booth fee might be $395 and travel expenses $600, for a total of $995. If your sales here were $3,500, your selling expenses would be running 28 percent of sales, which common sense tells you is too high for profitability. In comparing the two shows, you can see the smaller, nearby show was more profitable, even though overall sales were lower. When you do this show again, you might increase sales by improving your display and selling methods and taking a larger inventory of products, some priced a bit higher than before.

Here is a simple formula used by some craft show sellers. They look at what it costs to enter a show and figure they need to sell ten times that amount to cover all their expenses and yield a good profit. For example, if the entry fee for a show is $250, gross sales should be $2,500.

Although this rule-of-ten has long been common in retailing, I think few craftspeople today will be able to realize craft fair sales of ten times the amount of their entry fee. There are just too many shows and not enough buyers to go around. It never hurts to aim high, however, so start with this simple "profit formula" and see how it works for you. In the end, the most important thing is that you know what it costs to make and sell your products, so you can determine whether you're making a true profit or not. By keeping good records, you may find that some craft fairs are more or less profitable than others, that some of your products are far more profitable than others, and that perhaps you might be better off trying other sales outlets altogether.

Take Marj Bates, for example. She makes glass beads, jewelry, glass knobs and more. "By doing regular studies of my sales, I learned how to plan what to sell and where to sell it," she says. "The first time I asked myself if I was selling more (dollar-to-dollar) of glass beads or glass knobs, it was astounding. The answer was right there in my sales figures. My glass knobs were definitely the winner, and this ultimately led me into the production of Make-A-Knob kits as well as Make-A-Finial kits. These are sold both on my Web site at retail as well as to distributors."

The year Marj seriously began to analyze the profitability of individual shows, she also ruled out 60 percent of them. "Even though the money was okay, I felt my time could be used better elsewhere," she concluded. "I also admitted that I was just getting tired of doing shows. There are a few shows I love because I'm with my peers, but other shows are drudgery, even though the money is good. It took courage to drop some of the shows, but I felt that new doors of opportunity would open, and they did. I've now learned that you can't open a new door until you close one."

One new and very profitable door that opened for Marj when she cut down on her shows was the door to her own house. Read her success story in the next chapter to learn how she sells thousands of dollars' worth of products every year from her homebased gallery.

Chapter Eight

Selling Handcrafts from Home

If you must stay close to home or don't want all the work in involved in doing craft fairs, selling from your home or that of a friend may be the perfect solution for you.

*D*o you dream of owning a little craft shop of your own up on Main Street? If so, you're not alone. Most crafters think a gift or craft shop would be lots of fun, but few have any real understanding of how much time and money it takes to start and operate a retail store. Instead, they tend to see the romantic side of retailing, imagining themselves at work at their art or craft behind the counter, talking to customers from time to time as they browse in the shop. They look forward to decorating for holidays and figure they will rack up extra profits from the sale of their own work. Unfortunately, it doesn't work that way. Running a shop is a full-time job, and constant interruptions from customers make craft production difficult if not impossible. Because some of my readers have managed to do this with success, however, I've added some guidelines for would-be retail shop owners at the end of this chapter.

While I would not encourage the average crafter working alone to open a shop uptown (or downtown, as the case may be), a cooperative craft shop owned and managed by several artisans is another matter entirely and a topic I've discussed in Chapter Eleven. For now, however, let's explore ways you can have the fun of retailing without the financial responsibilities and worries of a regular retail shop, through

- A homebased shop or studio
- Open house sales
- Home parties (Party Plan Style)
- Holiday boutiques

Shops and Studios

Before opening a shop in your home or in an outside structure on your property, you need to consider legal matters such as zoning (see sidebar) and think about how a homebased shop will disrupt your personal or family life. Some artisans open year-round shops in their home and invite shoppers during regular business hours, but most seem to prefer working on a "by appointment only" basis. That is, the general public can't just walk in any time they choose, but preferred customers know they can always call and ask to come over most any time if they want to buy something. In other words, you might work in your shop or studio from 10 to 5 every day, but simply discourage drop-in shoppers by asking people to call first before coming round.

A couple in New York who had a shop in their home for a while sold at craft fairs and kept their shop open only at night and on weekends. There was a lot of business during the summer months when tourists were in town, but in time the couple found their shop sales to be less profitable than craft fairs. After moving to a new location, they decided to stop wasting their time and space with a home shop and began to sell through a local consignment shop instead.

This is just a reminder that while home shops may be fun, they do take up space in your home that your family might like to be using. And, you may quickly tire of giving up your evenings and weekends and always being at your customers' beck and call. Carefully weigh the advantages and disadvantages of your own shop versus renting space in a craft mall or other retail shop.

Attracting Customers to a Home Shop or Studio

When zoning isn't a problem, and your homebased shop or studio is open to the public at all times, you may have a different problem. "How do you get the public to accept an in-home shop?" asks Peggy in Louisiana. "In my experience, people do not like to come to a private home to shop. I have a small sign out front and you walk directly into my shop, not my home. My living room is wall-to-wall shelves and is definitely set up as a shop, yet I have watched people drive in and then leave when they see the shop is in my home."

Peggy ventures a guess as to why people react this way. "They may feel they are going to go in and a little old lady is going to pull out several items in a box from under the bed and try to sell them," she says. "Or they may think they will be pressured to buy, or that they are intruding into your privacy."

This problem will resolve itself in time if you work to bring visibility to your shop. In the end, the success of most home shops will turn not on how much paid advertising is done, but on how much word-of-mouth advertising you get.

Tip

To build local visibility for a home shop, get involved in community affairs, which often leads to publicity in the local paper. Donate items for raffles, asking that your home shop be mentioned as the contributor. Send special invitations to local clubs and organizations, offering them a "private showing" and a special discount on purchases. Make it easy for satisfied customers to give you word-of- mouth advertising by asking if they would like a few business cards, flyers or brochures they can pass on to friends.

Check Zoning Regulations

Before opening any kind of shop in your home, check with local zoning officials to see what's allowed or disallowed in your community. Even in residential areas that prohibit business signs and homebased business activity, many artists and craftspeople sell from private studios or workshops, present one-day open houses, give home parties or run weekend boutiques, but this is not something you can take for granted. (Refer back to my earlier discussion of zoning in Chapter Three, and my warning about sales in one's home.)

Before opening her retail crafts and gift shop (see end of this chapter), Susan Young operated her Peach Kitty Studio from her back yard, in a 12- × 16-foot wood structure she designed and had built to her specifications. "I did not have zoning problems and I learned I wouldn't even need a building permit if I didn't build a permanent structure on a concrete slab," she told me. Although the structure was considered impermanent (meaning it could be picked up and moved if necessary), it had all the comforts of home, including a tile floor, baseboard heaters and air conditioning. "Some people might have called it a glorified garden shed just perfect for the riding lawn mower," Susan jokes, "but it was exactly what I wanted and needed at the time."

The Peach Kitty Studio
Decorative Painting
and Folk Art

Since most zoning problems occur when officials receive complaints from neighbors, a big key to success in selling from home is never to annoy neighbors with too much traffic or noise. If your community's zoning laws are outdated, you may be able to get a zoning variance or "special use" permit. For example, a couple who had operated a pottery studio for several years wanted to expand their business by adding a bed-and-breakfast operation. Because this business was desirable to the community, their village board changed the zoning ordinance to accommodate them.

Selling from Your Front Yard

A number of people have written to me about the successful sales they have had simply by setting up shop in their front yard. This is a great way to sell last year's unsold merchandise, seconds, damaged merchandise that has been returned from shops or malls, and imperfect items you've created. While still operating her backyard studio, Susan Young began to have front yard sales on a regular basis. "The first time I tried it was to get rid of prototypes and experimental painting projects that I more or less made a mess of or had a product failure," she says. "I couldn't see tossing painted wood items into the landfill, so I set up folding tables on the driveway—nothing fancy—and put up a sign at the end of my street and in the front yard that read, DRIVEWAY DAZE! CRAFTS! STUDIO SAMPLES TODAY ONLY!

"The funny part of it was that it worked. Once I saw I could snag people by setting up a clearance table, I got the idea of selling new seasonal items using the same tactic and I began to put on two- or three-day shows around Easter and Halloween. I would place things that were obviously chipped or dog-eared into baskets at the base of the maple tree or near the table legs (at ground level) with a sign that said CLEARANCE—AS IS. People went through those baskets like they were looking for gold! One year I put all the seconds into the garden cart which I'd lined with an old blanket, and it got more attention than my carefully set-up tables. When I noticed the cart was getting empty, I began taking stuff off the tables and put it into the cart, where it sold at the original prices. I've learned that when it comes to anticipating the public's reaction, the best tactic is not to try, but instead to go with what you see happening when people step up to buy."

Selling to Clubs and Tour Groups

Many different groups—book clubs, garden clubs, civic home associations and library clubs—are likely to be interested in craftspeople as speakers. The more unusual your work, the better. In an article for *The Crafts Report*, potter, writer and speaker Susan Fox Hirschmann explained how she uses her studio as a meeting place for charity, hobby or religious organizations. She provides an

This sign graces the entrance of the driveway to the Charles and Liz Davis home in Dundee, Kentucky, where Dolls by Liz are handmade.

A "Kentucky Crafted" hang tag used by Liz.

This is a juried craft of the Kentucky Craft Marketing Program and was skillfully crafted by

Ky Folk Artist

Liz Davis

10978 State Route 69 North
DUNDEE, KY 42338

Phone (502) 276-5018

A small "artist information card" Liz includes with all purchases and also uses as a general promotional tool. Shown full-size, it is printed in black ink on tan card stock.

Liz Davis has been designing and producing hand-made dolls for over 25 years. An Ohio Countian, her work is being collected across the U.S. and internationally. Liz's dolls are said to "reflect a healthy respect for the past, and a contemporary sense of humor." Fiddleing Fifi is a limited edition—signed, numbered and dated by Liz. The doll is dressed in a cotton-blend print dress, holds a mahogany-toned wood fiddle and bow, and has a button music-box attached at her back. Fiddleing Fifi was created to honor bluegrass music's West Kentucky heritage.

evening's entertainment by showing a video of herself working at her crafts. (Lacking a video presentation, you could simply show people around your studio and give a brief demonstration of how you do your art or craft.)

"The idea is to bring people into your studio to educate them," she said. "I purposely leave my credit-card terminal and receipt book in plain view with a UPS shipping chart. I explain what services I provide, be it custom, phone order or special packing for one-of-a-kind pieces. They get the message. Often the attenders will not buy right away, but ask me to put a piece aside for them. Spending a few hours discussing your work can net you lots of new customers."

Tip

Susan donates 10 percent of club members' purchases to their organization. When she sends the commission check, she asks them to acknowledge her contribution in their newsletter, which gets her name out to the entire membership.

In addition to entertaining local clubs and organizations, consider opening your studio or shop to tour groups. While they operated a Rosemaling studio in Wisconsin, Audrey and Ray Punzel got tremendous word-of-mouth advertising in their area by inviting tour groups into their home shop when they weren't out selling at craft fairs. Situated on a rustic road by a lake, their home shop was inviting and they entertained many a busload of visitors before they finally retired. The strategy they used is still timely, however, and may be an idea you can use.

"Factories have sales meetings and other local groups are always looking for something interesting to see and do," Audrey told me. "We simply let it be known that we had an interesting attraction for visitors. As each bus arrived, I would give a little introductory talk before asking the group to split in half. Ray would take half the group into our home and invite them to relax with coffee and Norwegian pastries. He would show them our collection of articles from Norway and point out various ways we had decorated our home with Rosemaling. Meanwhile, I would be entertaining

151

Expanding Studio Profits with Classes

Many craft producers who sell finished crafts from a homebased studio or workshop increase their profits by offering classes and selling a line of related supplies and materials. (Bringing people into your studio for classes automatically builds word-of-mouth advertising for your products.)

Bobbie Irwin, a weaver who has lived in many parts of the country, learned something interesting when she offered her weaving classes in a small community of only a thousand people. "I thought I would quickly saturate the local market after teaching one or two classes," she said. "Instead, I found that one class perpetuated another. Friends see what folks are learning and then want to learn themselves. That's one advantage to living in such a small community. The locals are desperate for new things to do, and my classes are always well received."

the rest of the group in my shop and display room. After explaining the art of Rosemaling, I would answer questions and encourage people to browse and make purchases. When the morning was over, we had hundreds of dollars in sales and people from many states and Canada were taking brochures and going home to spread the word."

More Sales Through Open Houses

If the idea of a homebased shop is impractical or simply not appealing, how about an occasional open house to supplement your other craft sales? Many creative people have found this a profitable way to sell their products. You simply send information to those on your mailing list, inviting them to come at a specified time (or give them a range of hours when they may feel free to drop in). Just before the event, you might telephone several of your best customers to remind them to come and bring a friend. To get the word out to a larger audience, run an ad for two or three days in the local paper, or post brightly colored posters on all the community bulletin boards at local stores.

Open houses a couple of times a year are a great way to resell regular customers while acquainting new people with your art or craft and any custom design services you may offer. Whether you sell products during an open house or simply take orders for later delivery is a matter of choice unless such sales are strictly prohibited in your community.

Tip

Always check with local authorities before publicizing an open house event. In some areas, zoning laws prohibit any kind of business that involves inventory. In others, a seller may take orders in the home, but it would be a violation of the law if the customers walked out the door with merchandise they bought during the open house. (Later deliveries are a simple solution to this problem.)

Some sellers present open house sales before all the major holidays, but when you hold them is entirely up to you. Soapmaker Tammy Hodson, who works with her mother, Shirley Harrison, in their business, aptly named Mother and Daughter, LLC, says open house sales are a good way to make money after the craft fair season ends, as well as around holidays. "We usually have an open house in December to get extra Christmas sales, and Mother's Day is incredibly busy for us," says Tammy. "But what can you expect with a name like Mother and Daughter?"

Tammy sends flyers to her local mailing list of about a thousand names, many of them acquired and shared by another crafter in her area. The open house runs from noon to six, and customers are invited to place orders in advance if they want to pop in and pick them up on their way home from work. "We display soap products in the family room, on the dining room table, and the counter that separates the kitchen from the family room," she says. "Fancy gift baskets are placed in the living room area. All open house shoppers get a small freebie, such as a little heart-shaped bar of soap, a discount of 10–15 percent off regular craft fair prices, and free gift wrapping."

"These open house shows automatically generate repeat sales," Tammy adds.

"Repeat customers come to my home and purchase from us. They buy gifts for friends. They *bring* their friends. And these purchases don't carry any entrance fees or percentages. This is *cream!* These customers ask me to e-mail them whenever I add new scents and products, and when I do, they buy them."

Marj Bates, whom you first met in Chapter Two ("Pursuing Your Dream"), has a thriving glass bead and jewelry business that's perfect for the open house method of selling. She lives in a tourist area in a charming house on the ocean with a lighthouse nearby. Just driving to this location makes people happy, she says, so it's easy for her to attract new shoppers every year. Marj's special talents enable her to command top dollar for her products, and she can easily sell $5,000 worth of merchandise in an open house sale. (Some of Marj's lampwork beads sell for up to $85, and she also sells a line of findings so shoppers can create their own jewelry.)

"I used to invite my pottery and fiber artist friends to do an open house with me," says Marj, "but I'm now doing them alone, except that I let some of my students sell their beads at these sales. I like this kind of selling because I get to see people I don't have time for otherwise. And there's something delicious about making all this money without leaving your house and having fun besides."

Marj puts all her first-class wares in her gallery, and offers lower-priced items in a display area in another room. "At shows, when people remark that they love my work but can't afford it, I tell them to come to one of my open house sales," she explains. "Here they can buy samples—similar in quality, but at lower prices. I often have to make half a dozen practice pieces when I'm working on a special order or when I'm simply experimenting with new colors or techniques, so I sell these pieces as samples or seconds."

To bring in buyers, Marj sends invitations to all her customers, posts notices at the art center, and sends news releases to local papers. Since she is literally opening her house to strangers, she hires three or four people for each open house sale. Except for her cashier, who is paid in cash, Marj usually hires students who work in exchange for extra class time. One is positioned at the door so she can ask everyone how they heard about the event, one is in charge of refreshments, and another just keeps an eye on people as they move through the house. This allows Marj to relax and enjoy visiting with her customers and friends.

Tip

Opening your house to many people you do not know carries a degree of risk. You can never be sure who's going to walk in the door when you advertise this kind of event, so if you can't limit customer traffic to one or two rooms, be sure to have someone in every room at all times to keep an eye on people as they move about. Also make sure you have liability insurance to cover any accidents visitors might have while on your premises.

Open Houses in Other People's Homes

An open house sale doesn't have to be in your own home, nor do you have to host this kind of sale alone. Deena Nixon enjoyed considerable success for three years with her "Li'l Country Nook Home Parties," an interesting mix of a home party and open house. She worked on a simple arrangement with friends who offered the use of their home for a sale. "The hostess mailed invitations that I provided—25 to start with, more if needed," says Deena. "Guests were invited to shop anytime between six and eight o'clock, and the hostess received a sales commission that she could take either in cash or merchandise." Unlike traditional party plans where all the guests show up at the same time, stay for an hour or two and place orders for later delivery, Deena sold directly, taking orders only for custom-designed items. "I liked this kind of selling because I didn't have to give a talk or sales spiel like party plan presenters." she says. "Shoppers seemed to prefer it, too, because they didn't have to wait three weeks for their merchandise. They could drop in anytime during the open house period, buy what they wanted, and leave."

Each year, Deena presented ten open houses during October and November. Initially, she offered her hostesses 10 percent of sales, but she found they worked harder to bring in guests when she gave them a greater profit incentive of 20 percent of sales. One year, Deena worked with a partner. "Her items were different enough from mine that it added to the show and just made it better," she says. "It was a busy year for both of us, so by working together, neither of us had to produce quite as much as we had in other years." (Illustration is one of Deena's products.)

Tip

The hours you set for your open house may have a lot to do with the number of shoppers you get. Fewer people may show up if you limit your event to a specific one or two-hours' time. By giving shoppers a larger window of time (such as noon till six), they have the flexibility of dropping in at their convenience rather than yours, and you'll also catch shoppers on their way home from work. As one seller put it, "Since all my presentations are at the homes of friends or family members with whom I can sit and talk all day, the open house style of selling is perfect for me."

Formula for Calculating Open House Sales

A potter who announced a private exhibit of work in her home told me she sent postcard invitations to 100 customers on her mailing list. Thirty people came to see her creations, and 18 of them made purchases.

Take another look at those figures. This seller got a 30 percent response to her mailing, which is excellent, but she got a 60 percent sales response, which is extraordinary. Not everyone will do this well, so here is a simple, more conservative three-step formula to help you estimate how much you might make from an open house of your own:

a party in the future (and get a similar thank-you gift).

5. Give a little spiel about yourself and describe the products on display, suggesting how they might be used as gifts and passing them around whenever possible. (Label each product with its name, item number, price, and notations about other colors or sizes that may be available.)

Tip

Explain that there may be slight variations between the samples you are exhibiting and what people will receive, since no two handmade items will ever be the same.

6. Halfway through your presentation take a "fun break" to play little games and award some of your inexpensive craft items as prizes.

7. Wind down your presentation with information about how guests may order your products, the amount of deposit you require and who to make the check out to (you, not the hostess). If you have brochures, flyers or price lists, bring them to the attention of guests.

Tip

Some sellers ask guests to pay the full amount of purchase prior to receiving goods, but most people would be reluctant to do this. Having to pay only half up front will encourage more sales.

8. Close with information on how and when you will deliver their order, explaining that custom-design orders will take a little longer.

Advantages of Home Party Selling

"The biggest advantage of selling your crafts through home parties is that you control how much you work by spacing out the party dates," says Chris Peters, a longtime home party presenter. "Of course you will have great parties and not-so-great parties, but this is no riskier than selling your work at craft shows. While you have to tote tons of items to a craft show and bring them all home again if they don't sell, at a home party you only have to make an item *after* you get the order for it."

Tip

Some sellers promise delivery in two weeks while others take as long as three to six weeks to deliver custom-design orders. The closer you get to Christmas, however, the quicker most folks will want their merchandise.

9. While the hostess serves refreshments of cake and coffee, you take orders, chat with guests, answer questions and encourage them to book a party. (Take your date book with you.)

10. Later, tally the evening's sales and calculate the amount the hostess has earned (between 10 to 20 percent of sales, payable in gift merchandise, not cash). If you have booked some parties at this point, it is customary to give the hostess an extra $5 to $10 credit for each party.

NOTE: Some party plan presenters deliver merchandise to the hostess, who in turn delivers it to customers. For this extra service, they increase the hostess percentage from 10 to 20 percent (generally taken out in merchandise). Others give a certain percentage on sales up to a specific amount, and a larger percentage for orders totaling more than this.

Home Parties Lead to How-to Book

Opal Leasure, a mother of five and a craftsperson for over twenty-five years, started her Apron Strings crafts business in 1992 after her mother said, "You can do it, I know you can!"

After considering her many marketing options, Opal decided she liked the idea of doing home parties best. Everything that could go wrong did go wrong in that first party, but Opal's sales were good enough to keep going. In time, she became so successful at giving parties that she wrote and published a how-to book on this topic titled *The Apron Strings Lady Did It . . . So Can You!* (see Resource Chapter). It includes Opal's success story, business start-up guidelines, party planning and sales success tips, plus samples of printed materials needed in this kind of selling. (These include flyers, information sheets, thank-you letters, receipts, order forms, summary sheets and more.)

Opal's Apron Strings Country Home Parties were presented in the Madera, California, area between 1992 and 1998 where the average guest then spent at least $20, and often a lot more. Opal successfully sold both a country and a southwestern line of products, with her best sellers being Eucalyptus sprays, raffia swags and wreaths. Other products included birdhouses, dolls, hats, wooden and novelty items and a line of Apron Strings "Cow Babies." Opal estimates that she gained over 600 customers in three years of doing parties, and she counted a party a success whenever it led to at least one new party.

Opal's roots are in the Ozarks, where she was taught the old-fashioned values that became an important part of her business. She stresses the importance of not taking on so much work that your family suffers. "Managing is the key and controlling your work load is essential," she says. "If part-time employment is your goal, schedule only one or two parties per week. Just one party per week may generate two full days of filling orders."

Opal has since moved on to other things, not because her party plan business wasn't a success, but because she had a bigger dream—that of becoming a full-time teacher. This kind of transition is common with creative people who start businesses at home. They rarely end up anywhere near where they started, and often could not have gotten there at all if not for their crafts business experience. (For more on how craft businesses change and diversify over the years, read *Creative Cash*.)

How to Organize a Successful Holiday Boutique

Holiday or seasonal boutiques provide an interesting and profitable alternative to selling at fairs or through local shops, and they are generally successful no matter where they are held. An individual may decide to present a holiday boutique alone (with the help of friends and family), or by working with a group of local artisans. In the latter case, it is not unusual for 25 to 30 sellers to gross $30,000 or more over a weekend, particularly if the boutique has become a regular annual event noted for high-quality merchandise. Usually presented in the spring or fall, boutiques are generally tied to such holidays as Valentine's Day, Easter, Halloween and Christmas, the most profitable selling season of all.

Boutiques can be something as simple as your own work displayed in a shoplike atmosphere in one room of your home, or a major exhibit of products spread throughout several rooms, such as Susan Larberg's boutique described below. Although such shows usually start in someone's home, some become so successful in time that they must be moved to a school, church or other large building in the community. (See sidebar on this topic.) Wherever you decide to hold it, always give your boutique a name, as this will help you build a solid customer base for it.

An Open House Christmas Boutique

Every year since 1992, Susan Maggio Larberg of Brooksville, Florida, has presented her much awaited Open House Christmas Boutique to hundreds of guests in surrounding communities. The show opens with a four-day sale (Thursday through Sunday) in mid-November, and continues every weekend

162

Moving a Home Boutique to Larger Quarters

In thinking about moving a show out of your home, consider that you will have increased expenses from room rental and extra advertising to announce the change of location. One boutique organizer thought she would see significant increases in sales and customer turnout if she moved her boutique to the banquet facilities at a local restaurant/motel. Surprisingly, sales were no higher and many previous customers didn't realize the show at the restaurant was the same quality show they had been attending in this individual's home. Also, because products were spread out over a larger space, those who did attend felt the show was smaller.

In looking for a new site for your boutique, don't limit your thinking to schools, churches and restaurants. With so many vacant retail stores in shopping malls these days, it might be very easy to rent such a store in a prime location for a weekend or week-long boutique. Ten artists who had been doing in-home shows for eight years decided one year to rent the senior citizen library building for two days. Many boutiques have been presented in new homes for sale. (Realtors are delighted to have so many people see a home in such an attractive light.) One boutique presenter told me about her boutique, held in an old Victorian house on the National Historic Register that happened to be on sale at the time. Another said a historical mansion in her area was interested in hosting her show in the future because this would draw favorable publicity to the mansion.

after that until the week before Christmas. Susan's method of operation will give you many ideas.

House Setup and Decorating

Unlike some boutique presenters who limit their shows to one or two rooms of the house, Susan sells in every room of her home, except the master bedroom, bath, and her computer room/studio. "We literally turn our entire home into a Winter Wonderland," she says. "Every room has its own special theme and decorated trees—sixteen in all, big and small—each trimmed with handmade ornaments priced between $1 and $8. It takes us nearly a month to move furniture to make room for the Christmas trees and decorate them, set up display shelves, string thousands of white lights around railings, doorways and windows (inside and out), hang other decorations, and display all the products themselves."

Now 51, Susan has reluctantly accepted the fact that she can no longer do all this work alone and cautions others to enlist help from friends and family. "They can't duplicate your creativity," she says, "but they can set up and decorate trees, string lights, hang wreaths, bake cookies, and help with sales and bagging." Susan pays her helpers either with cash or a craft they have admired.

Products Offered

Hundreds of products are offered for sale, all grouped to fit a room's atmosphere. Elegant creations—formal centerpieces, swags, Victorian crafts and beaded ornaments—are displayed in the living and dining room area; wreaths of all sizes and kinds are hung on both sides of the long hall; garden crafts and stuffed animals fill the spare bedroom; seashell items, mirrors and treasure boxes are displayed in the bathrooms, and country furniture, sleighs and folk art crafts are situated in the pool area. Even the kitchen is loaded with products, from food gift baskets and flavored vinegars and oils to fruit and flower topiaries and kitchen decorations.

Everyone in Susan's family makes products for sale, except her husband. "He's not crafty but he does all the heavy work and is my best supporter," she says. Susan makes a variety of products, but she is best known for her "Woodsman Santas," no two of which are alike. Positioned on a slice of tree trunk from the Larberg's wooded property, each Santa is covered in fur from head to toe (usually rabbit fur purchased at thrift shops or Goodwill). Depending on size and materials, Santas are priced between $50 and $300, and each is signed, dated and numbered. "I especially enjoy making personalized heirloom Santas for buyers who provide an old mink or family fur," she says. "Some of my customers have started their own collections and now order a new Santa every year."

Added Attractions

Guests are treated to Christmas music, fresh-baked cookies, coffee, tea and punch. Susan raffles four gift baskets (a large one valued at $150 and three smaller ones) containing small handcrafts, candles, ornaments, gourmet cookies, candies, coffees, teas, flavored oil and vinegar and bath items. Tickets are sold for a dollar apiece with the understanding that all proceeds go to needy families in the area. "This is our way of giving something back to the Lord for blessing us so much," says Susan.

Advertising

A teenage neighbor loves the extra money she earns by delivering Susan's flyers to hundreds of homes in surrounding neighborhoods, but this isn't enough to draw a good crowd.

"I spend more on advertising every year because I've learned it really does pay off," says Susan. "I now advertise not only in the local papers, but in nearby large cities. I try to ask all new customers each year how they heard about the Boutique, and regular customers often remark about the advertising that they received. Most of my traffic comes from cities within an hour's drive, so this is where I put my advertising focus."

Tip

Do not stick flyers anywhere on or around people's mailboxes, but place them behind doors or hang them on doorknobs. After Susan's helper distributed a thousand flyers this way, she received a stern warning from the post office saying that what she was doing was illegal, and if she persisted, she would be charged $.34 for each flyer. This was directly related to a new law passed shortly after the 9/11/01 terrorist attack and the mail/anthrax problems that immediately followed it.)

Accepting Credit Cards

"Adding VISA/MasterCard privileges has increased my business by about 30 percent," says Susan, who got her merchant account through her local bank. She rents it for only three months a year for a reasonable setup fee and so much a month (fees that will vary from bank to bank). "I set it up at the front door where everyone comes in and checks out (one way in, one way out)," she says. "Most people pay with checks or cash, but I have noticed an increase in sales of the larger, more expensive items being purchased with a credit card. Before I had merchant status, however, whenever people indicated they couldn't buy if I didn't take credit cards, I would quietly tell them they could pay something now and pay the rest when they could, and they always did so."

Susan adds that she has never had a problem with theft because "it seems that people who attend this sort of show are a good class of people who appreciate fine craftsmanship and may even be crafters themselves." She has never asked people who write checks to provide identification, and she has received only one bad check in thirteen years—for $6.

I love a success story like Susan's, and it was gratifying to me to learn that I had played a role in her business. "Years ago when I first discovered your books," she told me, "I got so inspired! I always knew I was creative, but didn't know exactly how much I could do, or how diversified I could be until I was encouraged by your books to keep trying new things, and not be afraid to step into unknown territory."

Holiday Boutique Planning Checklist

Some crafters who work together to present a holiday boutique have firmly established operating guidelines similar to those of craft cooperatives (discussed in Chapter Eleven). Most, however, have no formal legal structure and different people may be involved in a boutique from year to year. It takes a lot of planning and hard work to organize and present a successful boutique, and plans for a Christmas event should begin no later than

Working with Other Crafters

If you know several craftspeople in your area, it would be easy enough to find several who would like to use your holiday boutique as a seasonal consignment shop, with you taking a percentage of their sales. But there can be pitfalls here. One boutique organizer who prefers anonymity told me about the tough lesson she learned about working with crafters. After five years of presenting her annual Christmas boutique—with her doing all the work and just bringing in additional crafters' merchandise for the show—she had a rude awakening the sixth year when ten of the seventeen crafters who originally signed up for her boutique backed out at the last minute. "They had a lot of excuses," she said, "but I found them all unprofessional and very upsetting. They were either too busy, too over committed, or too tired to produce extra merchandise for this show. I did present the boutique, and the seven of us made as much money as always, but I was so discouraged by the 'I don't care' attitude of those crafters who left me hanging that I didn't hold a show the following year. However, the many moans and groans I got from my customers have encouraged me to reconsider doing future shows. If I do, the rules for craft sellers will certainly change."

In this case, the boutique organizer charged crafters an admission fee of $15 (far too small for anyone to worry about losing). If she plans to continue operating this way, she might attract more reliable sellers by charging a $50 admission fee, which would automatically eliminate hobby sellers. The other option, of course, is to work cooperatively with a group of dedicated craft professionals, who would take an active role in making the annual boutique a success. See "Holiday Boutique Planning Checklist" below for guidelines on how to do this.

March. Assuming you will be working with a few crafter friends, here is a checklist of things that must be done (not necessarily in this order):

❏ *Decide in whose home the event will be held, and in which rooms of the house.* If no one wants their house open to the public, consider using someone's two-car garage. One boutique presenter gave her garage an antique flavor through the use of old lamps, cabinets and tables covered with color-coordinated sheets. She decorated one wall with quilts, another with pegboard for hanging crafts, and another with the end rolls of newspaper acquired from the local paper.

❏ *Select an interesting name for your event.* Examples from my files include "Cottage Collection—Only by Hand," "Harvest Time Craft Sale," "Christmas by Candlelight," "Santa's Helpers Boutique," and "Down a Country Road." Marketing consultant Silvana Clark suggests "The Mistletoe Marketplace," "Holiday Highlights" or "Trinkets and Treasures Boutique."

❏ *Take care of tax, legal and insurance matters.* Check with local zoning officials to make sure your event won't violate local laws. Contact your state's Department of Revenue, Sales Tax Division, to learn how to collect and pay all required taxes. Check with insurance agents about liability insurance in case a customer is injured while on the homeowner's property. Make sure all crafters understand they must obtain their own insurance on merchandise consigned to the show.

Tip

Keep neighbors happy by giving them special early-entrance passes to the boutique and perhaps a 10 percent discount on purchases.

❏ *Decide who's going to do what.* The group organizing the boutique needs someone who will act as boss, taking the responsibility of overseeing and coordinating all the work being done by others. This will include the making and distributing of posters and flyers, writing and placing advertisements, planning, buying and serving refreshments, obtaining special decorations or display props, recording and marking incoming merchandise, arranging it for sale, setting up a cashier's table, arranging for Visa/MasterCard charge services, recording sales, and capturing customer's names and addresses in an address book. Someone will also have to take care of putting up and taking down directional signs on the day of the event.

Tip

Have at least two cashiers who do nothing but take money. Someone else should remove price tags and wrap parcels. To avoid having too much money sitting around, someone might need to make a couple of trips to the bank during the sale.

❏ *Decide how exhibitors will be selected.* Will you limit participation to your immediate circle of friends or invite other artists and crafters to exhibit and sell? Those who only sell and do not take part in organizing the event should be charged an exhibitor's fee or a percentage of sales similar to what they would have to pay in a local consignment or rent-a-space shop.

❏ *Decide what kind of crafts you will sell.* Will you jury outside sellers to avoid duplication of products or place limits on certain categories of items for sale? Remember that not all crafters are dependable suppliers, so it would be wise to get a commitment as to the type and volume of merchandise each seller plans to display. Otherwise there may be either too little or too much merchandise for available space. Once volume of merchandise is determined, you can more easily decide how much display space you will need and how long the boutique should run.

❏ *Estimate expenses.* Expenses not covered by fees or sales commissions from sellers outside the core group will have to be divided accordingly. These would include postage, advertising and sign making; printing of flyers, posters and invitations; bags, tags, and wrapping materials; sales books; guest book; decorations and refreshments. You may want to mark the house with balloons or banners or string lighting outdoors. An extra amount should be paid to the person who lends her home for the event to cover electricity and phone expense. To avoid damage to carpets (in case of wet weather), floor runners may be needed. (Allow for the possibility of accidental damage to furniture or other possessions in the home and perhaps the need to have carpeting cleaned afterward.)

❑ *Decide how you will promote and advertise your event.* Common advertising methods include distributing flyers, sending post-card announcements to a customer list, placing ads in local papers (including "Pennysaver" publications), displaying posters with tear-off, take-along reminders attached, seeking announcements on cable television and sending press releases to area newspapers.

One boutique organizer said she rented a billboard at the fairgrounds for a week. Silvana Clark suggests publicizing your event by making colorful bookmarks that the library and local bookstores could place on their counters.

❑ *Set up an inventory system that accurately records all items consigned to the show.* For example, you might assign a letter code to each seller and a number code to each craft item. Note these letters and numbers on price tags and later transfer them to the sales slip at the time of purchase. You could then tally any sales commissions due you at the end of the show. (Several boutique organizers have told me that, in a one- or two-day show, it is common to sell at least half of everything on display.)

❑ *Plan how crafts will be displayed for sale.* Excluding furniture and lighting, remove from the sales area everything that isn't for sale. Display ideas that work at craft fairs also work in a home boutique. For example, avoid placing items flat on tabletops. Intermix items according to color, texture and size or arrange products in a mix that gives buyers an idea of how they would look if displayed in their own homes. Use interesting pieces of furniture for contrast, baskets for small items, bookcases for collections of small items. Put only large items on the floor.

Tip

During the show, increase sales by moving things around to make sure all items are seen, especially if crowds are heavy. Buyers aren't receptive when it looks like everything has been picked over, so make sure that holes on tables or shelves are quickly filled in with additional craft items or rearranged to look full.

❑ **Plan future events.** Holiday boutiques are rarely one-year events. Instead, they generally run for years, becoming more profitable with time. In New Jersey, a one-day boutique that began in a woman's home soon grew to two-day sales in a local store. The last I heard the boutique was running for a full two weeks, and gross sales were at the $80,000 level. Over 200 craftspeople were selling through this boutique and paying the organizer 20 percent of their sales.

Opening Your Own Crafts Shop

Once when I did a survey of the readers of my magazine column in *Crafts*, hundreds of them said that their dream was to own a shop of their own. But as I said at the beginning of this chapter, I do not recommend retailing to the average crafter, particularly today when retail shops everywhere are having a difficult time surviving. But if this is your dream—and you believe you are ready to take this step—I won't shoot you down, but I do want to give you a realistic view of what you're in for here. If you're making plans to open your own shop, you can learn much from the experiences of Susan Young and Gina Casey, two crafters-turned-retailers. Let me briefly introduce them here.

After selling thousands of miniatures in craft malls every year for four years (refer back to Chapter Nine), Gina Casey made enough money to open her own shop in Remington, Indiana, in September 1998. Although she retained the same name she had been using for her miniatures business—Mini Measures—her shop line now includes antiques, collectibles and handcrafts. "People do ask how I came up with the name," she says. "After I explain about my past dollhouse crafting, no one seems to think it odd. In time, I hope to add a miniature dollhouse line, but since selling out my entire inventory, I haven't had time to replace it."

For twenty-five years, Susan Young dreamed of owning her own crafts shop, and she realized that dream in part when she quit a high-paying corporate job several years ago to open her backyard Peach Kitty Studio. But she wanted more. She wanted a *real* shop, and she finally opened Peach Kitty Studio Crafts and Gifts in Madison, Alabama, in December 2000.

"I documented my personal and financial game plans and goals seven years before I actually began operation," she says. "Finally I knew I was ready and the time was right for me, personally, and I gathered my courage and leased an old farmhouse I'd had my eye on for years, spent three months renovating it, and turned it into a dream-come-true. Indeed, it was a neglected and sad-looking building, and I nearly backed down when I saw what I'd be dealing with. But, remembering a motivational quote I'd found on Barbara's Web site, I listened to the inner voice that said, 'If you don't do this now, you'll regret it the rest of your life.' I knew from the day I leased the building it would be six days a week and sometimes seven; also that it would be eight hours a day minimum and sometimes fifteen. Getting the building in shape, getting the shop decorated and stocked, finding suppliers and building traffic has been the most challenging work I've ever done; also the most satisfying. Retailing being what it is, I might fail, but at least I won't go to my grave wondering 'what if.'"

♦ ***Building Considerations.*** Both Susan and Gina selected run-down buildings, figuring they could fix them up easier than they could pay a higher monthly rent. Gina decided to buy her building outright. "It was a dump that needed a lot of work," she says, "but I figured if the business wasn't a success, I could sell the restored building to someone else. Fortunately, I have a handyman husband who made all the improvements to my building, and I will forever be thankful for his support."

172

Susan's landlord wouldn't sell the property, so she had no option but to lease, but she worked a deal with the owner to fix up the place in return for a lower monthly rent. "I then spent the next three months cleaning, painting, ripping up old carpeting, getting the building rewired, scrubbing the brickwork in the old kitchen, fixing the porch, hanging curtains, installing exterior lighting and a large illuminated sign at the highway, and much more. It was an incredible amount of work, but it's now paying off in very low overhead costs."

♦ **_Financial and Legal Considerations._** Both Susan and Gina had a bankroll of their own. "Do not borrow more than you feel comfortable paying back," Gina cautions. Susan thinks one should have a minimum of $10,000, although the square footage of your shop will have much to do with how much money you need for inventory and fixtures. "If you have a lot of gaps or holes on your shelves, you won't look successful," she says. "Few new shop owners have a clue as to how much inventory it will take to fill up a shop, or what it will cost. I hear and read stories all the time of independent shop owners who max out their credit cards to the tune of $25,000 the first year, and then close before they can pay off their bills. What a terrible spot in which to put the whole family and household."

Additional money will also be needed for shelving, display units, special attention-getting props, holiday decorations and display lighting. Susan adds: "People who dream of their own shop are often so busy dreaming they fail to consider they will also need liability insurance (in case a customer falls on the front steps or a tree limb falls on a car in the parking lot) and content coverage on inventory (tornado, fire, water leaks, etc.)."

♦ **_Shop Operation._** Susan's shop features her own decorative painting and folk art, carries a few items on consignment from selected outstanding artisans, and includes a growing line of painting and craft supplies for those who prefer to "do it themselves."

To make sure that she could meet expenses in the early days of the shop, Gina decided to rent space to a few craft sellers, being quite selective as to quality and variety of products. "I was picky about who could come in," she says. "My contract gives a dealer a three-month trial period to see how we get along. My husband eventually wants me to take over the whole shop and forget about renters, but I like the variety these additional sellers bring to the shop. They each have a 6- x 8-foot display area that they decorate and maintain themselves, and they add a lot of creativity to the store."

"Set shop hours that are comfortable to you and stick to them," says Gina. "Customers who drive 35 miles to shop expect your shop to be open on time. Gina's hours are Tuesday through Saturday, 10 A.M. to 4 P.M.; Susan's are Monday through Saturday, 10 A.M. to 6 P.M. (although she says she is always there from seven to seven every day).

♦ *Display Techniques.* Susan stresses the need for "attention-getters," things that will draw people to certain areas of the shop. "In every corner," she says, "I have a large display item. Depending on the season, I may feature large Santas, angels, Easter bunnies, or cats. People also expect appropriate holiday decorations—lots of lights during the Christmas holidays, pumpkins on the porch at Halloween, etc. Visitors to my shop often comment on how restful and peaceful my shop is, with its lovely decorations and displays, soft music playing in the background and scents in the air from liquid potpourri or scented candles."

Gina stresses the importance of changing window displays. "I have two large window display areas, and the display changes every month. Everyone in the shop gets to put items in the window by theme, and I sell a lot of merchandise just from the window display. In fact, I have this one old man who constantly buys from the window—I can't get him to walk through the whole store! He just stops by and says 'I want that item in the window' and leaves. I always suggest that he needs to take a stroll through the shop, and he says 'Just keep putting things in the window.'"

Always remember the four R's of retailing, says Gina: "RESTOCK merchandise that sells; ROTATE your items within your display to keep things looking fresh; REDUCE any items that just are not moving by having a sale basket or shelf; REMOVE old stale items that just won't sell, admit defeat and move on."

♦ **_Advertising._** Both Gina and Susan live in small towns, so their advertising methods are similar. Gina's constant goal is to draw traffic from the many nearby small towns as well as the nearest large city (Lafayette), about 45 minutes away, so she does a lot of advertising. Radio is the only form of advertising that hasn't worked for Gina, but she has had success with local newspaper ads, Yellow Page ads, flyers, and word-of-mouth. Gina prints flyers offering a 10 percent discount if brought into the shop. "I give these to folks who do craft shows, and they work well," she says. "I also get a lot of travelers from my ad in _Antique Weekly,_ which is circulated in the Midwest."

Susan's most effective advertising has been her large hand-painted sign on the highway. Eight-feet wide by four feet high, it stands on posts that bring its height to six feet, and it's lit by spotlights all night long. "Based on the comments I get from shoppers," says Susan, "I'd guess that 50 percent of my new business has come directly from this sign. While some shop owners might balk at putting up such a large sign, it is certainly working for me." (Note: Susan also has a Web site that promotes her work and shop. See the Resource Chapter for the Web site addresses of everyone featured in this book.)

♦ **Promotional Ideas.** Since she opened in the month of September, Gina always runs a September anniversary sale where everything in the shop is 10 percent off. Many dealers in the shop also offer the discount."This gives us a jump on the Christmas season, we are able to rid ourselves of slow moving inventory, and it gives us good cash flow for new inventory," she says.

Susan promotes through ads in coupon booklets that offer shoppers a free gift just for browsing, as well as $5 off on any purchase of $25 or more. People who sign her guest book receive special promotions whenever she wants to move certain merchandise at a discount. Although she's a computer whiz, she also sends hand-written thank-you notes to repeat buyers, and hand-written invitations to lure people back in a second time, always with some kind of special offer. "Technology aside," says Susan, "I believe the more personalized you can make your service, and your gratitude to customers, the better it's going to work for you. So many people have told me how much they liked getting my little thank-you notes and special invitations to shop and save money."

♦ **Working in the Shop.** Remember that retailing is a full-time job all by itself, so if you dream of spending most of your day creating products for sale in the shop, think again. "The extra walk-in traffic I originally anticipated was more of a headache than it was worth," says one crafter who opened her own shop after years of selling monogrammed products from home. "Being a sole proprietor, I found it difficult to work with the interruptions during the day, and working outside my home was definitely a hardship for my family. That's why I moved my business back home."

Like so many others, Gina thought she would have time to continue making miniatures during store hours, but says there are always various distractions that make it impossible for her to mass produce the way she used to do. Susan, on the other hand, gets a lot of painting done during shop hours. "I call my shop a working studio, and I paint whenever I don't have other shop work to do," she says. "One nice thing about having a place to work in your own shop is that on days when business is slow, you can still feel productive and create products you'll sell later."

Susan's farmhouse building has three front rooms that are her main display areas, but she also merchandises and sells out of what was the former kitchen, and the bathroom as well. (Yes, people really do buy products displayed in bathrooms, she says.) She has worked out a comfortable routine for dealing with all shoppers. "When I hear someone come in to the shop, I walk to the front door to greet them and ask if they have anything particular in mind," says Susan. "I tell them to have fun browsing, explain that I'm painting in the back room, and invite them to come back and look at my studio if they wish. Those who do walk back to see me at work seem thrilled to know I'm actually the artist who has painted many of the items for sale, and this always gives me an opportunity to promote the custom painting that is my specialty. If they don't seek me out after ten or fifteen minutes, I walk back out to see if they need any help or are ready to check out."

◆ *Shoplifting.* I thought shoplifting might be a real problem for Susan, since she obviously can't watch shoppers while she's in another room painting. In her first year of operation, however, she says she has lost only a couple of items worth about $25. "I think of these as my 'five-finger discount items,' and forget about them," she says. "I don't believe in bird-dogging my customers. A bit of shoplifting goes with the territory, and if someone feels they have to steal an item from me, I figure they need it worse than I do."

In summary, Susan emphasizes that everyone has to draw their own conclusions as to when they might be ready to move into retailing full time. "Being ready personally might include your level of family responsibilities, how many hours you can afford to dedicate yourself to your business, and whether it's going to tee off your husband if dinner isn't served until 9 P.M. Will the kids splatter three plates of leftover spaghetti in the microwave for you to clean up when you get home from the shop and, if so, can you deal with it without self-recrimination about your decisions? Running an off-site shop is nothing like 'working from home'—at least there I could run the laundry while I was painting snowmen, or write an article while a roast cooked."

You can make all kinds of plans when you start a new venture, but there will always be what Susan calls "extraneous circumstances" you can neither predict nor control. Susan never dreamed that during her first year of business operation—when she was planning on dedicating her every waking minute to her business—she would be faced with burying her youngest brother, weeks of unexpected house guests, having to relocate her mother, attend to other unexpected family concerns, and weather the total upheaval of the economy due to the 9/11/01 terrorist attack.

Owning a craft business is certainly a dream of thousands, but there are many details to think through before you begin this kind of venture. "One needs to have plenty of time and help (physical, moral, financial) and only minimal other responsibilities in their daily lives or they'll never make it," says Susan. "They also need a better than average penchant for handling finances, dealing with vendors, suppliers and the public, and a tremendous ability to keep the day-to-day activities fully organized—from filing sales taxes to paying the rent on time and everything in-between. Frankly, I've met very few people who can carry it off. It's so easy to daydream about a cute little shop and the world beating a path to your door, yet so difficult to actually accomplish."

Adds Gina: "Opening a shop has been a great learning and growing experience, and I'm happy I took the step forward. My advice to others is have a positive attitude always! You'll never know what might have been if you never try."

Chapter Nine

Craft Malls and Rent-a-Space Shops

Today's craft mall scene is quite different than it was in the 90s, but craft malls and rent-a-space shops remain a profitable outlet for thousands of crafters.

This chapter explores the current craft mall scene, offering both pro and con viewpoints of this method of selling. You'll learn how the craft mall scene has changed in recent years, why some crafters love malls, and why others are leaving them. After digesting all this information, you'll be able to decide whether craft mall selling is right for you or not.

Rental space has been available to artisans, flea market dealers and antique sellers for years, but everything changed in 1988 when Rufus Coomer opened the first Coomers Craft Mall in Azle, Texas. He was the first to refine the unique craft marketing concept that would sweep America in the 1990s and forever changed the way craftspeople sold at the retail level. At the turn of the century, Coomers still remained the nation's largest

Some 8,000 crafters currently sell through Coomers malls. "Most are hobby sellers operating from their kitchen table," says Linda Coomer, "but we also have many craft professionals, some of whom are selling more than $100,000 per year through our malls alone."

Coomers Web site, introduced in March 1996, includes photographs of store locations available for exhibiting crafts. To learn how to sell your crafts through any of the malls in the Coomers chain, mention this book when you ask for their "National Crafters Network" package. (See Resource Chapter.) (Illustration by Nancy Hester.)

retailer of American handmade crafts, gifts and decorations for home and offices, with 26 malls in nine states and annual sales of over $23 million.

As retailing entrepreneurs across the country began to copy Rufus Coomer's profitable idea, the popularity of craft malls spawned similar, yet different, types of retail handcraft shops that are discussed later in this chapter. Artisans were quick to see the advantages of selling in malls and other rent-a-space retail outlets. Now, instead of selling only at craft fairs or consigning merchandise to craft shops, they could:

- Rent an affordable amount of shelf or booth space and get the benefit of a shop atmosphere without the problems of consignment selling;

- Have control over how their wares were displayed;

- Enjoy year-round sales and regular monthly payments without the hassles involved in setting up fair exhibits;

- Sell in many different stores across the country and deal with mall owners and operators entirely by mail through special remote stocking programs.

Industry Overview

Most craft malls are individually owned and operated. Only a few have expanded with outlets in other locations, and there are no other chains in America similar to Coomers, except for American Craft Malls, now a chain of six (see nearby sidebar).

No one knows how many craft malls there are or how many have come and gone, because there has never been any central organization to monitor this industry's growth or police the way individual malls are operated. Where there is no control, there are bound to be problems. Because there has never been a guidebook on how to start and operate a crafts mall, everyone who has ventured into this field has had to fly by the seat of their pants, making up rules as they went along. It is not surprising, then, that there are no standards in the industry as to rental fees, booth sizes or service charges. Because each mall or group of malls has established its own fees, services and method of operation, craft sellers should investigate several malls before signing a lease. Coomers malls have set a high standard for the industry, but not every mall operates so professionally or efficiently.

When craft malls first appeared on the scene, crafters saw them as the greatest thing ever to come down the pike, but now the bloom is off the rose. Much has changed since 1995 when I first began to write about selling through malls. There are some exceptions, of course, but for the most part, professionals who take pride in offering quality handcrafts are mov-

American Craft Malls

Two of the first Coomers malls in Azle and Burleson, Texas, are now known as American Craft Malls and are owned and managed by Phillip Coomer. This chain of malls now includes four additional malls in Oklahoma and Texas. The illustration below shows how booths are arranged in the mall in Azle, Texas. Floor plans of the other malls can be found on Craftmark.com. Phillip was the first mall owner to promote his crafters with a site on the Internet, and he says many of his vendors (currently 960) have found his malls through the Web site. Whereas the number of remote sellers in most malls is about 5 to 20 percent of the total, in American Craft Malls, that percentage is between 25 and 30 percent.

"These out-of-town people have really got the pack-and-ship stuff down pat," he says. "They are true professionals who produce in quantity and deliver the kind of products we want to sell. We're delighted to have them because their sales tend to be higher than those of local craftspeople, many of whom sell only for extra income."

American Craft Mall sellers also have the option of being represented in their own online catalog. "CraftMark.com was the first online craft mall in Internet history," says Phillip. "We feature the work of outstanding crafters, and our catalog of handcrafts is the largest of any on the Web." A companion site, ProCrafter.com features articles, supply sources and crafter links. (See Resource Chapter for more information.)

ing out of the malls and into other markets because they can't compete with the cheap imports and commercial gift lines being carried in most malls today. Coomers' statistics offer an indication of what is probably also happening in independent malls across the country.

In 1995, some 8,000 crafters were selling through 30 Coomers malls. In 2001, those numbers had dropped to 6,000 crafters selling in 26 malls. These are still impressive figures, of course, and craft malls remain a viable market for many. It's just that today's craft mall scene is different than it was a few years ago and you need to understand this to properly evaluate malls as a possible market for your work.

Tip

Beware of "Crafters Wanted" ads for malls not yet open, and don't give anyone up-front money to reserve a space. There have been reports of crafters who have lost their deposit money to unscrupulous individuals who didn't follow through on their promise of opening a craft mall.

How to Select a Good Craft Mall

Craft malls come in all sizes, from small shops of 3,000 square feet to super malls of 20,000 square feet. All malls operate alike in that they rent space by the square foot, but that's where the similarity ends. Monthly rental fees, service fees and sales commissions vary considerably, along with size of exhibit space and benefits offered to sellers. In comparing craft malls, consider the following things:

Location and Size of Mall

If you are checking out a local mall, visit it to see how many people are shopping there at different hours on different days of the week. Is the store in a heavily trafficked area? Does it regularly attract tourists? Is it a new community? (Coomers has found that it's good for business to locate a mall in neighborhoods where new homes are going up, because people like to decorate them with arts and crafts.)

Consider the size of the mall not only in relation to its location but in terms of number of booths. In reading craft mall descriptions, I found a mall of 17,000 square feet with 250 spaces, one with 11,000 square feet and 500 spaces and another with 3,000 square feet and 200 spaces. What this tells me is that the display spaces in some malls are much smaller than in others. Always ask yourself whether the size of the mall and number of exhibitors seem right, whether the display space is large enough for your kind of crafts and whether shoppers have enough room to move about.

Booth Size and Monthly Rent

Some basic booth sizes are 3 × 3, 4 × 4 and 8 × 8 feet. To increase profits, however, some malls may try to squeeze extra booths into a space just to get the additional rent from crafters. You might think a 3 × 3-foot space at $85 is a better deal than a 4 × 4-foot space at $115, but is it? By comparing the square footage of a booth to the monthly rent, you will find that the 3 × 3 space costs $9.44 per square foot while the 4 × 4 space is $7.19 per square foot (3 × 3 = 9 square feet; $85 ÷ 9 = $9.44 per square foot). It's interesting to compare figures like this, but you also need to consider a mall's location. Ultimately, what crafters are charged for rent is directly tied to what a mall owner must pay to operate the building itself. The higher these costs, the higher the monthly rental fee will be. In some cases, a smaller-size booth in an expensive, higher-traffic area could be two or three times as profitable as a larger booth in a mall with lower rent fees.

Number and Types of Sellers

If a mall can accommodate 200 artisans, find out how many are presently represented by the mall. If it has been open for some time and is filled only to 75 percent capacity, there may be a problem. One sure sign of a successful mall is its being filled to capacity with a long waiting list.

Some malls will rent space to any seller, including antique dealers and others who sell commercial goods, making them less desirable outlets for high-quality handcrafts. A mall that sells only handcrafts is likely to jury all its sellers by asking to see samples or photographs of products that will be offered. (Most high-quality craft fairs are juried, so you should expect this in a high-quality mall.)

Lease

Read the lease carefully before you sign it to make sure you understand your responsibilities and legal obligations. You'll have to pay the rent whether your crafts sell or not. Initially, most malls require a three- to six-month lease and ask for a deposit to cover the last month's rent. Some malls require renewal for the same length of time while others allow it on a month-to-month basis after the initial lease period. If you have never sold in a crafts mall before, you might lessen your financial risk by leasing your first booth before the holiday or peak tourist season.

Sales Commission

This seems to vary from 4 to 8 percent. A low percentage here may be offset, however, by extra fees (discussed below). One mall owner I spoke with takes 7 percent, but only after crafters have made two times their rent.

Service Fees

Some malls charge for every little thing. There might be a 3.5 to 4 percent charge on credit card purchases, plus an additional fee for advertising or other special services. In comparison, Coomers charges an 8 percent service fee that covers all bad checks, credit charges, their Checkpoint Security System, and computerized checkout. If you think any of the service fees are unfair, check out some new malls. One seller reported that she and several fellow artisans pulled out of a shop in Vermont when the owner suddenly decided to impose a flat fee for processing credit card sales whether a crafter's purchases were charged or not. The shop owner figured this was fair since 70 percent of her sales were on credit cards. The crafters didn't agree. In the end, the shop suffered.

Payment/Sales Reports

All sales are made by the mall; crafters do no selling. Some malls make monthly payments; others pay every two weeks. Some malls have computerized their business and offer detailed sales reports of what has sold while others are doing sales reports manually.

Merchandising Assistance

Most craft malls leave it up to crafters to decorate their booth, but if you're not good at this, look for a mall with a merchandising specialist who can advise and assist you. All malls have some kind of remote stocking program set up to enable them to work with sellers outside their area, but there are some problems here. (See lengthy discussion on this topic elsewhere in this chapter.) Some malls will restock a booth at no extra charge, but most seem to be charging a flat $10 restocking fee.

Insurance

Unless a craft mall is located in a shopping center, you are not likely to have any fire insurance coverage on the handcrafts you are displaying there. (Shopping malls mandate all stores to buy liability and fire insurance on their contents whether they own the merchandise or not.) While the chance of fire may be slim, this is a risk you will have to take unless you can secure coverage on your own. If not, it would be prudent to limit the amount of merchandise you put into a single mall.

Security System

Is the mall well lit? Does it have a camera-security system or at least a strategic floor plan that discourages shoplifting? Are children allowed to roam freely and play havoc with displays? Bless the mall owner who has set up a special area for children to play in while Mom shops! (See discussion, "Two Problems You Must Deal With.")

186

Restrictions

I was astonished to learn that some malls do not allow crafters to use hang tags bearing their name and address because they are afraid other shop owners will come in and steal away their renters. Instead, they make crafters use the shop's tags. If you are renting space, you should be able to display your products as you wish. Hang tags add a professional touch that increases sales, so if a mall makes this kind of demand, it is actually harming your ability to make sales. If a mall tells you that you can't put hang tags on your products or put your business cards on display in your exhibit, find another mall.

Tip

Once you get started selling in different states, mall owners are likely to start coming to you. "Other mall owners pose as shoppers when they check out the competition," says a successful seller. "When they see products they like, they look for hang tags and business cards so they can contact craftspeople directly and invite them to sell in their mall.

Ask a mall if you are restricted to selling only your own merchandise. If the space being offered is too expensive or too large for you to keep filled, you may be able to sell with a friend whose work is compatible with yours. Some sellers have increased their profits by becoming a vendor for several crafters who don't want the responsibility of maintaining their own rental space in a mall.

Crafter Benefits

Are you getting any special benefits from the mall owner? "Some craft malls offer you space and wish you luck," says Coomers. "Look for a mall with expertise to help you develop your business."

For example, crafters in the Coomers stores are now able to check their sales daily and keep up with their inventory via the Internet. They can also lease mall space through Coomers' Web site (see Resource Chapter) instead of working with the mall by phone or sending for a brochure. Crafters receive merchandising assistance, booth setup and quarterly meetings on crafter development. Barcode software enables mall sellers to inventory and label their product with Coomers' exclusive barcode system. Coomers also provides marketing assistance for crafters by providing flyers and coupons for distribution at craft shows and events in which they are involved.

Craft Mall Merchandise

Crafters everywhere are complaining about the fact that most malls are now carrying imports or adding commercial products to the mix. In most cases, however, the malls have had no choice. It was either go this route or go out of business. When I questioned Rufus Coomer about why they were now carrying imported items in some of their stores, he said they were trying to fill some nooks and crannies. He confirmed that they also buy occasional truckloads of craft supplies from Wang's, and that their crafters love being able to buy such items in bulk at prices lower than they can find anywhere else. "They buy such things as unpainted birdhouses, candles that can be decorated, miniature teddy bears, and so on," Rufus explains, "then combine or enhance these items in a variety of ways to create products for sale in our stores."

Thus, some of the "imports" now appearing in Coomers malls are actually being put together by Coomers vendors themselves. But this is nothing new. As discussed in an earlier chapter, a growing number of crafters are also selling items at fairs that include component parts and supplies made in other countries. People are simply doing whatever they can to make money, and they can't be faulted for that. The crafts industry is changing, and there are many different categories of "crafters" today. Those who sell only products made 100 percent by their own hands will never be able to see eye to eye with those who sell products that have been "put together" in some way or merely purchased and "enhanced" for resale. Fortunately, this is still a free country, and every seller has the right to make and sell (or buy and resell) anything he or she wishes. Professional crafters also have the option of passing on craft malls and fairs that allow such sales and searching out the special sales outlets that are right for their particular wares.

To increase their profits, some mall sellers are adding commercial lines to their handcrafted product line. Ruth Magee and her partner, Connie Whitehill, are in the wedding/event decorating business, producing silk florals and other items related to this industry. They believe it is impractical for today's mall sellers to be purists about their work. "It just makes good sense to take on some other items as 'rent-payers' for those times of the year when crafts are not selling well," says Ruth. "Our current mall is the size of an old small-town dry goods store (which in fact is what it used to be) and we produce one-of-a-kind floral pieces. Earlier, when Connie and I were renting space in an antique mall, we realized a couple of dealers had steady sellers there in refrigerator dish towels and Rada cutlery. So we became Rada dealers and started producing dish towels for sale in the new rent-a-space, and these items are now helping to carry us through when the silk floral business is slow. Our antique dealer friend shares the space and the rent with me and Connie, and her antique furniture comes in handy for display pieces for our floral products. Occasionally, Connie and I also put a few antiques in the booth space—items usually priced under $10."

Craft Mall Arithmetic

Some well-meaning but inexperienced mall owners have opened stores that are too large for their market area. They may figure their profits will be higher if they have more spaces to rent, but they don't stop to consider that there may not be enough customers for the number of crafters interested in selling. Before signing a lease with a new mall, check to see how much traffic it has, then do a little arithmetic.

Let's say a new mall opens in a small community, offering 200 spaces to local crafters at an average rental fee of $95 per month. At full capacity, the owners would figure to gross $19,000 a month, or $228,000 a year. This may sound like a good way to get rich quick, but it doesn't work that way. If a mall can't attract enough buyers, its crafters won't stay. If everyone in a mall this size made even twice their rent in sales—and a lot of sellers don't do this well—the mall would have to sell $38,000 worth of crafts every month. For sellers to make four times their rent (which is the minimum professionals say is needed for a good profit), the mall would have to sell $76,000 worth of product every month, or more than $2,500 a day. If a mall's average sale is $25, to sell $38,000 worth of crafts every month, it would need to pull in an average of 50 buyers every day.

Here is another way to look at it. If a mall has 200 crafters and has monthly sales of $38,000 per month, it suggests that sellers are averaging only $6.34 a day or $190/month. ($38,000 ÷ 200 = $190/month). A few sellers may be realizing sales of ten times their booth cost, but most will be lucky to get three or four times their rent in sales. In other words, if you are paying $40 per space in a small craft mall, you would be doing well to have sales of $120-$160 per month. If you were paying $150 for space in a larger mall, you would need sales of $375 to $500 per month. To sell at this volume, however, you might need to display three or four thousand dollars' worth of merchandise.

"We consider sales that equal four times our rent to be a good result," says quiltmaker Joan Bleakly, who has sold in several craft malls in the Tucson area over the years. "Because it takes a while for a mall to attract a loyal customer base, one may have to sell in a new store for a couple of years to achieve this sales ratio. Although many craft mall vendors are happy if they just cover their rent, this seems to be an unprofitable business to us. But people sell their craft work for a huge number of different reasons and have equally as many different goals."

As a crafts mall seller, you have a lot of power because a mall can't stay in business without satisfied exhibitors. Its financial success depends not only on the quality of suppliers it can attract, but the number and quality of shoppers it can bring into the store. "We realize that without the quality crafter, our business would be nothing," confirms a mall owner in business for four years. "Therefore, our mission is to provide a quality environment for artisans and crafters to sell their quality creations. We know that if our crafters aren't successful, then we won't be either, so we make every effort to bring in qualified customers to buy our crafters' work."

Unless you're dealing with an established craft mall chain such as Coomers or American Craft Malls, be cautious when dealing with new independently owned craft malls outside your area where you cannot personally visit the facility. Do some research on the mall owner's background, and limit the amount of merchandise you put into any new mall unless you have favorable recommendations from other sellers in that mall, or until you've established a good working relationship with the owner or store manager. Finally, be sure you have the owner's full name and phone number in your files—not just the store manager's name or the shop's telephone number (which would be disconnected in the event of a shop's financial failure).

What Sells Best in Craft Malls

Craft malls are providing an important additional outlet for people who have a good deal of product to sell. Although most malls have suppliers from other parts of the country, their primary goal is to bring their area's buyers and sellers together. If you have been selling with success at local fairs or holiday boutiques, it stands to reason that you will do well in a crafts mall in the same area. Try to offer items that are not being offered by other crafters in the mall, however, and also try to find the "magic selling price" that is low enough to be attractive to buyers and high enough to give you a true profit.

The trick to success in the craft mall industry is to carefully match your product with the kind of buyers who frequent craft malls. You aren't going to do well if you offer products that sell well only during a particular season.

You probably won't do well in malls if you offer high-priced items that have a cheap counterpart in discount or craft stores. "I've not done well in malls," says Christine Zipps. "I've been told my home decor silk and floral items are too high end. The particular Coomers craft mall I tried didn't attract the kind of buyer who would pay $85 for a wreath when they could get a cheap version of same at the local crafts supply shop for $37.99. Also, the mall atmosphere seemed to be mostly 'country-cutesy' theme with their items. Nothing wrong with it, just not my style."

While many crafters are selling with success in craft malls, others have lost money. After signing a four-month lease with a Coomers mall, an artisan specializing in Victorian crafts reported on her unsatisfactory sales experience. "During the biggest shopping week of the year, I sold absolutely nothing," she said. "The only thing that seemed to be selling was cows and sunflowers, spray-painted coffee cans with cardboard tree cutouts and seashells glued into angel shapes."

The fact that Victorian crafts are popular in some areas of the country—and receive rave reviews from a craft mall jury—doesn't mean they will sell everywhere. Renting space in a prestigious store doesn't guarantee sales, either. When you specialize in a particular type of craft, you must pay careful attention to where and how you offer it for sale. Generally, the following items seem to be selling well in malls across the country:

- Seasonal items
- Traditional crafts and furnishings
- Country crafts, folk art and Americana products
- Small decorative accessories for home and office
- Dolls, toys and miniatures
- Crafty wearables, jewelry and accessories
- Novelty items and whimsical creations

For every crafter who complains of no sales, there will always be others in the same place who are selling everything they make. It always comes down to the same thing: to make sales you must make products that people *in that area* want to buy. "Too many crafters make what they want to make with little regard for what people want to buy, " says Linda Coomer. "They don't change with the times. They're still doing crafts that went out of fashion months or years ago, still using colors no longer in vogue or patterns and techniques that are old-hat."

Good pricing is essential to financial success at a crafts fair, but it's vital for success at a crafts mall because you've got to lay out the monthly rental fee whether you sell anything or not. Linda Coomer says the hottest sellers in Coomers malls are items priced around $6. The average Coomers shopper spends $26 (compared to $34 in 1995), which means that higher-priced items in the $40 to $50 range are also selling well. "You need to have a variety of prices on your products," says Linda. "Try to have items priced for everyone's budget: low, medium and high-priced. For example, a lot of school kids come in to find something for their teachers for $5."

Tip

The walls of a craft mall exhibit area are generally of white pegboard but may be painted or decorated in any way the crafter desires. Use colors that complement your crafts. Put small items in planter boxes and display others on glass shelves hung on the pegboard walls. Don't ever put anything on the floor—use wicker shelves or wooden crates instead. Drape fabric for accent.

Setting Up a Mall Display

How products are displayed in a mall has everything to do with whether they will sell or not. All the display tips and ideas you found for craft fairs in Chapter Six are applicable to a craft mall setup. In addition, it's important to regularly rotate your stock and freshen your exhibit. Some sellers report increased sales immediately after restocking or changing their display. That's because most malls have developed a loyal customer base that expects to see new merchandise every time they return. If your booth always looks the same, it will receive no attention from these repeat buyers. They not only want to see new products, but new products displayed in new and interesting ways. "Success starts with the way you present your booth," confirms Linda Coomer. "Keep it fully stocked—the more crafts you put in it, the better your sales."

Sells Thousands of Miniatures Annually

While it is difficult to make a true profit on low-priced items, some crafters have figured out how to do it. Take Gina Casey, for instance. By selling in craft malls for four years, she made enough money to open her own shop. (You'll recall reading about her in the preceding chapter.) She explains how she worked during her craft mall days: "I worked about four hours a day, six days a week to produce thousands of miniature hand-sculpted items each year from a special blend of Fimo and Sculpey mixtures. My line included fruits and vegetables, dolls, bears, cats and other items for dollhouses and people with shadow box collections. My best-selling item in craft malls was a 1½-inch teddy bear.

"From $10 worth of materials, I could gross $300 in sales. It took me only a couple of minutes to make one of my little teddy bears and I made hundreds at a time, pricing them at $2.50 each. At that time I was selling in five malls, which is all I could handle. I had a lot of requests to be in others, but I was also wholesaling at the time to a few shops in tourist areas, and doing a few craft shows as well."

Gina got her wholesale buyers by placing an ad in a consumer showcase magazine for handcrafts. Because her prices were so low, she gave only a 30 percent discount to wholesale buyers. She never knew what price shop owners were putting on her items, but I'll bet it was two or three times the price she was asking.

"When selling locally, visit the mall every month and rearrange all the items in your display," advises a successful seller. "If an item hasn't sold at the end of 90 days, take it home and either redo it or drop it from your line." Here are some ideas on how to add pizzazz to your craft mall display.

194

1. Do special displays for each holiday, featuring products appropriate for that particular holiday.

2. Change your color scheme periodically to reflect changing seasons.

3. Change the way products are displayed by rearranging shelves or hangers.

4. Rotate any display containers in use (baskets, boxes, crates, etc.).

5. Experiment with paint, wallpaper, curtains, swags or mirrors.

6. To attract more buyers, display your best sellers or higher-priced items at eye level.

7. If sales are sluggish, move your display to a different area of the store (rent a different booth space). Otherwise stay in the same place so regular buyers always know where to find your newest products.

8. Use signs to encourage sales (as discussed in Chapter Seven).

Two Problems You Must Deal With

Two display problems you need to address are the possibility of damaged merchandise and theft.

Damaged Merchandise

If you make expensive items that can't be handled without damage, don't put them in a craft mall. "You cannot expect a manager of a gallery or craft mall to guard your work," says a soft sculpture artist.

In every grocery store and shopping center, we see parents who let their children run wild, so you must take this into consideration when setting up a craft mall display. Goods within reach of young children are going to be handled. Other goods will naturally become shopworn as they are handled by adults. (You may want to reread the tips in Chapter Six for reminders on how craft fair sellers protect their work from excessive handling.)

Shoplifting

Be prepared to lose some merchandise to theft, especially in malls that are poorly lit, inadequately staffed or without camera security. Of course the only way to know if you have lost merchandise or not is to set up an inventory system, and I'll bet only a handful of craft mall sellers have done this. You should keep track of how many of each item you place on display, and as you receive payments from the mall with a list of items that have sold, mark your records accordingly. Periodically, take a physical inventory to see how many items are unaccounted for.

When a product turns up missing, check other booths. I can easily imagine a shopper picking up an item from booth 23, walking the aisle and then deciding when she's in front of booth 37 that she doesn't want that item after all. Is she going to walk back to booth 23 or even know it's important to replace the item there? I doubt it. Instead, she may lay it down in someone else's booth.

You would think that Gina Casey, the miniaturist mentioned earlier, would have had terrible shoplifting problems in the four years she sold in malls, but she felt her losses were reasonable, given the nature of retailing. "I lost an average of $400 a year against sales of $25,000, or .016 percent," she told me. Since most of Gina's items were priced at $2.50, this worked out to a loss of about 160 pieces a year, or about 32 pieces a year per mall. "Shoplifting comes with the territory," she says, "and I figured this was a loss I could accept."

You might compare your own losses to Gina's to see how you're doing, percentage-wise. Because Gina regularly took inventory at all the malls she was selling through, she always knew exactly how many items were missing from each store. All of the malls were within 200 miles of Gina's home, which was close enough to justify the cost of taking regular physical inventories. During the fall and through the Christmas season, she checked all of them once a month. During slower periods, she visited each mall every two months. "Curiously, fewer items were stolen during the heavy selling seasons," she recalls. "Most seemed to disappear during the slow seasons when there were fewer shoppers in the store."

Most malls offer security tags or labels that can be attached to merchandise to deter shoplifters. There are different kinds, but each is imbedded with a magnetic strip that sets off an alarm when people try to leave the store with a stolen object. At five to ten cents apiece, this is cheap insurance. Unfortunately, it doesn't work for everyone. The problem Gina had was that her items were too small to be tagged. "The 1 × 2-inch labels had to be stuck on a piece of cardboard before being attached to my products," she says. "This took a lot of extra time and was no guarantee of protection because they could easily be removed. For that reason, I never bothered to tag the low-priced items."

Gina tried selling items in plastic bags, but she made fewer sales, so she stopped doing it. "I think people want to be able to pick up and hold items before they buy, and putting them in plastic bags makes them seem more commercial," she reasoned.

This sounds reasonable, but Ginger Chamberlain would disagree. She, too, sells polymer clay miniatures in a mall. "I would like to see more craft malls offer glass cabinets to accommodate artists who make small things," she says. "After I experienced a loss of $300 from theft of my items, the mall owner supplied a glass case for them. It has worked out great for everyone involved (except the thieves). Now, no more thefts, sales are super, and the bonus is that the lighting in these glass cases encourages sales."

Ginger urges mall sellers not to be shy about asking for this kind of protection. "Mall owners may not know the need is there unless we tell them why we hesitate to do business with them," she says. "I am convinced that if more stores provided locked display cases, we would see a great change in crafters' attitudes concerning craft malls and shops."

Note that having your small items displayed in a large glass case near the checkout counter is apt to work much better than putting them in a small locked case in your crafts booth. This could cost you some sales since some buyers may be too impatient to wait for someone to unlock your case. Even then, you would need to establish rigid rules for how the case was to be handled. As one seller pointed out to me, "You would be surprised at how many people think it's okay to unlock a case, hand the item to the customer, and let them carry it around with them while they shop. This defeats the whole purpose of having your valuables locked up."

One solution to this problem is to have a sign on your locked display case that says items removed from it must be held at the check-out counter until the customer has finished shopping.

Remote Stocking Programs

Most craft malls offer a remote stocking program that enables crafters from other parts of the country to sell through their malls. This is a great service if you happen to live in an area that is devoid of craft malls, rent-a-space shops or good local craft fairs. It's also a good way to get your crafts into an area that may be hungry for your type of product. Some crafts have only regional appeal, however, so you always need to research a new market area to learn what's selling there. Two disadvantages of running a remote booth, however, are increased costs (shipping expense and phone calls) and problems in controlling your display.

The experience of Beverly O'Hara offers perspective on this topic. Now retired from the crafts industry, Beverly remains a legend in craft mall circles where everyone then knew her as "Beverly Durant, The Angel Lady." Her first products were four angel dolls seven inches in size, made of embroidery floss or mop yarn and finished with ribbon, lace and other items. In addition to these dolls, she had about a dozen other craft items in her line, all priced between $5.95 to $14.95. Beverly became a whiz at figuring out how to turn out items assembly-line style, and her whole family and three outside employees were once involved in her business. At one point she was selling more than 70,000 angel dolls a year in 35 malls, most of them out-of-state, and this was possible only because of remote stocking programs. Each time she opened a new mall, she would send a diagram and a photograph to the mall's remote representative, who would set up the display and send Beverly a picture to see if she liked it.

"Initially, I found remote stocking programs to be a godsend," she recalls. "I couldn't complain about the service I received because the mall managers did everything to accommodate me. They notified me when my stock was low and restocked my display each time I sent a new supply of merchandise. Problems developed over time, however. I would get a picture of my display every three months, and as time passed I became more dissatisfied with the way it looked. The people who were maintaining my display were trying, but they seemed to lack design sense and just couldn't comprehend how I wanted things set up."

In time, sales dropped in all of Beverly's out-of-state malls, convincing her of the importance of displays to sales. She gradually closed all of these outlets to concentrate on selling through fifteen malls (nine of which were Coomers) within a hundred miles from home. Although she appreciated the remote representatives who continually restocked her displays as merchandise sold, Beverly learned the importance of personally maintaining her displays with regular visits to each mall.

"If you can't maintain your craft mall display personally, you may get better service from a smaller mall," advises Gina Casey. "It always seemed to me that the bigger and larger the mall, the less attention my exhibit received. In my four years of craft mall selling and using the remote stocking programs offered by each mall, I found that items shipped in between times to replace stock were often haphazardly placed on shelves or in the type-tray boxes I use instead of being grouped by kind, color or theme."

In summary, stocking programs are important because they enable crafters to ship in new merchandise when it can't be delivered in person. Greater sales may be realized, however, if you keep a close eye on the quality of your display through regular visits to each mall in which you're selling.

When a Craft Mall Fails

Whether a craft mall closes because of poor management or market conditions, craftspeople are the ones who suffer most. Many malls have failed in the past, and more are likely to come and go in the future, so remain alert to avoid loss here.

Like some consignment shop owners in years past, some entrepreneurs who initially jumped on the "craft mall bandwagon" were inexperienced retailers or business managers, and a few were less than ethical. I won't include details here, but over the years, I've received several reports from crafters about independent mall owners who stole away in the middle of the night, taking with them crafters' hard-earned profits and sometimes all of their inventory as well.

One craft mall seller told me about a case she was involved in, where the owner of three failed craft malls ended up owing his craft vendors more than $300,000 (not to mention all the sales tax he collected and didn't pay to the state). "We all met to discuss the legal advice we had been given," my reader reported, "but it soon became evident that we were unlikely to get our money back."

Unfortunately, crafters don't have much clout in a case like this. Most will be lucky to get all their unsold merchandise back. In some cases, inventory may be subject to the claims of creditors and be seized. While many states have special laws to protect artisans when a consignment shop goes into bankruptcy (see next chapter), craft malls and rent-a-space shops fall into a gray area that is not currently covered by state consignment laws. About the only way to protect yourself against this problem is to keep a keen eye on the malls in which you sell and watch for warning signs of a mall in trouble. These might include:

▼ Less than 75 percent occupancy
▼ No advertising being done
▼ Too little traffic
▼ Crafters pulling out

▼ Poor accounting of sales

▼ Inadequate explanation of charges being made

▼ Late payments

Rent-a-Space Shops and Co-ops

The rent-a-space retailing concept has enabled many entrepreneurs to open shops that could not have opened as straight consignment shops. A few consignment craft shop owners were experimenting with this type of retailing as early as 1975, but crafters didn't catch on to the benefits of renting retail space until craft malls took the country by storm fifteen years later. Although craft malls and rent-a-space shops are similar in that they both rent space to individual sellers, there are some interesting differences.

First, rent-a-space craft shops are generally smaller than craft malls. Some are laid out like a mall (one display area after another), while others are set up like a regular gift or craft shop, with display controlled by the shop owner or manager. Shops that don't rent standard display areas may rent shelf space, wall space or a corner nook. They may also take handcrafts on consignment or sell a line of commercial goods. In many instances, craft vendors are given the option of working in the shop for a few hours each month in exchange for paying a lower commission on sales. Monthly rental fees and sales commissions may vary considerably from shop to shop.

Some rent-a-space shops might better be called "variety shops" since crafts are only a small part of the merchandise one will find in them. Linda Kindle, owner of Porhouse Crafts, has been selling in this kind of outlet for ten years, under five different owners, each of whom changed the personality of the store and the type of products offered for sale. "The Old and Nu Mini Mall in Martinsville, Indiana (which has had other names in the past), has gone through an amazing cycle of change," says Linda. "It began as an antique mall, then changed to an antique/variety store, then an antique/Victorian decorating shop, then an antique/Victorian/primitive shop. Now it offers all of these things plus yard sale and flea market junk. It's one of those weird little places lots of people love to dig through because you can find just about anything, and I do very well there."

Linda has been doing primitive crafts for seventeen years, and she's done well enough that she's about ready to give up her day job. Currently, she has three booths in the above-mentioned mall, plus a rented booth in a variety shop in a nearby town. Art primitives are her specialty, and she sells a combination of her own work plus other items she buys for resale. "I refinish or rework small decor items I find at yard sales and flea markets and offer them with my own painted items such as game boards, Christmas ornaments and Americana signs. Along with this, I also mix in a variety of items bought at wholesale that complement all my other products, such as homespun towels and candles. Although the climate and focus of the shop has changed with every owner, I have stayed the same and now have a following of customers who love primitive decor."

Craft co-op shops are similar in operation to craft malls and rent-a-space shops, except that they are owned by a group of crafters. (For information on how to start a cooperative shop, see Chapter Eleven.) In addition to featuring the work of co-op members, this type of outlet may also rent space to outside vendors. Saguaro Artisans Gallery is a business in downtown Tucson owned by two women who have been in business together for close to twenty years. The store functions as a co-op with more than forty sellers in the store who take turns running it on a day-to-day basis. The merchandise is all southwest themed and 90 percent of it is handcrafted locally. The balance is imported merchandise, mostly from Mexico. Joan Bleakly and her husband have been with this group for over a dozen years and have sizeable display areas in the seven rooms in the shop.

"Co-op members pay a monthly rent of $30 and 25 percent commission on all sales, which go toward paying store operating costs," she says. "Each co-op member must also work in the store one day a month. Those who have been with the store for the longest time have keys to the store and newer participants are assigned to work with the current 'key holders.' We do the opening and closing on the days we work. We have fun working our one day a month at the store because so many interesting people come in to browse or buy. Foreign tourists are always interested in finding something from our region to take home and we have sent pieces of our work to countries all over the world."

In Summary

Many crafters leave malls or rent-a-space shops because the rental fees are too high for the amount of sales being made. "I'm one of those that did well in craft malls for awhile, then stopped doing well and got out," says Lisa Risler, who now sells a variety of products on her six Web sites (see Chapter Twelve). "In one mall, sales were great when the mall featured only handcrafted items, and the rental price of $50 for a 10 × 10-foot spot was reasonable. But when the mall hired a bookkeeper, prices went up, the spaces got smaller ($65 for a 2 × 3-foot spot), and before long, they were selling antiques and 'junk' from dollar-type stores and imports. At that point, my sales dropped to nothing and out I went. Imports have really hurt the crafters here in Texas (where quality handcrafts are hard to find), as well as the major discount stores that sell mass quantities of 'similar' items at cheap prices."

I have wondered whether professional crafters, who now have new opportunities on the Internet, will continue to sell in craft malls and shops or gradually get out of them altogether. "That's a hard question," says soapmaker Tammy Hodson. "I don't think we will do craft malls anymore because of the cost of doing business. Selling on the Internet is costly, but craft mall fees have gone up, too. I just checked out a new spot that looked really promising and this one charged a fee per square foot. It came to a rather hair-raising figure when you consider there are additional fees besides. My main selling product is a $4 pickup. Many people do pick up several items, but still it is not like a $90, one-shot floral wreath. My gift baskets are usually not more than $30. Plus, to get a realistic view of how you are doing, you need to average your selling months. Holiday months may be big selling times, but there are other months that are much, much slower. Then there is drive time, plus the costs of trying to keep your area looking nice and seasonal."

Even when sales are not terrific, some crafters remain in malls for other reasons. In addition to marketing through her own Web site, Gwen Taylor Lord sells her trademarked "Eppie the Pew Baby" dolls, patchwork quilts, carry-all bags, coloring books and puppet pals in Coomers malls. "Over the past twelve years, I've sold in eleven different locations but have only five going now," she says. "I kept moving inventory around until I found the highest selling locations for my products. Although I have not made significant income through these outlets, I will continue with Coomers as long as there is marginal profit because I consider these stores a great marketing and advertising tool. They offer a place where my customers can get a 'hands on' feel for my products. There are several stores I haven't tried yet, so I'll probably branch out again next year to increase my territory."

I've tried to present a balanced view of both the good and bad side of craft mall and rent-a-space selling, so now you must decide if it's right for you or not. Compare these types of marketing outlets to the consignment shops and galleries discussed in the following chapter (which have their own unique pros and cons), and also consider your marketing options on the Web, as discussed in Chapter Twelve.

Chapter Ten

Selling on Consignment

Selling on consignment is one of the oldest and most successful methods of marketing art and handcrafts. It is also the most controversial.

Many professional crafters would advise you against consignment selling, arguing that shop owners who won't (or can't afford to) buy your merchandise outright will not work very hard to sell it and will often ruin it in the process. Yet, for the beginner who can locate a good consignment shop, this is a great way to gain experience in the retail marketplace with less financial risk than with craft malls or rent-a-space shops. After reading this chapter and considering the pros and cons of selling on consignment, decide for yourself if this is the route you want to go.

First you need to understand the difference between selling your work outright and consigning it to a retail shop or a gallery. When you sell outright (wholesale), you relinquish all control over your merchandise. Once you have been paid for it, the shop owns it and can sell it for any price it wishes. When you consign merchandise, however, you are merely transferring it to another who will act as your sales representative. You remain the legal owner of all consigned goods. If and when it sells, the retailer will withhold its standard sales commission and send you the balance. This can often take months, which is why some craftspeople prefer to wholesale their work. Although profits may be smaller, at least they get their money in hand quickly.

If you have previously sold only through craft fairs, you may think it is more profitable to sell directly to the consumer than through a shop that takes a sales commission of 35 to 40 percent. But is it? Much will depend on what you are selling, what it costs to make, and how quickly you can produce it. As I've emphasized earlier, if you were to take the time normally spent at fairs and use this time for production instead, you might find that your increased volume would more than offset the sales commission paid to shops and give you a larger profit at year's end.

Different Types of Shops and Galleries

Although no one has ever been able to keep track of all the consignment shops that have come and gone, reports from my readers suggest that true consignment craft shops are a rare species today. Although not yet gone, they are steadily declining in number, much like craft malls and craft fairs. In time, the Internet or changing market conditions are likely to cause the total demise of the 100 percent traditional consignment craft shop, leaving only a curious mixture of interesting shops with operating methods as varied as their individual owners, and merchandise that runs the gamut from fine handcrafts to commercial gift lines, imports, antiques and flea market "junk."

Years ago, consignment shops were all the same: Sellers left handcrafted items on consignment and when they sold, the shop owner retained a small percentage of sales and gave the rest to the seller. In the 90s, however, a new breed of consignment shop emerged, due in part to the popularity of (and competition from) craft malls and rent-a-space shops, and partly because of ever-increasing overhead costs. Today, in addition to taking a higher percentage of sales, most consignment shops are also charging overhead or management fees, and consignors are sometimes asked to work in the shop a day or two a month (like the cooperative shops discussed earlier), or pay a higher percentage on their sales. Some have simply throw in the towel and become rent-a-space shops. There are still some good consignment craft shops today, but you may have to search hard to find them. (See "How to Find Good Consignment Shops" below.)

Sales Commissions and Other Costs

Once you get involved in consignment selling, you will find yourself dealing with shops that have different commission arrangements. One seller asks:

> "I work with two consignment shops. One works on a 60/40 percent arrangement, the other on 75/25 percent. If I offer my crafts to both shops at the same price, the second shop will sell my work for much less. Is that fair to the first shop? If I raise the price of my work to sell to the second shop, to keep both shops equal in their selling price, is that fair to the second shop?"

What's important here is that you establish a firm retail price on all the items you plan to consign or sell in shops or any other retail outlets. Don't be concerned about what is fair to the shops; instead, be concerned about what is fair to buyers. Set firm retail prices based on the true worth of the product, and if you can make more profit from one outlet than another, consider it gravy.

Susan Gearing, who has sold in consignment shops for twenty-five years (see nearby sidebar), says the average sales commission she has paid through the years has been 30 percent, but some shops today are taking as much as 50 percent of the sale price. I sympathize with shop owners who are being faced with increasing overhead costs, but craft sellers have too many marketing options today to give 50 percent of the retail price to a consignment shop. This might make sense if you make mostly one-of-a-kind items and don't have any other outlet for them, but it makes no sense at all if you are producing multiples of a line of products that could be sold just as easily through fairs, boutiques, craft malls or rent-a-space shops. When wholesaling to gift shops, it is standard practice to offer them a 50 percent discount off the retail price, so why give the same amount to a consignment shop that may not sell your products for months?

NOTE: It is common for art and craft *galleries* to operate on a 50/50 consignment basis because their overhead costs are high and the products they carry tend to be unique, expensive, one-of-a-kind works of art that can't be wholesaled or even sold any other way. Some galleries offer only fine art while others sell both fine art and crafts, including sculpture, weaving, woodworking, pottery, glass, metalwork, and stitchery. Special exhibitions and sales are often held in galleries to promote the work of the artists and designers they represent. Commissions from architects and interior designers and custom orders from private collectors are just some of the special benefits connected with gallery exhibitions. Prestige is another.

Rebekah Rowe sells soft sculptures that hang on the wall, from magic wands to stars, moons and hearts, plus small framed and decorated mirrors. She sells almost exclusively on consignment and does very well with it. "I consign my work long distance and locally," she says. "The main reason I started with consignment is that my work is a bit different (not very mainstream) and the shops are not always sure if it will catch on, so it eases some of those 'I-don't-want-to-get-stuck-with-it' jitters. Also, a lot of stores cannot afford a big investment any more, so this also helps to get my work out there and get it exposed."

Rebekah has been paying a sales commission of between 25 to 35 percent, with the latter rate being most common. As I was writing this edition of the book, she wrote to say that one shop she was in had a fire, and she lost over $800 worth of work—a new line of products that had just been dropped off the night before. What a devastating experience for any artist or crafter, even when the loss is covered by insurance! Rebekah said the store did have insurance on contents (which is unusual for consigned merchandise), and she believed she would be reimbursed. "It's important to have a good consignment agreement with your shops," she emphasizes, "and you should pay particular attention to the matter of insurance against loss." Fortunately, Rebekah has always made it a point to keep very accurate records of what she has consigned where in case a store's consignment records are lost or damaged by fire or other disaster.

How to Find Good Consignment Shops

The best recommendations will always come from your fellow crafters as you network at craft shows, craft organization meetings or business seminars. Another good way to network with professional sellers is to join one of the many mailing lists on the Internet. (Check those on eGroups.com for starters.)

Other good shops can be found through ads in print magazines that serve professional crafters, such as *The Crafts Report*. Since most every art gallery and fine crafts shop now has its own Web site, a good search engine (I like Google.com) will turn up some interesting shop leads. Type "art/craft galleries" in the search box to come up with over 3,000 listings to explore. When searching for consignment shops, be sure to specify "craft consignment shops" to avoid pulling up listings for general resale shops.

Sometimes a shop finds Rebekah Rowe through the local art league to which she belongs, but mostly she finds her new shops by word of mouth or by reading about places and researching them online. "I check the shops out online to see what they carry, and see if my work would be a good fit. I tend to choose Main Street/Boutique type towns with actively

The Widget Queen

Prior to moving her business almost 100 percent to the Web, Susan Gearing of Susie's Crafts successfully sold to consignment shops for twenty-five years. Her friends long ago dubbed her "The Widget Queen" because of her ability to constantly come up with inexpensive items that consistently sell. Her consignment line included pins of all kinds, painted cups and pots, magnets and keychains, potholders and granny crafts in contemporary designs and color, fabric gift bags and more. Each of her products cost between 12 and 20 cents to make, and she retailed them for $2.50 to $4 each, selling thousands of items every year. "I always found I could sell fifty $2 items a lot faster than one $100 item," she says.

In years past, Susan generally consigned items ranging from $2 to $40, and kept track of current inventory by hand on a chart. "I usually sent just a small amount to a new shop to see if my things would sell well there," she says, "and to test/check on the honesty, accuracy and efficiency of the shop in paying on time. After the first couple of months, if all went well, I would expand my inventory and line accordingly. I usually gave a shop close to a year to see if it was going to work for me or not. In January of each year, I reevaluated and dropped those shops which were marginal. I tried to jury into a new shop each month or two, but I could not expand much faster than that and keep existing shops supplied. I usually shipped to current shops once a month after I got my check and sales records for the previous month. The key to success in consignment selling is keeping outlets well stocked. Many crafters complain of not doing well when they aren't replacing inventory and sending new things. If you try to sell the same old products, eventually they just won't sell."

Although Susan still sells through a couple of consignment shops today, she now finds marketing on eBay to be more profitable and more fun. (See Chapter Twelve for more from Susan on this topic.)

growing arts districts. I also find shops through The Crafts Report. I network a lot, too. When contacting a local shop, I just go in with samples. For shops out of my area, I send photos and a catalog and also direct them to a few places on the Web where my work can be seen."

When Sherrill Lewis gets a good lead, she picks up the phone and describes her products and interest in consigning to the shop. "I offer to send photos or set up an appointment if the shop is within two hours' drive time from home," she says. "Sometimes I visit a shop personally to see the layout, check out the enthusiasm of shop personnel (or lack thereof), and generally 'scope the place' to determine if it's a reasonable environment in which my work would sell."

Although Irene Haddow no longer consigns her quilted products, she suggests some research into who is running a shop. "It has been my experience that the best people to deal with are former or currently practicing craftspeople," she says. "They have been in your shoes and they recognize that you like to be dealt with in a businesslike manner including receiving payment when due, and being notified when stock is running low. They may also inform you if customers have special requests. Those that are in it strictly as a business, however, tend to be more lax, and you have to keep on top of them for payment or to find out how your stock is doing."

The Benefits of Consignment Selling

The great advantage of consignment is that it enables individuals with limited capital to open shops that may provide important marketing outlets for local producers. None of today's most successful handcraft shops could have opened if, like regular gift shops, they had to buy all goods outright to begin with. The benefits to crafters are threefold. They can

1. Consign merchandise of their choice without the pressure of meeting a deadline date
2. Control the retail selling price of their work
3. Test the marketability of new or untried items

In fact, consignment selling is often the best or only way to market work of limited production or expensive, one-of-a-kind crafts and needlework. On the minus side, consignment selling means increased bookkeeping and paperwork for both shop and seller and, for the latter, merchandise is tied up but not sold, which presents cash-flow problems.

It will be easier to work with consignment shops outside your area if you have professional printed materials that include illustrations or pictures of your work (see Chapter Fourteen). If not, be prepared to send a photograph that illustrates the quality of your work. Instead of sending a batch of unprofessional shapshots that have been developed at the local drug store, ask a friend with photographic skill to take a professional picture of a collection of your best items. Arrange them artistically against an appropriate background. Once you have a good negative, find a company that prints photographs in quantity.

Tip

Consider the cost of photographs part of your advertising and selling costs and don't whine if you don't get them back. You can enclose a SASE and ask a shop to return a photograph, but when you do this, you automatically mark yourself as a hobby seller that few shops will want to deal with.

What does "SASE" mean? It doesn't mean a "self-absorbed stuffed elephant," as I once heard someone say on radio. It means you are to include a Self-Addressed Stamped Envelope with your request for information or other reply.

Avoiding Consignment Pitfalls

Don't ignore new craft consignment shops as a market for your work, especially if you are still trying to "get your feet wet," but do be cautious about dealing with them until you're satisfied you have a good thing going. One hazard is that some new shop owners are as inexperienced as the sellers with whom they are dealing. Often, it's a case of the blind leading the blind.

You can greatly expand the number of shops you sell to by dealing with them by mail. On the other hand, you need to be careful in deciding whom to trust with your handcrafts because you can't personally monitor what's happening to them in a far-distant shop. The longer a shop has been in business, the more comfortable you will feel about dealing with them, so always ask how long the shop has been in business before you ship your first order.

After writing on the Internet about the many craft mall owners who have stolen away in the middle of the night, taking crafters' merchandise and profits with them, a consignment shop owner wrote, "I am distressed to hear sad stories of mall owners who stiff the people they claim to be helping, but worse, I hate the bad publicity this gives the rest of us who do not do such things." Her remarks reminded me to emphasize that craft malls and consignment shops are "two different animals." Different kinds of people operate both types of outlets and some care more about craftspeople than others. These two types of outlets also present different problems and pitfalls to sellers. Do not let the bad reputation of some malls or shops turn you off entirely to either type of selling.

At the same time, keep a close eye on any shop where you have consigned your crafts, and *always* insist on knowing the name and telephone number of the shop's owner (not just the shop manager). If a shop ever fails and suddenly closes with your crafts locked inside, having this information could make the difference as to whether or not you'll get your merchandise back.

"Working through consignment shops has been profitable for me over the years," says Susan Gearing. "But I found that the privately owned shops

213

Damaged Goods

A seller who offered beaded earrings and needlepoint tapestries through consignment stores told me about the problem she had encountered. "I have had work that didn't sell in consignment stores returned to me in poor shape," she says. "In one case, my work was displayed in a window. That sounded great at first, until the unsold work was returned badly faded by the sun. In another case work had been handled by many customers and was returned to me very dirty."

A crafter who avoids consignment shops adds: "If you can afford to get damaged merchandise back and have low sales, then consignment is for you. Some shoppers try to tear a product apart to see how it was made so they can try to make it themselves. The resulting damage is the responsibility of the crafter and not the store owner. That's why I now sell only to wholesale buyers."

really came and went at an alarming rate, sometimes without paying or returning merchandise. It became a game of always looking for new shops and I had a lot of merchandise out there not earning money. I found the most reliable shops to be those run by nonprofit organizations, such as Women's Exchanges, which are in it for the long haul and thus run in a more businesslike manner. In my experience, few consignment shops are computerized today, and many do not keep good records or send good sales reports with checks, so it's very important for craftspeople who sell this way to keep their own records of everything that has been shipped, sold and paid for."

Susan always accepted the fact that, when consigning merchandise, some things would be lost, damaged or shopworn. "I've always just written off such losses as the cost of doing business this way," she says. (See nearby sidebar on this topic.) As discussed in the craft mall chapter, theft is also something you have to consider when you consign merchandise to a shop.

"I like consignment in nice boutiques or galleries because my work is on view all the time," says bead artist Sherrill Lewis, Eximiously Yours! "But I've learned to take precautions. I make sure I have the name of the owner and all pertinent information, and I try to always meet the owner and establish some rapport before consigning merchandise. Even so, I've had a problem with theft. I decided to consign some of my beaded jewelry to a nice designer clothing store here in town, but a week later, someone stole a $275 necklace, so I immediately pulled my things out. In future, I will put items on consignment only if they can be in a secure environment—in a locked case or under a glass counter. My husband, Gene, has made a small display case for me so I can now provide it to any store that does not have adequate facilities."

Here are some additional tips to help you avoid common pitfalls:

▼ Never consign merchandise without a consignment agreement. Reputable shops will use a standard consignment form. (See "Preparing a Consignment Agreement" below.)

▼ Avoid consignment to shops that normally buy most of their merchandise at wholesale. Such shops who offer to take your work only on consignment may believe that your products are unsalable for one reason or another, and they will not work very hard to sell them for you.

▼ Never consign more than a few items to a new or unknown shop until you have developed a satisfactory relationship with the owner or manager (based on prompt payment after the first merchandise has been sold) and see other indications that the shop is being well managed.

▼ Your products will sell better in any shop when several pieces are displayed. If the choice is between several shops that want only a few pieces, and one or two that will take a good supply, pick the latter and offer a wide price range in the articles you consign. Obviously, the less expensive pieces will sell first, but your higher-priced pieces will encourage sales of the lower-priced items.

▼ When you make a shipment to a shop, prepare two copies of a packing list that describes each item you're sending. Keep one copy and include the other in the shipping carton for the shopowner. This should prevent later disagreements about what

Get It in Writing!

"No matter how much you want to believe what you are being told and what you think you see, get it all in writing," cautions another crafter who learned the hard way. "Be sure every area of your consignment agreement is spelled out in clear English. Don't leave anything to chance or rely on verbal agreements. This includes doing business with friends. Don't ruin a friendship or take a chance with a stranger."

A seller in Pennsylvania warns against working with new consignment shops. "Get the consignment commission details in writing," she says. "I started in a shop that had no set fee and nothing in writing. After being there for a few years and becoming friends with the owner, I found it very hard to leave after she decided to double all the prices. It took me two years to find the courage to tell her I was leaving, and why. We are still friends, but this spring when she opens her shop again I won't be there unless we agree on a much lower fee and I get it in writing."

was sent and received by the owner. If you ship more than one carton, reference on each the total number of cartons being shipped, and number each accordingly. Make sure your packing list shows which items have been included in each carton in case you need to make a claim for a carton that gets lost or damaged during delivery. (Insure each box accordingly.)

Preparing a Consignment Agreement

A good consignment agreement will cover all situations that are likely to come up in your relationship with a shop. If any of the following points are not included in the contract you are offered, it may be that you are dealing with an inexperienced shop owner. In that case, you should get answers to all of the following questions and add appropriate clauses to the consignment agreement before you sign it.

Shopowner's Name

When you establish a relationship with a new shop, insist on getting the name of the owner, not just the manager. Shops have sometimes been known to close suddenly with owners and stock disappearing overnight and sellers left holding the bag. Other shops simply go bankrupt, with consigned goods being seized by creditors. If you don't know the owner's name, you won't have a chance of reclaiming your merchandise. (See "State Consignment Laws" sidebar.)

Shipment of Merchandise

Who pays the freight? Buyers are generally expected to pay shipping charges on goods they buy outright (at wholesale prices), but a consignment shop may expect you to absorb the expense for both the shipping and insurance. (If you ship by UPS, your shipments are automatically insured to $100 without additional cost.)

Display of Merchandise

Will your crafts be properly displayed and not left in the storeroom after you bring them in (or ship them) on consignment? What guarantee do you have that they will not be carelessly placed in a display window for weeks at a time, to be faded by the sun? Discuss the matter of display in advance, noting in your agreement any special requirements you may have.

Insurance

What happens if your work is damaged, completely ruined, stolen, or destroyed by a fire or flood? Be sure to ask if the shop's insurance policy covers such loss. If not, you may wish to purchase your own insurance policy to protect against such loss or limit the amount of merchandise consigned to a particular shop.

Return of Unsold Merchandise

Ask how long your work will be on display and how unsold work will eventually be returned to you. Will it be returned at your expense? Must you claim unsold goods by a certain date or forfeit ownership entirely? (Some shops have a clause stating that if unsold merchandise is not claimed within 30 to 60 days after a notice has been sent, the shop can assume ownership of it and dispose of it any way it wishes.)

Pricing and Sales Commission

Consignors are usually expected to set the retail price on their merchandise, but sometimes a shop will ask consignors simply to tell them how much they want for an item and they will set the retail price accordingly. This arrangement, or the exact percentage the shop will retain as its sales commission, should be clearly stated in your agreement.

Payment Dates

How and when will you be paid? Monthly payments to craftspeople are customary for many shops, but there are many ways to keep consignment sales records, and the method of payment should therefore be spelled out in your agreement. In addition to a check each month, you should receive a report of the specific items sold so you can adjust your inventory records accordingly.

In Summary

Consignment selling is neither fish nor fowl in that it is neither retail nor wholesale selling. It is, however, an effective way to test the market for products you might consider wholesaling in the future. Interestingly, switching from consignment to wholesale selling may be more profitable

State Consignment Laws

Theoretically, consigned goods remain the property of the seller until they are sold to the retail customer. In normal situations there are no problems. If an establishment goes bankrupt, however, consigned goods may be subject to the claims of creditors, and may be seized by such creditors unless certain protective steps have been taken by consignors. (This is according to the Uniform Commercial Code that has been adopted by most states.)

A standard consignment contract will not offer sufficient protection in a bankruptcy case. In some states, artists and craftspeople have lost all their merchandise due to such seizures. (In one case I recall, an artist actually had to pay $10,000 to retrieve her own paintings from a bankrupt gallery.) Fortunately, most states now have consignment laws designed to protect artists and craftspeople. Those known to me include Alaska, Arizona, Arkansas, California, Colorado, Connecticut, Florida, Idaho, Illinois, Iowa, Kentucky, Maryland, Massachusetts, Michigan, Minnesota, Missouri, Montana, New Hampshire, New Mexico, New York, North Carolina, Ohio, Oregon, Pennsylvania, Tennessee, Texas, Washington, and Wisconsin. There may be others I am not aware of.

If your state is not listed above, contact your state legislature to find out if it has a consignment law. If so, be sure to ask what kind of merchandise that law protects from seizure by creditors. Even when a consignment law exists, there may be a pitfall. Some states protect only "art," and handcrafts may not be included if they fall outside the area of painting, sculpture, drawing, graphic art, pottery, weaving, batik, macrame, quilting, or other commonly recognized art forms.

than you realize. You may think you will make less money because you'll get only half the suggested retail price instead of the usual 60 to 75 percent you ordinarily get from consignment. However, you will gain in other ways, especially in the time department, and you will have fewer cash flow problems as well.

As one crafter explained it to me, "Instead of consigning $300 worth of merchandise to one shop and receiving $10 to $75 monthly checks trickling in over a year's time, I can now send three shipments, each worth $100 to three different shops and within a month have $300 in hand." She added that, within a couple of months after switching to wholesale, her monthly gross sales had doubled and her bookwork decreased by 80 percent.

Chapter Eleven

Innovative Marketing Methods

Opportunities to promote your business and sell at retail are everywhere. You need only stretch your imagination a bit to see them.

*I*n previous chapters you have learned how to sell handmade products through eight of the most common arts and crafts retail outlets (1–8 on list below). This chapter discusses seven additional, unusual ways to market arts and crafts in your own community (9–15). Closing the chapter is a discussion of ten low-cost marketing and promotional ideas. The following list will serve as a reminder of the retail markets discussed at length in this book:

1. Art and craft fairs and festivals
2. Home shops and studios
3. Open houses
4. Party plan selling
5. Holiday boutiques

6. Consignment shops

7. Craft malls

8. Rent-a-space shops

9. Local businesses

10. Schools

11. Hospitals and clinics

12. Retirement centers and nursing homes

13. Military base

14. Pushcart merchandising

15. Informal marketing cooperatives

Selling to the last seven markets on this list will require extra effort and creative thinking on your part, but I think you will find them worth exploring. Success here will depend on your ability to take the initiative, make sales presentations, set up special displays or form cooperative marketing arrangements with others.

Working with Local Businesses

You may be surprised to learn how many marketing opportunities await you in your own back yard. Begin by taking a look at all the small retail businesses in your community—the hardware store, butcher shop, sports store, beauty shop, drug store, clothing shop, convenience store, etc.—and note the kind of sideline merchandise they offer. The owners of such businesses aren't likely to come to you in search of products, but if you can show them how they can make money by offering your products to their customers, you've just opened the door to mutual profit. Ideally, you will offer products that complement a particular merchant's line.

Many local businesses also need employee or client gifts, so study your line and select one special item that you could make in quantity at reasonable cost to buyers. Then call some larger businesses in your area and make an appointment to discuss their needs. Here are other examples of how you might work with local businesses to sell your products:

Gift Shops. Gift shops are always interested in buying handcrafts at wholesale prices, but if you can't sell at wholesale or a shop isn't interested in buying from you, they might consider renting you a bit of display space. A gift basket seller expanded her mail order business by asking a local gift shop if they would showcase a selection of her baskets and decorative woodenware in exchange for a 30 percent commission on sales. They were happy to do this, and she sold quite a few baskets this way. A sign in the exhibit area informed buyers that they could special-order a basket or create their own baskets by filling them with items in the shop.

Floral Shops. Some floral shops now sell handcrafts as a sideline, and a few have jumped on the "crafts mall bandwagon" by making space available to crafters on a rent-a-shelf basis. Visit local floral shops to see if handcrafts are currently offered. If not, ask if the shop owner has any interest in renting you some space for your products. (In case you're thinking of offering your crafts to florists at wholesale prices, remember that floral shops traditionally buy only through distributors in this industry, or from exhibitors in floral trade shows. While you can probably sell to local florists through a personal sales call, a direct mailing to a national list of floral shops is unlikely to produce any orders.)

Any Store with a Big Window. An article in a crafts newsletter told of a crafter in a small rural community in Minnesota who discovered a great way to market her crafts. She rented local store windows for $25 a month and decorated them with her products, using themes appropriate for the season. She said beauty shops were best because they have windows just begging for decorations. (See also "Beauty Shops" below.)

Many retailers are hurting for business these days, and some might be happy to clear a window, or at least a portion of it, for a special crafts display. Such a display would be beneficial to the store because it would attract attention from people who might otherwise walk on by, and once they get into the store to take a closer look at a crafter's products, they might buy something else from the retailer. This kind of win-win arrangement certainly seems worth exploring. If you try this idea, you will have to work out the details on how shoppers can actually buy your products. Will they call you to place an order you will deliver in person or ship by mail, or will the store owner sell items right out of the window, collecting the money and appropriate sales tax for you?

Ad Agency. One crafter was thrilled when an ad agency hired her to make a thousand dough Santas to be used as employee and client Christmas gifts. The fact that her Santa had an Old World look and specially designed enclosure card helped cinch the sale.

Corporate Clients. Many crafters diversify their businesses by adding gift baskets of one kind or another. Susan Larberg sells a variety of crafts, but finds there is considerable demand for her food baskets, most of which are sold through her annual holiday boutique. When she wants extra business, however, she simply visits local businesses in the area, offering them beautifully decorated 18- to 20-inch gift baskets loaded with her homemade cookies, gourmet teas and coffees. Some clients order several for their employees or business associates. Priced at $50, they cost Susan about $20 to make. Although comparable baskets usually cost more than this, Susan loves making up these baskets and is happy with her profits on this item.

And here's an interesting idea that might work for some readers who have a "corporate connection." I heard about a clever woman who gives presentations during lunch hours in corporate cafeterias. The benefit to the corporation is that she donates 10 percent of her sales to the corporation's favorite charity. She sets up a table for two or three days, and makes about $500 a day selling costume jewelry, watches and selected craft items before moving on to the next location.

Realtors. Randall Barr, who used to sell his Birdhouse Clocks at craft fairs, said his first large order was from a realtor who wanted to use his product as client gifts. Realtors also buy a variety of promotional giveaway items to remind people in their community to call them first when they're thinking of buying or selling a home. One realtor in our area drops off home-baked pumpkin bread to dozens of homes in our neighborhood every Christmas. (A nice crafts item might cost him even less—a small Christmas ornament, perhaps?)

Local Builders. As Susan Larberg and her husband, Denny, were designing their new home in Brooksville, Florida, their builder admired and inquired about the handcrafted items Susan had made to decorate their new home. He offered to supply all his new customers with her card and flyer in his new-home packets, and this brought her many orders for custom floral arrangements, centerpieces, wall decor, and even some interior decorating jobs (thanks to the builder's personal recommendations).

A holiday boutique Deena Nixon used to be in would get permission from a builder to house the show in one of his display homes for two weekends (and the week in between) every year. The builder, who was showing homes in the area, would find one item at the show when it was first being set up, and use it as the prize for a drawing for people who came and looked through a house or two and signed up. "The craft show brought about a thousand people to the builder's new neighborhood," says Deena, "and people who came to see the homes often went to the craft show. It was a very good combination that worked well for many years, but it hinged on timing. The whole thing fell apart the year they couldn't find a builder or house in time."

Beauty Shops. Have you ever though of taking a sample of your work to your favorite beauty shop? In rural communities and small towns where gift shops do not abound, this idea could be extremely profitable. To maximize sales in this market, concentrate on solving a gift need facing busy women, such as an upcoming graduation, birthday, anniversary, wedding or baby shower. Scout local beauty shops to see which ones have space for product displays, then show them your stuff and make an offer. In negotiating with the shop owner, first suggest a merchandise incentive (more economical than cash), but if this doesn't work, offer a 25 percent commission.

One successful seller says there are four reasons why this kind of marketing works:

1. Women in a shop seem predisposed to buy things;

2. Hairdressers are excellent saleswomen;

3. Many of the same people come in each week, which allows them time to think about buying something and another opportunity to purchase;

4. Repeat business is assured as friends ask about the products and order their own through the original customers.

Selling through beauty shops is also a good way to do market research. Knowing the hairdresser personally will be a plus because you can get feedback from her about your products.

Other Community Markets to Explore

Here are more innovative ideas on how to sell through schools, hospitals, clinics, retirement centers and nursing homes:

Schools. Yvonne Ward is a teacher in a Catholic elementary school who writes and paints on the side. When she began to show her work to other teachers in her school, she found a new market for her work when her colleagues became excited about purchasing her paintings. TC Ferrito, who specializes in polarfleece hats and jackets, sells a lot of product through her kids' schools. "The teachers and other parents see my kids wearing my stuff and want it for themselves," she says. "So my kids are part of my advertising force."

Melody, another teacher, once told me how she sold 40 straw-burlap scarecrows without even trying. She got the idea of taking a display scarecrow with her to different schools where she placed it in the teacher's lounge with a sign-up sheet for orders and colors preferred. "I was amazed to discover how many teachers, librarians, bus drivers and principals wanted not just one, but two or three," she said.

The easiest way to get a display of your products in a school is to know a teacher who can put in a good word for you with the principal. To get his approval, show how a display of your products will benefit the teachers (make holiday shopping easier) or the school (donate a percentage of sales to a special school fund).

Hospitals. Eileen, who offered a country line of antique lace and pot-pourri, told me of her interesting experience doing fund-raising shows for a hospital that had no gift shop. Initially, she did this three times a year, but the idea proved so successful that she ended up doing monthly exhibits. "I set up shop for one or two days and sold to employees and visitors," she explained. Eileen donated 15 percent of her sales to the auxiliary department, and raised over $1,300 for them—a selling point many hospitals would find interesting.

Clinics. From her own children, Andrea Warner learned that kids want things they have touched or played with. "The true test of a toy is if it can make a child happy when he or she is scared or sick—both big possibilities in any doctor's office," she told me. "Parents will buy something that pleases a child under stress, particularly if the child shows great interest in it."

Following this logic, Andrea contacted a clinic in her area and asked if they would like donated toys for their waiting rooms. The only catch was that they had to post a list where their patients could see it, telling who made each toy and how it could be ordered from the craftsperson. The clinic did this and orders began to pour in. Later, when a new clinic opened, Andrea was asked to set up a similar arrangement for them. Craftspeople who donated toys handled their own sales and deliveries, and the items they donated stayed donated, even if no orders resulted. "When you consider that you are getting unlimited publicity for the cost of one sample, it's a good idea," Andrea says. "Well-made items sell well because the parents can see that they are holding up to repeated playing."

NOTE: I've lost touch with Andrea, but her innovative marketing ideas need to be shared. See another idea from her in "Informal Marketing Cooperatives" later in this chapter.

Retirement Centers. Prior to moving into wholesaling, Joyce Roark found a terrific way to sell her custom-made jewelry. She told me her sales increased by 400 percent the year she raised her prices and began to sell her products at senior living retirement centers (not nursing homes).

"The people I sold to had difficulty going shopping," she explains. "They tired easily and they feared being knocked down by kids running in the stores and malls. The retirement centers furnished me with tables and advertising, and did not charge me a fee. I was only there for a couple of hours at a time."

The products Joyce developed for this niche market included decorated mini–tote bags for room keys, bingo money and other items, tissue holders for the pocket, eyeglass cases and custom-made jewelry. She made earrings and necklaces to match special outfits and often modified jewelry pieces owned by the residents. She adapted earrings, changed clasps on chains and necklaces that were hard for arthritic hands to manipulate, and cut pendant chains to specific lengths wanted.

"My customers appreciated the fact that they didn't have to spend hours shopping for the right piece of jewelry," says Joyce. "They often brought a special outfit to me and if I didn't have something already made, I would customize a piece of jewelry for it at no extra charge. People repaid me by purchasing more of my products!"

The first time at a facility, Joyce might realize about $50 in sales, but each time she returned, her sales increased until she was making at least $200 in a two-hour period. "Once people got to know me and my merchandise, they were repeat customers," she says.

This idea proved to be so popular in Joyce's area that she was asked to return to those facilities from October to December so residents could do some of their Christmas shopping. Because those with arthritic hands have a hard time wrapping gifts, Joyce began to offer a selection of paper and ribbon and a gift-wrapping service, and that idea eventually led to her being invited to offer the same service in area nursing homes.

Nursing Homes. Ruth Magee has had success in selling holiday florals to the nursing home where she and her partner used to work. "They use them as centerpieces for their employee Christmas party, then give them as door prizes," she says. "This has prompted us to discuss similar arrangements with two other nursing homes in the area."

Selling Crafts on a Military Base

If you happen to live on a military base, here is an idea that might work for you. While in West Germany, Denise Hall found jobs to be scarce. When she looked to crafts to earn some extra money, she also found a way to provide a profitable service to the community. After learning there was no consignment shop in the area, Denise suggested the idea of a craft shop to the manager of the local thrift shop run by the Army Community Services. Since there was no shopping center on the army post, she was given some space within the hospital.

To generate interest in The Craft Boutique, Denise ran ads on the local American radio station and distributed flyers in apartment buildings. The shop began with only six consignors selling off a table in the hospital one day a week. As more consignors brought in merchandise, the Boutique was given longer hours and a room of its own. In time, this idea proved so successful that a second consignment shop was established to serve more than a hundred crafters in the area.

"The volunteer association that runs the shop retains 17 percent of the sales price of merchandise," Denise explains. "This money pays expenses and purchases things for the hospital and the entire military community that cannot be purchased with government funds. The other 83 percent of the sales price goes to consignors, most of whom are military spouses."

Pushcart Merchandising

If you are a prolific crafts producer who yearns for a shop of your own but can't afford the high investment of a retail shop or the time it would take to run it, pushcart merchandising is an idea you might consider.

"Many shopping malls offer attractive pushcarts or other structures on a temporary basis and are willing to strike deals with artists and craftspeo-ple," says Gail Bird, a pushcart merchandiser for fifteen years and self-pub-lished author of *Cart Your Way to Success.* "But this kind of retailing is only for those who can produce in limited volume."

Pushcart merchandising is an interesting and more profitable alternative to wholesaling because the seller as a part-time shopowner keeps a greater percentage of the profits and can test market the line directly to the con-sumer. Its advantage over marketing through a craft mall or rent-a-space store is that more merchandise can be moved in a shorter period of time because you're not competing for attention with other sellers, and your customer doesn't have to walk through a door. (Impulse items and demon-strations are very helpful.) The rent on a pushcart is usually higher and is based on the number of daily potential buyers that pass by your business each day. Before you take this kind of financial risk, be certain that your products are appealing to the thousands of people who regularly visit shopping malls. A good track record of sales success at craft fairs, malls or shops is one indication that you might do well with your own pushcart in a busy mall.

The nice thing about pushcarts is that they can be rented for one week, two weeks or a month once or twice a year. How much merchandise would you need to sell this way? Gail suggests that, to sell $3,000 worth of products a week, you would need about $5,000 worth of inventory. She says one of the secrets to success in this kind of retailing is knowing how to negotiate a pushcart lease with the temporary tenant leasing manager. "There is no temporary tenant organization (networking or help) for the pushcart/kiosk industry, so all leasing agencies have different rules and rental fees," she says. "One big problem usually is that the leasing manager is an entry level position of a large leasing organization, and the turnover in this job is rapid because everyone wants to move up the corporate lad-der as quickly as possible. You spend time and energy developing a good working relationship with your leasing manager only to find a new one in his or her place the next time you go in."

For this kind of retailing to be profitable, your lease costs (rental) should not be more than 10 to 15 percent gross sales, Gail advises. Thus, if your goal is to sell $6,000 worth of goods over a two-week period, you should pay no more than $900 total in rent, including percentage. "Avoid renting a pushcart over the Christmas holidays unless you can triple your sales because the rent usually triples at that time," says Gail. "Leasing agents have a standard rental fee, but they are not set in stone. If you have the right product mix they are looking for and you have your facts and figures at hand, you can usually negotiate with them. You'll have some leverage if you act like you know what you're doing."

Gail no longer does pushcart retailing because she has found it more profitable to sell on the Internet and in international and short-term target market consumer shows. "I opened GailBird.com in 1999 and now do as many sales in these markets in three or four days as I used to do in a week in a pushcart," she says. "My newest idea in profits is per pound or square inch. Doing this is an art I can't easily explain, but in order to maximize my profits, I have to keep my operation cost way down. I have a pretty good idea what I will sell for sure, and that is all I'm willing to pay UPS ground shipping on. The 70-pound trunks I take on the airplane are my allowable luggage, containing models, display, sales supplies, fragile items and retail items. Since I manufacture most of my line, I design with specific size and minimum weight in mind. I have also learned how to pack twice as much in a small space so not an inch of space is wasted."

Informal Marketing Cooperatives

Crafters all over the country have formed craft cooperatives to gain marketing power and increase annual profits. Following are several examples of informal marketing co-ops organized by groups of crafters.

Entering Fairs as an Organized Group

I once heard from a group of six craftswomen who had formed an informal cooperative so they could do craft fairs as a group and also batch their supply orders to get quantity prices. They said they never had any problems in gaining entry to a show because each seller presented her work individually. They did as many as eight shows a year, including their own Christmas boutique in December. At shows, they mixed their work to create an old-fashioned store image. A large sign, country painted with the name of their group, was prominently displayed on an artist's easel. Each seller, who offered country items that did not compete with others in the group, wore an apron with the name of her business either embroidered or painted on it.

Here is the strategy these women used to sell to customers at a fair. A designated "catcher" would stand in front of the exhibit to welcome customers and assist them in making a selection. Her job was to emphasize product benefits while providing interesting tidbits of information about the artist or her technique. Of course, customers loved this kind of attention. When a sale was made, the "writer" would take over to write the sales ticket and get the buyer's name and address in a guest book. In the meantime, the "wrapper" was busy packaging the item. Enclosed with each purchase were the business cards of each seller and a flyer about the craft group.

This cooperative idea worked well for four years. Problems developed only when new members were added to the group. Personality clashes began to occur and some crafters began to sell similar items, competing with others in the group. In the end, the six who started this cooperative decided to go back to selling solo.

Displaying and Selling Crafts in a Restaurant

One of the most innovative marketing ideas I've come across was reported to me several years ago by Andrea Warner, who conceived the idea of a unique crafts marketing cooperative that helped many talented people in her area realize greater sales.

Noticing that a new restaurant had some terrific display space in its window and a lot of blank space on its walls, Andrea contacted the owner and ultimately arranged for changing displays of fine craftwork that could be purchased by restaurant patrons on a custom-order basis. She emphasized that the restaurant owner would not only save money on

decorating expenses but make money by renting space to local artisans. No special permit was needed since goods were merely being displayed, not sold. All the restaurant owner had to do was buy insurance to cover the merchandise on display. (Andrea said that when the insurance agent came by to write the policy, he left with $300 worth of crafts.)

Here is how the co-op worked. Co-op members were given a number as they joined, and these numbers were rotated so everyone had an equal chance for space for periods of three months at a time. "Space" included two large windows in the front, walls and some floor space. Twenty people were allowed wall space, and ten were allowed floor space. Each paid a flat monthly fee for each item displayed, paying three months in advance. These fees were taken by the restaurant owner who used it for extra advertising and insurance on items displayed.

Displays were changed the last Sunday of the third month, and everyone had to come in at a certain specified time to remove their displays so the next group could get set up. Neither the restaurant owner nor his waitresses did any selling. Instead, craftspeople simply hung a framed 3 X 5 card near their work giving price and availability information, telephone and address. Interested buyers jotted down this information during lunch or dinner and dealt directly with the craftsperson thereafter. A deposit of 25 percent was requested on all custom orders with balance due on delivery of merchandise.

This idea was an immediate hit with restaurant patrons. Business boomed as soon as people learned there was a place in town where they could have lunch and shop at the same time. Doctors, lawyers and other business people, to whom time is money, especially appreciated this kind of shopping service.

Local craftspeople saved money by paying a flat fee per month, rather than a commission on every item sold through local consignment shops. They made more sales with less effort, increased their visibility in the community and enjoyed some control in how their work was displayed and sold. Several members of the co-op got enough orders to keep them busy for months after their initial display, and two of them got enough business to enable them to cut down on their outside work and spend more time on craft production.

The co-op was forced to disband a couple of years later when the restaurant was sold to someone who had no interest in this idea, but it had a lasting effect on the community. Before its formation, local consignment shops were taking 45 to 55 percent of sales and charging insurance fees and penalties for too-low monthly sales. The success of the co-op forced them to lower their fee to 25 percent to compete for the quality items they wanted for their shops. In time, most switched to renting display space instead of charging commissions, which resulted in greater profits for the shop and increased sales of crafts whose prices could now be lowered.

I think this idea would work in many communities today, particularly in smaller towns that lack a good gift or handcraft shop. It might even fly in larger, more affluent communities because of the special advantage it offers to busy people who have no time to shop.

How to Start a Cooperative Crafts Shop

The job of establishing a cooperative crafts shop is rarely easy. It takes a considerable amount of time, effort, patience and cooperation for a group of individuals to get together and figure out a cooperative's legal structure, membership guidelines, bylaws and other details such as finding and financing the actual opening of a retail shop.

Launching a co-op is one thing; maintaining it over a long period of time is another. Some co-ops survive only by undergoing periods of change (see "The Laurel Tree Crafts Cooperative" below), while others simply go out of business, such as Bobbie's Shop of Shops, which was a success story in the first edition of this book.

Annie Lang, a former member of this cooperative, filled me in on what went wrong there. The shop was originally started by the owner of a craft supply shop that wasn't able to bounce back after a recession. Instead of just selling the shop, however, the owner began to rent space to local crafters, and before long, they had a good thing going. The crafters formed a cooperative that was first managed by the original shop owner, and later by another individual with poor management abilities. She was asked to leave when it was discovered that several months of rent and retail sales money could not be accounted for. A new manager was then appointed, but the co-op was never able to recover.

"I think the failure of this co-op was a simple case of 'united we stand, divided we fall,'" says Annie. "When management decisions began to be made without group knowledge or permission, the co-op no longer functioned as originally intended. When I saw what was happening to the shop, I felt like I was up against a speeding train, so I opted to take my life in a different direction."

The Laurel Tree Crafts Cooperative

Here's an interesting example of how crafters can work together to launch a successful retail outlet for their work and survive periods of change. In the mid-90s, when the town of Butler, Pennsylvania, was suffering an economic slump, a group of crafters presented a show in the local mall where several stores had recently closed. After the show, the mall manager approached a few of the exhibitors asking if they would be interested in staying in one of the empty stores for a while longer. "A while longer" turned out to be twelve years.

Because Pennsylvania doesn't recognize anything but agricultural cooperatives, this group decided to incorporate as an S Corporation. They named it The Laurel Tree because a real tree stood in the middle of the store. Here is how the co-op was launched, and how it operates today after undergoing several changes.

Stock was sold and each owner put in $50, an amount that would be refunded if they left the co-op. (The number of owners is limited by S-Corporation law, but as long as there are openings in the co-op, an individual can join the corporation.) There is a board of directors, a store manager and committees to do everything from screening to cleaning. Co-op members are required to work so many hours a month in the store and they pay back 20 percent of their sales to the store to provide working capital. Individuals who want to sell in the store but not take an active part in the cooperative are welcome to sell on a 60/40 consignment basis. If they wish to work in the store, however, they can keep up to 75 percent of their sales.

"It took time and effort to get the co-op going," says Elaine M.

Obidowski, one of the original owners and current purchaser. "There were twenty of us in the beginning, and we had to devise our own forms, a bookkeeping system to handle craft sales, a work schedule for everyone involved, a co-op agreement that would satisfy everyone, a wholesale ordering system and numerous other procedures that needed to be tailor-made to fit an organization with so many people. It took a while for us to think of ourselves as a unit, but because of the desire and commitment of the women involved, we worked out our problems and moved on. To make the store successful, we had to learn how to give and take."

As the years passed, the mall in which the co-op was located continued to decline. When a decision was made to tear it down and replace it with a new strip mall, the co-op relocated in the downtown area in the basement of one of the oldest buildings in Butler. "Formerly a prominent department store, the building fell into disrepair when the store closed," says Elaine. "But a motorcycle shop purchased the building in 2000, and we rented the basement. After a massive amount of renovation and hard work, we opened to a much larger area.

"Times have changed, as have we," Elaine adds. "The influx of cheap manufactured items has affected our ability to sell at a marketable price. We have only ten members now, and we have allowed them to add a manufactured line to their stock to increase their profit base. We now offer remote crafter rents for folks from out of state who wish to ship their articles to us. We charge a monthly fee and a small percentage of their sales. To further supplement our income, we sell manufactured items such as coffees, candles, stuffed toys and candy to complement our merchandise, offer a limited number of booth rentals and are now expanding to include antique dealers. Through our Web site, which allows free hosting, we're venturing into Internet sales. We offer monthly newsletters and many promotions via the Internet and mail."

As you can see, forming and managing a cooperative is hard work, but the rewards are obvious. As one of the original co-op members told me when I interviewed her for the first edition of this book, "From the roots of cooperation and the sturdy trunk of hard work, the branches of friendship have grown to produce an opportunity for each of us at The Laurel Tree to achieve what we could not have done alone: own our own craft store."

Thank You

During the years when Alberta S. Johnson was selling her originally designed paper earrings or holiday ornaments, she always gave customers a special "Thank You" sheet designed to increase word-of-mouth advertising. She offered them a 15 percent discount off their next purchase if they would send her the names, addresses and phone numbers of five to ten friends or relatives. She gave each customer further incentive to do this by offering an additional 15 percent credit on total sales that might come from her referrals. To further qualify the new leads, Alberta asked her customers to check with friends first, to make sure they really wanted to receive such information. She then authorized the customer to offer her friends a 10 percent discount on their first purchase.

"This sheet not only let my retail customers know that I appreciated their business, but also rewarded them for telling their friends about me," says Alberta. "I generated many extra sales this way and one Thank You Sheet brought me several hundred dollars' worth of business when a customer passed it on to a friend who booked a home party that led to a second party later."

Ten Low-Cost Marketing and Promotional Ideas

Home business owners historically begin their businesses on a shoestring, and rarely have money for advertising. But that's okay because there are many things you can do to advance your business without spending a dime. Here are ten strategies you can use to build word-of-mouth advertising and increase your local visibility.

1. Talk It Up

Talk is not only the cheapest marketing strategy you can use but often the most effective way to advertise a business. You begin by talking and soon others begin to carry the word for you. It's called word-of-mouth advertising and in tine the benefits can be enormous. To get this rolling, tell your friends, family and small business associates about your crafts business. Give them a couple of business cards, flyers or brochures, one to keep, and one to pass along to a friend. (Do not, however, load people down with a big stack of printed materials.)

Your friends will be the first to buy from you, especially when you give them one of your handmade creations as a gift. By including a brochure with your gift, you let them know that you can help them solve their own gift-giving needs in the future. One year when I gave a friend one of my teddy bears for Christmas, she said she would love to buy several for Christmas gifts if I had time to make them. I found it amusing that, without even trying, I was back to selling my crafts again.

2. Ask for Referrals

Make it easy for your satisfied customers to help you get more business. Each time they refer you to someone who places an order, you might thank them by sending a 10 to 20 percent discount coupon they can apply to their next order.

3. Work Cooperatively with Other Craftspeople

Consider having an open house sale with a friend whose art or craftwork complements your own, or take a sampling of one another's products to craft fairs, keeping a small percentage of whatever sells. Keep a supply of each other's business cards on hand and send custom-order business to one another. If you have a Web site, exchange links with others in your field so you can all benefit from one another's traffic.

4. Show and Sell Your Products at Work

A nurse told me that she sold hundreds of dollars' worth of jewelry every month to nurses and doctors in the hospital where she worked. Several crafters have told me how they make sales simply by taking samples of their crafts to work with them and showing them to fellow workers during

---

Donate Something for a Raffle

When Stephanie Heavey became aware of the Quasquicentennial (125) Celebration in her city, Palantine, Illinois, she designed a special doll named "PalaTINA" and offered it to the centennial committee for promotional purposes. "They were delighted to exhibit her at several events before using her in a raffle," Stephanie reported. "Then the *Daily Herald* picked up on the doll and sent a reporter to do a feature. This generated several calls and letters, which led to sales for both PalaTINA and another doll that was pictured in the article."

---

coffee breaks or lunch hours. A friend or family member may also help you sell by taking a sample product to work with them.

In talking with Susan Young, who worked for a Fortune 500 company for ten years before starting her own business, I learned that so many office workers are selling products on the side these days that it's a wonder any work is getting done. "Somebody was always selling something in my office," she says, "from Avon, Shaklee and Tupperware products and Longaberger Baskets to jewelry and handpainted clothing. Everyone with children in school sells things to raise money for special school projects, from wrapping paper and ribbons to oranges and grapefruit to Girl Scout cookies."

Susan left her high-paying job at the end of 1995 to design and sell crafts full time, and it was the volume of crafts she sold in her office that helped convince her she didn't have to stay in that job to earn a living. "Four or five times a year, I would take 30 to 50 of what I thought were my most appealing little creations and put them on the credenza behind my desk where everyone could see them," she says. "Within three or four days' time, I could sell $600 worth of crafts without even trying. I began to see that I was really filling a need when my coworkers kept coming to me asking if I could solve a particular gift-giving need and save them a trip to the shopping mall after work.

5. Market to Strangers

A woman who designs birth announcements always has a supply of brochures with her when she goes out. When she sees a woman who is expecting, she just hands her the brochure, smiles and walks away. This has led to many sales, she says.

Whenever possible, wear the things you make. Some crafters report they have sold jewelry, vests, bags and other items while chatting with strangers as they stood in line at the movies or in the bank.

6. Set up a Local Display of Your Work

Bank lobbies, libraries and other public buildings are a natural for craft displays, especially when they can be tied to a holiday or upcoming community event or are in any way educational. Of course, such a display would include a sign that promotes your business and handcrafts.

7. Donate to a Community Event or Local Charity

Having your name mentioned as the one who has donated a special item for a raffle is a good way to get attention in your community and sometimes leads to good orders. A woman who makes personalized towels donated several to a fund raising drive. A child who got one of them happened to have a father in a barbershop quartet. That towel led to $4,000 in sales to a large group of barbershop singers.

After reading my advice on how to get publicity, 74-year-old Dessie Durham, who made sculpted Santas, wrote to tell me how well this strategy had worked for her. Every time she demonstrated her craft at a fair or shop, she drew a crowd by sending news releases to local newspapers and radio stations announcing that she would donate a percentage of her sales to charity. Once, when she donated a portion of her sales to a local shelter for the homeless, the headline on her feature newspaper story read, SENIOR HELPS FULFILL KIDS' HOLIDAY WISHES.

8. Develop a Promotional Freebie

Basketmaker Cathryn Peters asked artist Pam Edevold to do pen-and-ink renderings of four of her unusual basket creations. She then printed 2,500 of each design for sale in her home shop and at workshops and conventions. More important, the cards are used for advertising and  promotional purposes. "They carry my name and address and serve as a ood reminder of products and services I sell," says Cathryn. "All my basket customers get a complimentary package of note cards, and I frequently donate packages for the 'goodie bags' given to conference and workshop attendees." For raffles, Cathryn donates one of her basketry patterns along with any special accessories needed, such as the deer antler shown in illustration at right.

9. Give a Talk about Your Craft

If you have an unusual craft and the "gift of gab," many groups will be interested in seeing you demonstrate your craft and learning more about what you do. At first, you may not be paid for this kind of speaking, but it's a great way to promote yourself and it generally leads to product sales and other opportunities to speak.

10. Call Your Local Paper

Publicity in the local paper is often as easy as picking up the phone and asking to talk to a reporter. When you do any of the things described in points 6, 7, 8 and 9 above, either send a press release to the paper or telephone them with the news. Because newspapers are always scrambling to get enough news to fill an issue, they welcome human-interest stories and announcements of what people in the community are doing. A mention in

241

How to Get on Television

One year, when rumors began about the possibility of Halloween candy being poisoned, a designer interested in selling her patterns whipped up what she called a "60-Second Crocheted Pumpkin" that held a coin in its mouth. She phoned her local television station to see if they would be interested in announcing this alternative to candy, saying she'd give the pattern free to all those interested. The TV station sent out a video crew and did a 2½-minute tape that aired on the six and ten o'clock news. The station received many calls from people who wanted this clever crocheter's address.

your local paper isn't likely to bring you much business, but it sends an important signal to people in your community who may do business with you in the future. It also gives you a great ego boost and a clipping for your scrapbook.

It pays to read your paper carefully, noting special columns. A doll-maker who took my suggestion about sending a press release to her local paper got her unusual "Karrott Top Tots" featured in her paper's "Count Down to Christmas" shopping column. She sold many dolls as a result.

Sometimes the secret to getting local publicity is to get national publicity first in one of the home-business or craft marketing periodicals. One of my favorite publicity stories started when I mentioned in my newsletter that one of my subscribers who had a garment business on her farm had found a way to solve her independent contractor problems. A writer for the **Wall Street Journal** noticed my article and contacted the business owner for a few comments he could use in his column. After being recognized nationally in such a prestigious publication, the business owner called her local paper to tell them about it. The news that a local business had received national attention prompted them to send a reporter and photographer to her place of business. With a full-page color spread on her business, she became an overnight celebrity in the community and attracted many buyers who never knew about her business before.

Once you've had a taste of publicity at the local level, you'll hunger for some national publicity as well. One of the most common ways to get national publicity is through news releases sent to the media, but few artists and craftspeople ever take the time to master this type of marketing. It's a topic worth studying, however, because through publicity it is possible to get free advertising that would normally cost thousands of dollars. More important, publicity in the right place can generate hundreds or thousands of dollars' worth of business. When you're ready to explore the art and craft of writing a good news release, read one or more of the recommended books in the Resource Chapter.

Chapter Twelve

Selling on the World Wide Web

You may not need a Web site of your own to successfully sell art, handcrafts, stitchery and other related products and services, but as this chapter will prove, there are many advantages to having some kind of marketing presence on the World Wide Web.

oday's business world is changing almost daily now because of one new technological advance or another, and these changes are also affecting the way artists and crafters do business. There is no longer any guarantee that what works today will work tomorrow, so if you're serious about your crafts business, you must also get serious about using computer technology and exploring your marketing options on the Web. As your crafts business and personal goals change, you need to constantly rethink how you might use the Internet to your advantage.

Many crafters today are asking themselves whether they need a Web site or not, often concluding that, since everyone and his dog has a site, they

245

must need one, too. While many crafters on the Web aren't selling enough to cover the costs of maintaining their sites, others are making good money because they've taken the time to learn about this new way of doing business—and *learning* is the key word here. You'll have to do a considerable amount of self-study to succeed in this marketing medium.

Through interviews with several craft professionals in my network, I got frank comments about the practicality of being on the Web along with stories that will encourage you if you're Web-inclined, or give you reasons *not* to go on the Web if you're thinking this really isn't your cup of tea. Note that the amount of money you can earn from your own Web site (or sites—many sellers now have more than one) has very little to do with how much you spend to develop your Web presence. The whole secret to success on the Web is (1) having products or services people want or need, and (2) knowing how to get the word out that you can provide them.

In this chapter you will gain perspective on whether you need a Web site or not and, if so, what kind you should have. You'll learn how a few other beginners got their sites designed and published to the Web, how they maintain them, what it costs to do business this way, and whether sales justify the costs and the time it takes to manage a Web site. More important, you'll be alerted to financial pitfalls you can avoid in having a site designed and hosted and find out how to get started on the proverbial shoestring.

For those who are absolutely certain they do not want the responsibility of designing or maintaining their own site, this chapter also explains alternative ways to market on the Web through other established sites, as well as how to get started selling on eBay—a wonderful marketing outlet for many crafters today.

Contributors to This Chapter

Instead of constantly repeating information about each individual's business or Web site each time they are quoted in this chapter, I've listed the names of contributors below, along with their business name, product line and Web site URL (Uniform Resource Locator):

▼ Rochelle Beach, Cinna-Minnies Collectibles (dolls, ornaments and home decor items made from a cinnamon-based compound, and kits) www.cinna-minnies.com

▼ Carol Carlson, Kimmeric Studio (hang tags for crafts and gifts) www.kimmericstudio.com

▼ Cathy Colley, Cucuzza (handbags, totes, jewelry, notebooks, housewares)

▼ Jacqui Collins-Parker, Angel Craft Studio (lampworked glass beads and mini sculptures) www.angelcraftstudio.com

▼ John Dilbeck, Metalsmith ("The Rose that Never Wilts," T-shirts and other items) www.johndilbeck.com (links to his other five sites)

▼ James Dillehay, Warm Snow Publishers (books and articles for professional crafters) www.craftmarketer.com

▼ Tammy Hodson and Shirley Harrison, Mother and Daughter Glycerin Soap (soap, bath and body products) www.motherdaughtersoap.com

▼ Sue Krei, Wood Cellar Graphics (rubber stamps, stationery, recipe cards and other printed materials) www.WoodCellarGraphics.com

▼ Susan Larberg, Golden Touch Crafts (Woodsman Santas, florals, jewelry and other crafts) personal.lig.bellsouth.net/lig/s/l/slarberg

▼ Chris Maher, Art Web Works (Web site design and hosting) www.artwebworks.com

▼ Cheri Marsh, The SoapMeister (handmade soaps and related products) www.soapmeister.com

▼ Cathryn Peters, The Wicker Woman (informational/advertising site for her chair caning, wicker restoration and basketry services, teaching and lecturing) www.wickerwoman.com

▼ Lisa Risler, Interior Matters (doll patterns and classes) www.dollheaven.com (links to her other five Web sites)

▼ Debbie Spaulding (puppet patterns for ministry) www.puppetsforministry.com and www.puppetpatterns.com

▼ Susan Young, Peach Kitty Studio (an advertising/promotional site for products found in her retail shop) www.peachkittystudio.com

Free Web Pages

Anyone can have a free home page on the Web today, but such pages are for personal or hobby use, not for business. Many Internet Service Providers (ISPs) offer free Web pages to their customers, including America Online and WebTV, and there are now hundreds (if not thousands) of other places on the Web where you can get free space. (When I typed "free Web sites" into my browser's search engine, I got a listing of 170,000 pages with links to Web page providers, so I'll leave that research to you. A similar number of pages will turn up when you type "free Web hosting services" in the search engine.)

You could spend a couple of weeks just researching these sites, but before you do that, ask yourself whether a free site is suitable for your needs. If all you want is a free color brochure on the Web that you can point prospective buyers to, a free site may be sufficient. But if you want to sell products or services directly from the site, you're going to want—and eventually need—much more than that.

There are several problems with free Web sites. One reason they're free is because the Web host will run his ads on them—those annoying pop-up windows you're always running into on the Web. On a free site, you will have no control over the ads that appear on your site, which means you might get gambling or other undesirable ads that could give your visitors a bad impression of you or your business.

"Beginners who aren't sure about marketing on the Web are well advised to start on someone else's site until they can afford to set up their own domain," says Cathryn Peters, who piggybacked on some basketry Web sites and her own American Online home page before she bought her own domain in August of 1997. "The problem with working this way, however, is that search engines are not as likely to find you on the Web if you don't have your own domain name."

Another problem with free sites or Web pages on someone else's site are long domain names. The URL (Uniform Resource Locator) that results when your name gets tacked onto the host's URL is usually longer than the average person can type without an error, and impossible for anyone to

248

Domain Name Registration

Many places on the Web now offer domain name registration, and fees for this service vary from around $12 to $35 per name. All of these providers are merely resellers who are working through Network Solutions, which owns the database that contains all the dot-com, dot-net and dot-org names (called the SRS Database). All accredited registrars are doing for Web site owners is placing their domain name into the SRS database, which costs them only $6 to do. Anything over this amount becomes their profit, which explains why you see so many different prices for domain name registration.

If someone else registers your name for you, be absolutely sure that the registration is in your name and not that of your Web hosting company or some other individual, as this can cause serious problems if you later decide to move your Web site to another server. To have complete control over your domain name, you must be registered both as the owner *and* the administrative contact. It's fine to have another party listed as the technical or billing contact, however.

"Because domain names are not considered property, it's important that you read and understand the contract you sign," advises Chris Maher, my technical adviser for BarbaraBrabec.com. "Each registrar will give you certain specific rights when you sign a contract with them. If someone should steal your name, for example, you will find that you have no property rights to your domain name beyond what the contract says."

To find out if the domain name you'd like is still available, go to www.whois.net to do a name search and find answers to common questions about domain name registration. Also check out www.betterwhois.com, which offers the same search service, but provides a list of active domain name registrars if you want to compare costs and services.

If you want to get a site going on the Web, but all the technical stuff seems a bit too much for your creative spirit, I highly recommend Chris Maher's services and affordable prices (see Resource Chapter). When I was struggling to learn all this stuff, Chris's help by telephone was absolutely invaluable to me, and knowing there was someone I could always call when I got into trouble was an instant stress reliever.

remember. Take Susan Larberg's URL for example, which is http://personal.lig.bellsouth.net/lig/s/l/slarberg/. Whether a long name like this will work for you will largely be determined by what you hope to gain from being on the Web. Susan is happy with her site because she can send people there to see photos of her Woodsman Santas and other products and get details about her annual Christmas open house. "My site serves as a color brochure for my products," she says. "Through it, I've also gotten customers from other states who have visited our area during the time of the show and stopped by."

Jacqui Collins-Parker ran into a different kind of domain name problem with her first site, which had a long name. "Initially I signed up with at least a hundred free sites that let you have pages," she says, "only to find that either I couldn't post a commercial page or that my domain name was way too long."

Some free Web hosting sites like Tripod have reacted to the long domain name problem by offering shorter URLs that give the site owner's name first (www.membername.tripod.com), which is much easier to promote and easier to type or remember.

Selling Through Online Malls and Shops

"I think it's a good idea for serious craft business owners to have and maintain their own Web site," says Cathryn Peters, "but for the average crafter who works part-time and does only a few shows a year, I don't think it would benefit them enough to make the investment. Such crafters would be better off to test the waters with an established online craft mall or shop first. Then, if the money is there, they can branch out with their own domain."

John Dilbeck, who now manages six Web sites but began with space on someone else's site, also recommends this route to shaky beginners. "There's so much to learn about making Web sites that it will inevitably pull your time and energy (and creativity) away from what you're really wanting to do," he says. "In the long run, it's cheaper to pay someone else to showcase your products so you can concentrate on production."

Since I could not find any success stories about good sales being made through listings or ads in online craft malls, shops or galleries, my comments on this topic will be brief. "Online sites and galleries are good options for beginners," says Jacqui Collins-Parker, "but you have little control over how and where you are placed on the site." Cheri Marsh has built a solid business on the Web through her own site, but she never had any luck with online malls and shops. "I did try several different online shops, but I never received an order or even an inquiry from any of them," she says. "Credit card and commission fees are extremely high for online malls, and the owners aren't as customer oriented as I am. In my experience, they did no advertising and were slow to respond to questions or requests."

Because there are literally thousands of virtual shops and galleries on the Web, I must leave this "Internet legwork" to you and let you decide if this is a route you'd like to take. Begin by using your browser's search engine and typing in such key words as "craft malls," "online art galleries," and "craft shops." Some of these online shops rent space to sellers or charge an advertising fee to list products or link to one's Web site. On other sites, products are displayed for free with sellers paying the site owner a commission only when something sells.

Two Inexpensive Web Site Options

A beginning Web seller asks, "How can I find a low-cost startup program that is tailored to crafts, and one that will also let me accept credit card payments? I am getting so discouraged and feel I'd be running into a lot of debt if I go with some of the merchant/Web hosting/Web design companies out there. Can you put me in contact with someone who can help at a reasonable price?"

Craftspeople do have to be careful because the prices being quoted for merchant account and Web hosting services run the gamut from very reasonable to absolutely ridiculous (thousands of dollars), depending on who you connect with. If you're looking for something more than a place to run an ad for a few products, but aren't yet ready to commit to your own domain name and all the responsibilities that go with maintaining your own site, consider setting up shop on one of the following crafter sites that regularly draw a lot of traffic and clearly have crafters' best interests at heart:

- CraftMark is owned and operated by Phillip Coomer of American Craft Malls (refer back to Chapter Nine). Here, crafters have a number of Web packages they can choose from, priced from $10 a month and up, depending on features desired. You sign for a minimum of six months, payable in advance. Your pages will appear within an appropriate category of crafts in CraftMark's online catalog, which currently features the work of 300 crafters.

- The National Craft Association (NCA) can put your crafts business online within ten business days for between $89 and $129 for a year. This includes both site design and hosting fees, and you get attractive space in one of NCA's Shopping Malls with your page being under NCA's URL. If you want your own domain name and merchant card account, the initial cost will be higher, of course, yet still reasonable and affordable to professional crafters. Nearly 600 professional crafters now have space on this site.

"The Internet should be a part of every professional crafter's marketing strategy," says Barbara Arena, managing director of NCA. "It's a good way to balance out your sales program and, compared to exhibiting at craft shows, it's a real bargain. Artisans may pay between $75–$250 for one weekend show, or $38–$130 a day. When you compare these figures to a 24-hour-a-day Web site that costs only pennies a day, you can see that you don't have to make many sales to break even."

As many professional crafters are learning, the Internet is a good sales maximizer. While some crafters have been slow to grasp the importance of the Internet, those who are enjoying success here will confirm that a Web site does far more than just bring in extra orders. It is a great image enhancer and a convenience to established customers who may wish to visit a crafter's Web site after they've come from a crafts show. Crafters who wholesale can show off their wares in blazing color to prospective buyers, not to mention friends and family members across the country. "More important," adds Barbara Arena, "your own Web site is a great way to strengthen your customer relationships and build your business."

Working with Family, Friends or Freelancers

Many crafters elect to set up their own sites because they can get free or inexpensive help from family and friends. Take all the free help you can get, but be cautious about depending on well-meaning friends whose Web design skills may be limited. Soapmakers Tammy Hodson and her mother, Shirley Harrison, got started on the Web when a couple of friends put up a page for them. "That was nice, but not as professional as we wanted," says Tammy. "And when you're working on the 'friends and family plan,' it can take a while for your site to get updated. In the end, we went to a Web building company locally who could photograph our products for the site."

Tammy is right about friends and family members taking their time. I had this problem with my first Web site, which was part of the now-defunct crafter.com site. Initially, I appreciated that someone else was maintaining my Web pages for me, but as one who has always been in control of her business, it was frustrating to always have to wait for new pages to be published, or corrections to be made. I knew I could not operate that way for long. Like other professionals on the Web, I soon concluded that I had to have the ability to add new content, tweak pages, correct errors, fix broken links, or make other minor adjustments on a regular basis.

You may think that hiring a professional will solve all your problems, but many crafters have had problems here, too. Rochelle Beach recalls the bad experience she had in working with a freelance Web designer. "The most expensive mistake I made was to trust someone I met in one of my e-mail groups to do my first site," she says. "That cost me over $600 before I called it quits and decided to look for another designer. But she was not responsive to my needs and wouldn't do the things I asked her to do. She acted as if the site belonged to her, not me, and I felt very stifled and frustrated. In the end, after considerable research on the Internet, I hired The Old Drawin' Board to do my site. The folks there were responsive to my ideas and bent over backwards to service my needs and build a Web site I love. Even though it has been a greater expense than I had anticipated, I am getting a lot of hits and enough orders to be satisfied with the results at this time."

Debbie Spaulding hired a professional Web designer because she thought that designing and maintaining the site would be more then she wanted to get into and would take up too much of her time from designing puppets. But her experience with a freelance Web designer didn't work out. "After she had put in about fifteen hours of work on the site, I took a look at what she had and decided I was not going to be happy with what she was doing," says Debbie. "So I went out and bought *Front Page* software and gave myself a six-week crash course. The Web designer was so impressed with what I was able to design in so short a time that she dismissed the bill for my time and wished me luck with my business."

Lisa Risler hired someone to build her first site, but within three months, decided she would just have to learn on her own. She found a free Web site builder at Tripod.com with a link to Trellix, a free Web design program she downloaded. "It took me only a month to learn the program, which is by far the easiest thing I've tried for designing Web sites," she says.

Lisa later bought the paid version of this software because the free version locked her into hosting her site only on Tripod's Web server, which meant the inclusion of annoying ads she couldn't control. She now uses GlobalSCAPE's *CuteSiteBuilder 3.0* software. "It's almost the same as Trellix, with a few minor changes," she says. "With it, you can create a professional site without having to know HTML, FTP (file transfer protocol) or graphic design. You just add your content to a template of your choice, and publish to the Web with one click."

If you still don't want to get involved in site design, you are more likely to find people who understand your special needs and budget limitations if you work with designers in the crafts and home business industry. The best way is to get recommendations from other crafters on the Web, much the way you'd scout for a new doctor. Also check the Resource Chapter to find some reliable and affordable Web designers I know personally and can recommend. All will be happy to discuss your needs by phone or e-mail and give you a quote on request.

Tip

HTML (HyperText Markup Language) is the special language of the World Wide Web. It's easy for anyone to learn, and actually fun. See recommended books in the Resource Chapter, or check out the free tutorials on the Web, easily found with an "HTML tutorials" word search on your browser.

Learning to Do It All Yourself

Before you set up shop on the Web beyond space on someone else's site, you need to ask yourself what you hope to gain from being on the Internet. Do you just want to make friends, chat about your hobby interests, or *sell?* If you want to sell, you'll have to learn some Web site basics. You can do this either by buying books on the topic, taking a class, doing research on the Internet, hiring someone to assist you while you learn, or asking for help from family members or business friends.

"The biggest obstacle to Internet marketing for a craftsperson is not a lack of opportunities, but an overabundance of choices," says James Dillehay, author of *The Basic Guide to Selling Crafts on the Internet.* "To be profitable (as opposed to just being confused) you have to focus your activities in an organized plan that produces online sales and profits while measuring which activities are working and which aren't."

In his book, James discusses the time and costs involved in selling through your own Web site. Having set up my own site, I can tell you that there is a steep learning curve, so don't try to do this at a time when you are particularly stressed by your regular crafts business activities. Using Web site design software, such as *Front Page* or *Dreamweaver*, you can design your own domain or hire someone to design it for you with the idea that you'll learn to update it later. This is the route I took. Before I could learn Web site design, however, I had to first learn how to use Windows software after having been a DOS user for fifteen years. I bought computer manuals for each of my new software programs, a couple on HTML coding (which every Web site manager needs to know), and a couple on *Front Page 2000*. Although *Front Page* has a nice tutorial, I had to get my site up as quickly as possible and didn't have a month or more to learn everything through trial and experimentation, so I hired Chris Maher to work with me on the phone until I got the hang of everything. Many crafters without a lick of prior experience have done it all on their own, however.

"I knew nothing about computer Web site design, coding and maintenance when I first purchased my own domain," says Cathryn Peters, "so I searched out Internet tutorials and began that way. Later, I purchased a book or two, but the majority of what I learned was from the tutorials and examining the View Source code of just about every Web site I liked the looks of. Then I would use snippets of the sites I liked, adding my own touches with text and graphics and overall layout."

Tip

The "View Source" code can be seen on any Web site (except those that have blocked this information from public view) by right clicking the mouse and then clicking "View Source" on the menu that opens up. What you see at that point is HTML coding, which is the heart of Web site design. Sometimes, when you see an effect you like on someone's site, you can read the HTML coding to see how that effect was achieved. Even when you use sophisticated Web site management software, such as *Front Page* or *Dreamweaver,* you need to know basic HTML coding so you can fix little glitches that arise.

"After purchasing a couple of books on HTML, I designed the first layout for my site strictly writing the code by hand," says Cathy Colley. "I figured this would help me to better understand how some of the WYSIWYG (what-you-see-is-what-you-get) programs work. The second design of my site was created using *Dreamweaver* 2 and 4. It's much easier to keep the site current and fresh using this program and I highly recommend it to others."

Carol Carlson learned HTML at the local community college. "I was so lost when I first went in," she recalls. "The first day the teacher made a joke, saying 'If you don't know what a URL is, you're in the wrong class.' Everyone laughed. I had no idea what a URL was, but I laughed along with everybody else so I wouldn't look too dumb! I'm glad to say I've come a long way since then. I made a good friend in the class, and we talk often about our computer problems. I highly recommend having a computer buddy."

Some people become so good at hand coding that they don't even use Web site management software programs. Jacqui Collins-Parker manages her site with Top Page, which was free from the Web host. "It doesn't have scripts that confuse you and the server," she says. "It's a WYSIWYG program, but there are still many, many things that you have to do manually in HTML in order to get the site to function well."

Debbie Spaulding uses *Front Page 2000* to manage her site. "I found it easy to learn, but a bit on the flaky side at times. Overall, it is a good program with a few minor drawbacks—one being that it needs to be hosted by a Web server that supports Front Page Server Extensions. Sometimes when the ISP is making changes, the sites lose their extensions and they have to be reinstalled by the ISP. This can mean downtime for your site resulting in a loss of sales and also turning potential customers away when they can't access your page. As a result of these problems, I've considered switching to *Adobe Go Live*."

In talking with Chris Maher about this problem, he said that proper management of Front Page Extensions is related to the skill of the system administrator and how well he is managing the server. "If this is a constant problem for a Web site owner, it would be better to move the site to a different Web server than to learn new Web site management software."

Learning basic HTML and Web site management will take some time—a good month of effort, at least—but it will be well worth it to you in the long run if you enjoy this kind of work. "I'm glad I forced myself to take that extra step," says Debbie Spaulding, "because I can add new prod-

One of Debbie Spaulding's many puppet patterns.

257

Beginning on a Shoestring

Some businesses mentioned in this chapter spent a considerable amount to design and launch their Web sites, while others started on the proverbial shoestring.

Cheri Marsh started her soapmaking business in 1997 with $50 and a dream. A year later, working in partnership with her mother, Cheri launched SoapMeister.com. "I started with an eight-page site I created myself," she says, "but I hired a Webmaster a few months later and our site is now well over 200 pages. We market handmade soaps, bath salts, custom gift baskets, favors for weddings/bridal and baby showers, holidays and celebrations."

The site has attracted half a million visitors since it opened, and Cheri attracts additional visitors to her site every week by running contests. "We also do a weekly newsletter with information about soaps, oils, herbs and other topics of interest," she says, "including contest winners for that week. Approximately 10 percent of them become long-term customers. We cater to small businesses, create custom soap and salt blends and labels, as well as manufacture for other companies under their label. Our growth has been steady with revenues projected at $50,000 this year."

At the start of 2002, Cheri and her mother were advertising for sales reps and beginning a controlled expansion of the business, planning to relocate to a warehouse facility in the spring. When you consider this is a home-based business, the growth is impressive. Cheri thinks one key to her success is "quality products backed by phenomenal customer service."

ucts quickly, change prices or try out new layouts and colors without having to pay someone $40 to $100 an hour."

Over time, site management costs will add up if you don't learn to do this work yourself. Although one crafter says she can get changes made to her site every month for just $20, another says she is being billed $5 for every new photo she adds to her site. "This really added up when I initially added fifty new products to the site," she said. "Adding links to other sites costs me $2 per link. I knew the cost would be high for me in the beginning, and I can only hope I will generate enough sales the first year to cover my expenses and be profitable thereafter."

Web Hosting Companies and Merchant Account Providers

In interviewing Web sellers for this chapter, I found that most of them are paying between $15 and $30 a month to have their sites hosted, so it becomes immediately obvious that you can save a bundle if you pick the right Web hosting company for your site. Some companies offer hosting for as little as $4.95 a month, but should you select the lowest-priced service?

"You need to know if a company has a track record for reliability," says Chris Maher, who regularly monitors Web servers and frequently moves his clients from one place to another to make sure they are being properly served. "Some offer 15 megabytes of space while others offer up to 500, and some may charge a higher annual hosting fee because their package includes more Web space than one actually needs," he says. "Some offer service around the clock while others don't. Some have a better statistics package than others, and some mange their Front Page Extensions better than others."

Check the fine print to see what the hosting company does *not* offer. For example, one company Chris is currently recommending— ReadyHosting.com ($99 a year)—is offering 500 megabytes of space with unlimited bandwidth for no extra charge. But part of the terms of service are that you can't have any downloads. "Included in this annual fee, however, is a world class statistics reporting package in real time so you can see who is on your site at all times," he says.

Note that if you use *Front Page* software to design and manage your Web site, you must host with a company that has Front Page Extensions (a technical topic I can't get into here—just be sure to ask about this before you make this decision). If you have questions about where your site should be placed, or you want to move your site from one server to another but don't know how, e-mail Chris Maher (see Resource Chapter) and explain your needs.

259

$100 Web Investment Becomes $100,000 Business

Lisa Risler opened her first doll pattern Web site in September 1999 with an investment of just $100. Now she has five sites that are linked together by a hub site, www.dollheaven.com. She sells doll patterns, some handmade art/cloth dolls, other crafts on consignment, and craft-doll supplies. "The consignment areas are just to be helpful to doll artists and crafters who need to make a little money on the side," she says. "The patterns bring in the bulk of the money to support all of the sites, including DollClasses.com, a new venue I find intriguing and exciting. I take a percentage of the students' fees and the teacher gets the majority."

A year after she began, with sales already at the $40,000 mark, Lisa quit her job to work her business full time. By the end of 2001, sales were approaching $100,000 a year and she believes this income will continue to grow in the future as she expands into other areas on the Web. "I've never even done any real advertising yet," she says, adding that she's a natural born cheapskate. "It's amazing how much less you can spend and still have outrageous sales! I have a sign outside my house, and word-of-mouth advertising has been it so far. I do plan to make catalogs and flyers in the future, however, plus do some advertising in national magazines."

Free Web Hosting with Merchant Account. Many crafters automatically select their Web hosting company when they select the credit card service they plan to use on their site. In fact, this is the gimmick many hosting companies are using to attract clients—they make a monthly charge for the credit card service and throw in hosting for free. Actually, this is the way Lisa Risler got started on the Web for less than $100 a year (see nearby sidebar).

"After beginning with my sites on Tripod's free Web server," she says, "I later moved four of them to the Goemerchant.com site because they offer free Web hosting when you use their credit card program ($49.95 a month for each site). They take 2.29 percent of each sale, plus thirty cents per transaction, and pay me within 48 hours after I batch up sales."

Note that free ads you may not want are also part of the Tripod package. Although Lisa loved getting everything for free in the beginning, she was not happy with the annoying pop-up ads on her site, none of which she could control, and this was another reason she decided to move to Goemerchant.com.

The High Cost of a Regular Merchant Account.

Unless you think you can sell $1,200 a month or more from your Web site, forget about going the traditional route of getting merchant status from your bank or Costco or one of the many online merchant account providers because the costs are just too high.

One of my readers told me about the surprise she had when she set up her eCommerce site. When she signed the credit card contract she *thought* it covered a shopping cart on her site, but it didn't, so she had to pay someone $362 to design one for her. Then, her monthly charges to process credit cards cost $49.95 (basic fee); $3.30 (Batch Header Fee); $10 (Statement Fee); $9.98 (Minimum Processing Fee); plus a thirty-cent transaction fee for every sale.

As you can see, you must be *very careful* before you sign any kind of credit card contract so you understand exactly what your monthly charges will be. "New opportunities on the Internet are costly," says Tammy Hodson. "A professional looking Web site with a shopping cart, real time credit card processing, hosting fees, and business phone lines can really add up. We just experienced this and have decided not to accept credit cards for awhile after trying to absorb these costs. A crafter needs to be very careful. Just building a Web site does not mean they will come. The site needs to be properly submitted to the search engines and regularly updated. You have to give customers a reason to keep coming back. This has been a hard lesson learned for us. We have had to do a lot of rethinking, and are now formulating a new plan."

Logo from Tammy Hodson's Website, done in two shades of purple with swirls of green and pink accent touches (not shown here).

In her book, *The Complete Idiot's Guide to Making Money with Your Hobby*, Barbara Arena urges all crafters to gather at least five price quotes from prospective merchant account providers (MAPs) and suggests visiting Merchant Workz (www.MerchantWorkz.com). "Here you'll find a free and impartial listing of MAPs and their primary rates and fees," she says. "These rates and fees are negotiable," she says, "so don't hesitate to push MAPs into a bidding war."

If you belong to a business organization of any kind, you can probably get better discount rates through the program they offer than what you can get on your own. NCA, for example, offers its members complete merchant credit card programs at very competitive rates for both traditional and online businesses. (See Resource Chapter.)

Other Credit Card Options for Web Sellers. You don't
have to have credit card options to sell on the Web, but historically, this service will automatically increase sales. Many crafters simply include an order form on their site that customers can print out and mail with a check. In talking with Barbara Arena, I learned that 30 percent of NCA sales of memberships, books and directories are paid for by check. "What's important," she says, "is to offer your customers a variety of payment options. Even when you take credit cards, you might increase sales by giving customers the option of ordering by mail."

Many crafters now use PayPal as their credit card option, but it is my understanding that this company can hold your funds for up to a year after you stop using their service. And if you ask to increase your minimum clearing amounts (a maximum of $1,000 business per month) they can hold any amount over that original $1,000 for a year—interest free—before releasing it to you. *Be sure to read the fine print here.* Also realize that there is still some consumer resistance to PayPal because it requires people to open an account with PayPal before they can make their first purchase. If you use this service, you might encourage sales by explaining the benefits of using PayPal and reminding interested buyers that signup is a one-time thing that becomes a handy one-click purchasing option they can later use on other sites.

There are several options to PayPal, but they cost more. For starters, see

Tips for Getting a Merchant Account Locally

Cheri Marsh, who lost a couple of thousand dollars when her Web-based merchant account provider went out of business without paying her for sales that had cleared, decided to get merchant status locally the second time around. You can learn from her experience.

"If approaching a local bank, go with your financial statements in hand," she says. "If your business is fairly new, show the growth over the past months. You are, in essence, shopping for a loan. The banker will want to know you are stable, reliable and serious about the business. You may be required to keep an escrow fund in the event you have chargebacks or disputes on sales. That means you need to have extra funds to cover those that are 'locked up' in the escrow account. Read the fine print before you sign any account. If you have questions, put them in writing and request a written response to them. For example, some accounts limit the amount of money you can take in. (How can you grow if they put a cap on what you can take in on credit cards?) Make sure you can increase this amount when business grows and that there will be no fee or penalty for this.

"One drawback most Internet people will find is that banks will not carry their merchant account unless they have a shopping cart that automatically bills the credit card for the purchase. Banks do not want the vendor to have the ability to intervene. Due to the custom features of my business, I could not utilize my bank's program. I went instead with Costco because they have great rates and outstanding merchant assistance round the clock, seven days a week. The initial setup costs are expensive (printer/transmission hardware), but I recommend having your own equipment—not the software.

"The biggest benefit of the hardware is that you can take it with you if you go offsite to market. You can process cards immediately, which is imperative if you are selling product and the customer leaves with it. You know the card has cleared before they take the merchandise. With software, you take all the information, go home and process the charge. Only then do you know whether the card is good or not, and if not, it's too late to get the merchandise back."

the Resource Chapter for Web site addresses for a list of some I've looked at, including ProPay, CCNow, ClickBank and DigiBuy. In trying to decide which might be best for your needs, work up an estimation of what you think your monthly Web site sales might be over a period of three months (number of orders, dollar amounts, etc.), then visit each site above and compare what it would cost to use their services to handle your estimated order volume. In all cases, be sure to read the fine print to make sure you understand each company's charges, payment methods and cancellation options.

Shopping Carts. "You *have* to have a shopping cart if you are to have a successful online business," says Lisa Risler. "There is no way around it. Initially, my sales were $20 a month if I was lucky. But they quickly went to over a $1,000 a month once I got my shopping cart and credit card facility up and running."

The good news is that shopping carts are offered as part of the service when you use any of the electronic credit card options discussed above. If you decide to have a specially designed shopping cart system set up by your Web designer, be careful. (You'll recall my earlier mention of someone who paid $362 for this feature.) Make sure you know how the shopping cart will work. After Carol Carlson spent $600 to have what she called "a really bad site put together by one of the local hosting companies," she discovered that the shopping cart system they had installed had a "small order fee" of $3 that was automatically being tacked onto her customer's orders. "I thought this was highway robbery, so I had to absorb that cost, losing all my profit on small sales," she says. (Carol quickly got out of that bad situation by learning how to set up her own site.)

Selling on eBay

I've heard nothing but good reports from crafters who are selling on eBay, and this kind of Web marketing may be perfect for you. "I think that developing and maintaining a Web site would be a waste of time for the average crafter unless they can truly do all the work themselves, are willing to take orders, pack and ship," says Susan Young. "And even then, unless they've got a product no one has seen before or can offer a service no one is offering, they're going to become just one more fish in a big lake. I believe their time might be better spent learning how to market on eBay." I agree, so let's take a look at what three happy eBay sellers are offering and how they work.

▼ ***Rubber stamps, stationery, recipe cards and other printed materials.*** Sue Krei sells these items on her Web site and also through eBay, which she says is a great way to move excess inventory. "eBay sales help our cash flow and also send people to our Web site," she says. "Each auction that we list on eBay has a direct link to our site. Also, when I send out notices to the winning bidders, there is information on the notice about current sales, etc. As a result, we get a lot of add-on orders from the auctions."

▼ ***Fabric items (handmade tablecloths, napkins, throws, scarves, etc.).*** Susan Gearing sells almost 100 percent on eBay under the name of "Susiecraft." Although Susan's daughter could set her up with a Web site, she has resisted getting one because she has all the business she can handle just on eBay alone. "I'm an eBay Powerseller," she says, "which means that I make at least $2,000/month in auction sales.

"eBay appealed to me because here I would be making only things that were already sold. I could make up a prototype of something, then keep listing it and only make more when I had the payment in hand. What a deal! But the demands of running so many auctions meant that I ultimately had to turn to selling more goods and fewer handmades to make the kind of income I wanted to make on eBay. I am primarily in mail order right now, running well over 200 auctions at all times, and really working at full capacity, shipping over 100 packages a week. Everything I sell is flat and easy to ship.

"The mix I have right now is working well for me," she adds. "My profits are quite good—much more than keystone on everything, usually three to four times cost and sometimes much more than that. With the bulk of what I sell, there is no labor other than cutting and packaging. For example, I might buy some clearance fabric for $2 a yard and sell it for $7.95 to $8.95. Things that sell very slowly or not at all are put on 'Clearance Sale' after awhile, and then sell very quickly."

In addition to money from the auctions themselves, Susan says many customers then come back by e-mail to request extra fabric, more napkins or other products, which she sells direct to them. "So there are sales besides what is selling on eBay and, of course, no commissions are due on those. One thing about selling on eBay is that you are all 'out there' with your success or failure for the world to see. You can't fudge about sales being good if they're not because this is a very public venue. For a person in the business of arts/crafts/creativity, it is simply the best marketing method I have ever found!"

I haven't had time to mess with eBay yet, but Susan says it looks much easier than it is. Like everything else related to the Web, there is a learning curve. "To be successful on eBay," she says, "you need a really good eye and feel for what will sell, plus marketing ability and good copywriting skills. I can't emphasize enough that, while eBay is simple in concept, successful execution takes talent, a lot of different skills, organization and determination."

Susan uses Andale (www.andale.com) to manage her auctions and hold her pictures. "This is my secret for doing the kind of volume I do," she says.

▼ **Glass bead and related items.** Jacqui Collins-Parker has also had great success in selling on eBay. Her monthly income from her Web site and eBay has been as high as $1,200, though it does fluctuate through the year. She sells glass vessels priced at $75, and sets of ten beads that she offers with an opening bid of $17.00. "Sometimes I've had bidding wars for these sets that have ended at $95," she says. "Other eBay buyers include folks who simply collect art glass beads. I don't know what they do with them, but I always encourage buyers to e-mail me a picture of their finished items so I can see what they did with what

I created. This helps me to bond with my customers, whom I really care about.

"On eBay, customer service is everything! Ship when and how you say you will, and bend over backwards to accommodate your customers and answer any questions they may have. Internet buyers can be very, very picky. If they want to return an item for a refund, don't argue, but see if there is any way you can help them want to keep the item."

▼ *Selling a 'Stash of Goodies.'* Jacqui's glass beads have a good market, but she can't sell them consistently throughout the year, so when sales start to slump in early fall, she starts selling items from her mother's and grandmother's craft stashes. "My mom and grandmother were pack-rats," she says, "and I have craft supplies, mohair from England, blank sweatshirts, craft and sewing books, jewelry, ribbon and lace and a lot of other things I will never use, so I sell it on eBay as 'More Great Stuff!' I scan the individual items during the summer and list them in mid-October. Although these are smaller ticket items usually starting at less than $5, I have found that folks will bid on them and sometimes have small bidding wars over them.

Tip

To create an illustration, lay whatever you need to scan right on the scanning bed. For example, I scan iron-ons and beads, then tweak the size, crop, lighten and adjust contrast using my graphics software. (Since beads are so small, it's hard to get a good photo of them with a lot of clarity and detail. I tried an inexpensive digital which was loaned to me and an expensive 35mm camera, and neither of them did as good a job as the scanner.)

Advice for eBay Beginners
by Jacqui Collins-Parker

Getting Started. Selling on eBay is a very simple learning curve. You register using a credit card, debit card or your checking account. If paying with a credit or debit card, the fees accumulate during the month and are debited monthly around the 18th. If using a checking account, you're limited to $25 in fees per month (listing and percentage of sales).

Once your registration is complete, you click on the "Sell Your Item" link (which is at the top of every page), and the eBay links will walk you through the process of pictures, listing how-tos, and even a bit of HTML to spice up your listing. (Don't pay for highlighting, double categories, bold print title, etc. They're annoying!) Folks will find you by typing in a keyword, such as "cookie cutters," "sterling silver beads," "art primitives," etc., and once you've created a presence there, they will bookmark you to see what you have to offer on a regular basis. *Do* add your item to the "gallery" images to boost exposure.

Listing a Product. The eBay Web site has a "Community Area" that includes tips and hints on how to list a product. To increase sales, include good descriptive copy. If there is a story behind your item (its age, the fact that it belonged to Uncle Frederick during the Civil War, etc.) tell the story. For example, I sell old cookie cutters that belonged to my grandmother and came from the old Reading Terminal Market in Philadelphia. When I was listing them, I told the story of how my mom and grandmom took us to the farmers' market to shop and how they always bought more cookie cutters while there. As a result, some of those 59-cent cutters sold on eBay for $12 each! (I even printed the story, with dates of the terminal market and original use, and packed it with the cutters.)

Illustrating Your Products. No one wants to buy something that isn't illustrated, so provide as many pictures as possible. But don't buy an expensive digital camera—invest in a scanner instead. For around $100, you can get a basic scanner that will give you good pictures. Buy one with a lid that unhinges so you can lay three-dimensional objects on the glass. I didn't like the software that came with my scanner, so I went to a free software site and downloaded *PhotoSuite*, a graphics program I like. (Even shareware, which offers a thirty-day trial period, will work until you start making money.)

"When selling your stash, pay particular attention to pricing," Jacqui emphasizes. "Although some collectors will pay more for certain items, the majority of folks on eBay are looking for bargains similar to those found at a flea market. Let the buyers set the price initially, and you will be able to adjust them up or down as time goes by and you establish yourself. An item priced too low may cause buyers to think it's junk; too high, and they'll go to another seller whose prices are more within reason. Explore categories of like items to determine the 'going starting bid price' and try to stay within the market prices on eBay. For example, if someone is selling four yards of ribbon for $4, can you sell it for less and be satisfied? If it belonged to great-aunt Sarah in 1897, adjust your opening bid price accordingly."

See more eBay tips from Jacqui on the opposite page.

Time, Money and Fame

Long before I knew what I was talking about, I called the Internet the greatest time-waster ever invented. Now that I've spent the better part of two years exploring the Web and all its riches, I still think it's the greatest time-waster ever invented *unless* one learns to be discerning about what sites one spends time on, what mailing lists one subscribes to, what chat rooms one enters, etc.

You must be discerning about e-mail, too, or you'll end up spending half of every day chatting with friends and family members and not getting any work done. Once you get into the design and management of one or more Web sites, however, time literally flies out the window, and you'll never again have enough time for everything you want to do in a day. I've learned that I can't focus on writing a book and also focus on updating my Web site—both of which take enormous concentration—so I'm always struggling to find large chunks of time I can devote to these necessary tasks.

In doing an analysis of my time this year, prior to starting the writing of this book, I was astonished to find that I had spent 33 percent of my time doing e-mail, 37 percent working on my two Web sites, and only 25 percent on writing that generated income. Once I started writing this book, however, work on my Web sites simply ceased. I asked my book contributors how much time they spent a week doing e-mail and working on their sites, and their answers will give you a much better idea of what to expect if you decide to make this leap.

For example, John Dilbeck, who manages six sites, says he spends an average of 50 hours a week on e-mail and Web site work. Lisa Risler says she practically worked around the clock for a year to get her six sites going, but now has a better handle on time and can manage her established business in a 48-hour work week. Debbie Spaulding (two sites) works 10 to 14 hours a day, but devotes only five to seven hours a week to e-mail and Web site work and spends the rest on designing puppet patterns. Retail shop owner Susan Young says maintenance of her Web site requires a minimum of 4 hours a week and as much as 12 depending on the season and how important it is to her to change it.

"Keeping content fresh and updated is key," says Cathy Colley, "and I just haven't devoted enough time to it (currently around 32 hours a month). Of course, in life you juggle many balls at once and have to set priorities every day."

"My husband says I'm working on my Web site 24 hours a day even in my sleep," says Cathryn Peters, "but of course he exaggerates a bit. It's more like about five or six hours a day, tweaking the coding, doing research on how to improve the site, working on the pictures or answering e-mail. But that's due in a large part because I am not a professional Web site designer who knows what she's doing. I'm still on that big learning curve."

"I'm online about 30 hours a week doing e-mails, newsletters to my customers, listing on eBay, etc.," says Jacqui Collins-Parker. "That leaves time to prepare and ship my orders. I also spend some time shopping, cleaning, bathing the dog, and talking to hubby. I guess I work about the same 130 hours a week as I did when I worked as a nurse. Actually, I could use a clone."

Sales vs. Hours. And here's the part you've all been waiting for. You've seen that some site owners are doing a good business on the Web, but you may wonder, as I did, what percentage of sales are coming through the Internet, versus other marketing outlets? The answers I got from Web site owners quoted in this chapter ranged from one-half of one percent to 100 percent, and I think that if you asked a thousand Web site owners, you'd probably get a similar range of response.

Lisa Risler's income comes 100 percent from her Web sites. Tammy Hodson says most of her special orders and about a third of their total sales come through the Web site. Jacqui Collins-Parker (with both a Web site and strong eBay presence) brings in about 25 percent of her business directly from her Web site, but adds that it's her site and its high listing in the search engines that give her a lot of traffic to her eBay auctions. Even without a Web site, Susan Gearing now derives most of her income from eBay sales.

Of course, many new site owners are generating fewer sales because they simply haven't yet learned how to direct traffic to their sites. Search engine placement is only one way to do this (a technical topic I can't get into in this book). Advertisements and publicity in print publications will generate additional traffic, and you should also include your Web site address on all printed materials and make it part of your automatic e-mail signature.

Being on the Web isn't just about making sales, of course. For many of us, it's simply good image advertising that often leads to new opportunities. "Although I don't make sales through my Web site as such, my presence on the Internet has elevated my popularity as a wicker restoration, seat weaving and antler basket expert," says Cathryn Peters. "Because of this, I am scheduled to teach, lecture and demonstrate at many annual regional, state and national basketry events that I was never privy to before. Actually, I thought my little niche Web site wouldn't get much traffic, but with the addition of my free monthly newsletter, the wicker FAQ page, and tying in all the pictures from my online photo albums, it has really taken off."

Susan Young isn't concerned with Web site sales, either, but is using her site to draw traffic to her retail shop. "The percentage of people who have found me via my site is probably less than 5 percent," she says, "but this has spurred some people to drive the highways to find my shop, and once they get here physically, most of them purchase off the shelf or order a custom or personalized item."

271

Except for the eBook I published this year, I have nothing to sell on my Web sites either, although I am planning to publish a series of eReports in the future. I plan to keep my BarbaraBrabec.com site going until my brain goes dead or these old fingers can't type any more. My primary goal will always be to keep my name before the public and the media as I promote sales of my books at the bookstore level. I also want to make it easy for my readers to communicate with me. Although I never give free business advice by e-mail (else I'd never get any writing done), I'm always happy to hear from my fans and direct them to a needed source of information, whether in one of my books or somewhere on the Web.

Best of all, I like it that I can so easily be found by anyone who knows my name. As a result, I've recently reconnected with old acquaintances I'd lost touch with twenty years ago. Now all anyone has to do to find me is type my name in a search engine and, voila—there I am! Frankly, I love it, and so do a lot of other folks. It's great if you can make money on the Web, but just being there in the first place is a kind of fun and fame none of us could have imagined only a few years ago.

Chapter Thirteen

Your "Potential Opportunity" Box

Offering products by mail is a great way to diversify any home-based crafts business. It's also a near-perfect moneymaker for people who live in rural areas of the country or lack access to the traditional retail outlets discussed in earlier chapters.

What's the most interesting place thousands of people visit every day? I think it's their P.O. Box. Now you may think that "P.O." stands for "Post Office," but as a former mail order marketer, I always looked at those initials and saw "Potential Opportunity!"

Prior to moving my business onto the Web in 2000, I sold my books, reports and newsletter by mail for twenty-five years. It always gave me a kick to open our drawer at the post office and see a bunch of envelopes of all sizes, shapes and colors because I knew each one held a surprise of one kind or another. On any given day, my mail was likely to include

- ▼ Orders with payment enclosed
- ▼ Requests for information that, when mailed, would bring more orders
- ▼ Inquiries from wholesalers interested in selling my products
- ▼ Personal letters or thank-you notes from satisfied customers, which brightened my day
- ▼ Information useful to me as a writer, speaker or publisher
- ▼ Advertising mail loaded with marketing ideas and good design/copywriting examples

Once you begin to advertise and sell by mail, your name and address will be grabbed by countless companies interested in selling you something. While you may not appreciate all of the mail that will end up in your mailbox, some so-called junk mail can be quite valuable. By studying the advertising mail that regularly fell into my P.O. Box, I gave myself a good education in how to write successful advertising copy and design printed materials. I learned how other sellers like myself were marketing their wares and promoting their businesses, and I got ideas for more books than I will ever have time to write.

You may be wondering about whether you can use your home address as your mail order business address, or whether you should get a post office box for your mail. I strongly suggest the latter. If homebased businesses are outlawed in your area by outdated zoning laws, you may avoid problems by conducting your business through a box number. Even when a homebased business is deemed legal, some communities require the owner to secure a "special use permit" to do business. (This is something you will have to check out with local officials. A mail order seller once told me, however, that his local licensing bureau advised him to obtain a post office box number for his address because the post office is in a commercial zone, and that eliminates the need for any special use permit. Zoning matters aside, a post office box address is the best way I know to keep a

Dealing with Details

In addition to legalities and regulations that apply to any home-based business, mail order marketers must also collect and pay sales tax, something that is no longer simple because of new tax laws in many states. Mail order marketers must also comply with FTC rules and regulations related to truth-in-advertising and the "30-day Mail Order Rule." (Refer back to Chapter Three for more information on these topics and the address of this government agency.)

low profile in the community and discourage drop-in customers.)

If you have a Web site, it's all the more important to have a P.O. Box address. Many sellers have order forms on their sites that customers can print and mail with a check, and this mail should be directed to a P.O. Box so you can maintain your personal privacy.

Analyzing Your Options

According to researchers in the mail order industry, more than half the adult population orders merchandise by mail or phone every year. This suggests that many people would find your mail order offer of interest, too. Here are six ways crafters can break into mail order selling:

1. Take custom orders to be delivered later by mail or UPS;
2. Give all customers a copy of your brochure or catalog to encourage follow-up sales by mail;
3. Place classified ads offering your catalog or an inexpensive product by mail (only one product per ad);
4. Offer a small selection of related products in a display ad;
5. Periodically mail to your customer and prospect lists;
6. Advertise on the Web (as discussed in the previous chapter).

The kind of printed advertising materials you use will be determined by the number of products you have to sell. If you begin with only one or two, flyers or a brochure should work. Once you have a complete line of products, a multi-page, stapled catalog will enable you to do a better selling job and will also build customer confidence in your company.

As I stress in the following chapter, the quality of your printed materials will have much to do with the kind of response you will receive from mail order buyers. A flyer, brochure or catalog that is poorly designed or printed suggests that the products being offered for sale are not of high quality either. Some handcrafts have to be presented photographically (preferably in color) to sell well by mail, but many common items familiar to consumers can be sold with line drawings if the artwork and overall printing of the catalog are of high quality. Such items include:

▼ Teddy bears and dolls
▼ Wooden toys and decorative accessories
▼ Sweatshirts and bags
▼ Christmas ornaments
▼ Gift baskets
▼ Handmade soap and candles
▼ Dried items such as grapevine or pine cone wreaths

If you can offer your art or craft at wholesale prices (a topic I can only touch on in this book), you may find it surprisingly easy to market by mail to out-of-state shops and stores. If you cannot wholesale your crafts or you simply lack the ideas for things you might sell, think about related products or services that could be offered to individual buyers by mail, such as:

▼ Originally designed patterns or design books
▼ Newsletters, directories or how-to booklets
▼ Greeting cards, calendars and calligraphy products
▼ Hard-to-find supplies and materials or kits
▼ A craft or needlework related service
▼ Craft business or marketing information
▼ Audio- or videotapes

Selling Through Your Own Catalog

Joan Green is a plastic canvas needlework designer whose catalog is proving to be quite successful, in spite of its simplicity. "I've carved out a nice niche for myself offering hard-to-find yarns, design booklets and my own kits," she says. "Those who are able to find me are buying because they can no longer find decent supplies or any variety in the chain stores. July through December is my peak selling time, but sales are generally steady all year long."

Joan's twelve-page black-and-white catalog can be used as a self-mailer, but she often sends it along with extra flyers promoting special sales or new kits she has designed. "The catalog isn't fancy," she says, "which may put some people off because we live in an age of glorious color and slick brochures. But when people call to ask about it, I explain that I am primarily a designer who offers this small catalog to help them find much needed and hard-to-come-by supplies. Over the years I have managed to get editors to take my catalog seriously. Usually they will list me as a source along with how-to projects of mine they have published, partly because they don't want to have to field all the calls they would get when their readers can't find my recommended yarns. Among my best-selling yarns are metallic and specialty yarns from Rainbow Gallery. Some designs they have bought from me are posted on their Web site at TheStitchery.Com for consumers to download for free."

Over the years, Joan has run classified ads in the major craft magazines, offering a free pattern and catalog for an SASE. Now she's running display ads in the plastic canvas magazines because rates are so favorable. "I picture a design and offer the kit as a promotional deal to drum up business, hoping people will like the kit and reorder, and this has worked quite well for me," she says.

As this book was being written, Joan was making plans to open her Web site. She wants to increase her mail order business, but not to the extent that it consumes all her time. And that's the lovely thing about mail order. You can easily control the amount of orders you get simply by increasing or decreasing the number of ads you place, or the number of mailings you make.

▼ Crafty food items, such as home-grown nuts, jams, candy or seasoning mixes and blends

▼ Seasonal items, such as holiday decorations or party favors

Mail Order Brainstorming

Now that you have some general mail order guidelines under your belt, it's time to get specific. To brainstorm for products you might offer by mail, answer these three questions:

1. **What do you make that is unusual** (not readily available elsewhere) but not so unfamiliar that people would hesitate to buy it? (People won't buy a product by mail if they don't understand what it is or why they need it.) Exclude from your list any product consumers are likely to find at a local crafts fair, boutique or craft mall.

2. **Which of your products "go together"** (made from a common material or themed to a particular style, such as country, Victorian or contemporary)? Focus on offering a coordinated line of products instead of a hodgepodge of crafts.

3. **Which of your products solve a particular need** (gifts, decorative accessories, clothing, toys, etc.)? Also list them in categories under holidays (Valentine's Day, Easter, Mother's Day, Father's Day, Halloween, Thanksgiving, Christmas) and general gifts (birthdays, graduations, baby showers, wedding and anniversaries, etc.). This may help you decide when to make your first mailing or place your first advertisement.

Now look at all the products on your list and delete (1) any that will be difficult to package or are too fragile to travel well through the mail; (2) anything you are unwilling or unable to produce in quantity, and (3) any item whose manufacture is dependent on a single or questionable supply source. (Before you offer any product for sale by mail, you must be confident you can produce enough to fill all orders received, and that

278

you will have no difficulty in buying the necessary materials for their manufacture.)

Building Your Mailing List

Before you spend any money on advertising, pull together a mailing list of every customer you've ever sold anything to, along with the names and addresses of people who have expressed interest in your work but haven't bought anything yet. If you are not already collecting the names and addresses of individuals who see your work at craft fairs and other outlets, you should be. Keep a notebook or a tablet in your booth or display area with a small sign that says something like:

> **SIGN HERE ...**
> To receive information about
> my next craft show and
> new products.

"When you're just getting started in mail order, you main concern is to build your customer base," says John Schulte, chairman of the National Mail Order Association. "Each time you sell something, capture the buyer's name, address and phone number and note what they bought and how much they paid. Then, at regular intervals in the future, send these customers information about your newest products."

Although you can get started in mail order with just one product or service, substantial profits will not be realized until you begin to resell your customer base. As you continue to build your mailing list, your constant goal should be the addition of new products or services so you will always have something different to offer to satisfied customers and others who have expressed interest in your work. If you can't come up with new products and services, try to think of new ways to offer the same old merchandise.

Classified vs. Display Ads

A beginning designer started selling crochet patterns through classified ads in magazines. Her first ad cost $20, the second $120. For a total cost of $140, she got over $3,000 worth of business in six months. Then she took what she felt was a logical next step. She began to run ads in bigger magazines with higher advertising rates. It didn't work. "I never lost money, but I also didn't run to the bank," she reported. "After spending a fortune on one ad in a national magazine, I barely broke even. The lesson I learned was higher advertising rates and larger circulation numbers mean nothing if my product isn't right for that publication's audience. I'm back to $20 ads in crochet magazines, and they're still pulling."

Prospecting for New Business

Once you have developed a mailing list of interested prospects and satisfied buyers, you should constantly mine it for new business. Many inexperienced mail order sellers figure if someone doesn't order the first time information is sent to them, they will never order. This is not true. You might have to mail a consumer or wholesale buyer half a dozen times before you hit that prospect's hot button. At any given time, only a certain percentage of a percentage of those on your mailing list will be in the "right mood" to consider your advertising offer. Think about how often you have received and discarded advertising mail and catalogs. When it arrived, you may have been at the end of your income for the month, down with a cold or busy trying to get ready for weekend guests. If the same mailing were to arrive at a different time a few months later, your situation would have changed, and now you might be interested in the advertiser's offer.

The same logic should be applied to the placement of classified or display ads. One mail order advertiser says she never runs ads in December issues because she has found that what is happening in people's lives is directly reflected in her business. "April (income tax), June (school graduations and weddings) and September (school beginnings) have always been slow mail order months for me," she says. A pattern seller says summer is a bad time for her, but fall is usually good because people are then starting to think about Christmas gift needs. Since most magazines have a long life in libraries, doctor's offices and beauty shops, orders from any display ad you place could dribble in for a couple of years afterwards, so plan accordingly.

While the experience of others is always a helpful guide, only you can determine which months of the year will be most profitable for your direct mailings or magazine ads. Each seller has to do a lot of testing to figure out an average response, and it's essential that you keep good records of all your mailings—which list you've used, the quantity mailed, total cost of mailing and order response. So much depends upon what you're selling, how those on your mailing list perceive your products, and how good your follow-up printed materials are.

Industry research suggests that the average mailer may get an order response of only one or two percent, but your response will always be greater from mail lists you develop yourself (as opposed to mail lists you might rent or trade with other businesses). Again, I stress the importance of understanding basic advertising concepts when you get into direct response marketing. Having a good product or service is not enough. You must also learn what motivates people to buy, then incorporate this knowledge into all your advertising, publicity and mailing programs. (See "Display Ad Wisdom" later in this chapter for guidelines on the kind of response you might expect to get from a display ad in a crafts consumer magazine.)

Classified Advertising

To attract new prospects for your mailing list, try some of the publicity strategies mentioned in Chapter Eleven, plus a few classified ads. Begin by selecting two or three magazines that carry advertisements for products similar to what you want to sell, then use the "two-step advertising method" to hook prospects. The idea here is not to catch fish, but to merely go fishin'. When you get a nibble (a written request or phone call for more informa-

Clean Your List with Postcard Mailings

If your mailing list is even slightly out of date, you can "clean" it (get address updates from the post office) at no cost with a first class postcard that includes an "Address Correction Requested" line beneath your return address. (If you request address changes on a bulk mailing, you will have to pay extra for these corrections.) If you already have a bulk-mail permit number, you can get a first-class permit at no extra charge. The same number can be used for both kinds of mail. Ask your postmaster for details.

In one day's mail, I happened to receive two postcards from one small homebased business that had previously sent me catalogs. Both mailers said I must respond if a new catalog was wanted. One company asked that I return the postcard. The other asked me to return the postcard with an SASE with 52 cents postage. Although this is an inexpensive way to weed out disinterested people on your mailing list, be prepared to lose some potentially good customers who may simply be too busy to respond to your postcard reminder or annoyed about sending an SASE.

Before automatically deleting the names of people who do not respond, however, try another postcard mailing about six weeks later. This time, instead of offering your catalog again, feature a hot item from the catalog and emphasize new products. Offer a free catalog with purchase or sell it singly.

tion), send an appropriate response (sales letter and flyer, brochure, catalog, etc.). Answer inquiries immediately before prospects forget why they were interested in your offer.

There is a limit on what you can successfully sell directly through publicity or a classified ad because people won't buy a "pig in a poke." But they may buy from you once you've given them your best sales presentation. Each year for more than twenty-five years I generated thousands of

new prospect names for my mailing list and sold thousands of books and reports in the process. To keep my list to a manageable size, I periodically dropped older prospective names that had not responded to earlier mailings. (Once you've got a good mailing list going, the most important thing is to keep it up to date because constant remailings to your entire list are yet another secret to success in direct mail marketing.)

Seven Classified Ad Copywriting Tips

If you've never written a classified ad before, or if your present ads aren't pulling well, the following copywriting tips will save you money and help you generate a greater response.

1. **Keep your ad short** (20 to 30 words at most). Eliminate unnecessary words. Instead of writing, "Here's a wonderful way to store and carry all your needlecraft supplies," say instead: "Stores and carries needlecraft supplies efficiently." (Without changing the meaning, you've cut the ad cost in half while strengthening your product's benefit to the customer.)

2. **Offer only one product per ad.** Don't try to sell six kinds of potpourri each at a different price, then ask customers to specify order numbers, add sales tax, or include $3 for postage and handling. Any reader who made it this far would probably be too confused to order. However, anyone interested in potpourri would probably respond to a simple ad that states: "POTPOURRI 'Scentsational' sample and catalog, $1."

3. **Offer more information.** Don't try to sell a high-priced item directly in an ad. The higher the price of your product, the lower your response rate, unless you also offer additional information. If you can't afford to send free information, experiment with one of these closing lines: (1) For details, send SASE, (2) Brochure, $1, or (3) Catalog, $2 ($1 refundable).

   If you decide to offer a product direct to customers, keep the price under $10 and don't waste ad money on useless

SASEs: Good Idea or Not?

"SASE" stands for "Self-Addressed Stamped Envelope." While an SASE or small handling charge will help offset the cost of advertising, it also diminishes ad response. Some people won't respond if they have to bother with taping coins to a card or enclosing an SASE. Yet the advantage to the seller in asking for an SASE or some money is that it qualifies prospects and eliminates many curiosity seekers who send for things just because they're free. The person who does take the time to send an SASE and a sum of money or a dollar for information is at least truly interested and more likely to buy. Some mail order novices ask for both an SASE and a sum of money, but if you do this you could cut your total response by 35 percent or more.

Many businesses now charge from $1 to $5 to mail a descriptive brochure or catalog, and most consumers see this as a reasonable postage and handling cost for information. To increase the number of orders for a more expensive catalog, try advertising it together with something else, perhaps a sample pattern, swatch of material or yarn, a tip sheet about your craft, a list of recommended supply sources or a reprint of an informative article you've written. I recall the dollmaker who created a wonderful full-color poster of her product line, then advertised and publicized it for $3. The orders she received for the poster covered printing and advertising costs and enabled her to get her catalog into the hands of hundreds of interested consumers and wholesalers.

words. "Please send check or money order for $6.00 plus $2.50 postage and handling" is a thirteen-word statement that can also be stated in just three words: "$8.50 ppd. from . . ." With some classified ads costing $5 a word or more, this kind of tight copywriting could save you hundreds of dollars a year.

4. **Stress customer benefits.** An ad that offers a "Summer Special—Two-for-One Sale" suggests the benefit of ordering now to save money. "Bonus pattern with first order" promises a reward

to someone who requests your catalog and then orders something. "A catalog that solves gift-giving needs" will appeal to people who are too busy to shop, or who lack ideas on what to give as gifts.

In writing ad copy, avoid the use of opinionated words and phrases such as "beautiful" or "You'll love it." Instead, stress words that imply customer benefits such as "comfortable," "practical" or "lasting." The use of such persuasive words as "save," "new" and "guaranteed" may also increase your ad response. (Note that the Federal Trade Commission restricts use of the word "new" in advertising. Generally, a "new" product can be advertised as such for only six months.)

5. *Remember the AIDA formula.* It stands for Attract, Interest, Desire, and Action. ATTRACT readers with an appropriate two- or three-word heading, then INTEREST them by appealing to one of their needs or wants. Stimulate DESIRE for your product by listing benefits to be derived from it, then demand ACTION by telling readers to write, call, send for, order, etc.

6. *Test a special offer.* Try "Free gift for ordering within 30 days," or offer a sample or sampler package for a special price. A spinner who breeds Angora rabbits to make a line of hand-spun yarns offers her brochure and a dozen samples of her lush yarns for a dollar. To emphasize the benefits of her product in her brochure and publicity promotions, she points out that handplucked/handspun Angora does not shed like the commercial Angora imported from China. Sheared from rabbits, the China Angora gives short fibers and flat ends that work their way out of the yarn, she explains. (This is a great example of how to make a product stand out from the competition.)

7. *Analyze the ads of others.* Here is a homework assignment you can give yourself to learn how to write more effective ad copy. Pick a magazine that carries advertising similar to what you'd like to place. Analyze each ad in the magazine, noting things that grab your attention, pique your interest or make you want to reach for your checkbook. Apply to your own advertising copy the same techniques these advertisers are using.

Display Ad Wisdom

If you offer handcrafted items not commonly found at craft fairs and you want to break into mail order (and possibly wholesaling), you might consider placing a display ad in a consumer magazine that features handcrafts. You'll have to check your newsstand to find appropriate magazines since many have come and gone over the past few years. Also network with other crafters to get their advertising recommendations.

The first edition of this book included a detailed analysis of the results several artists and crafters received from their display ads in a *Better Homes & Gardens "Crafts Showcase"* magazine that is now out of print. Since I could not locate all of these advertisers to re-interview them for this edition of the book, I decided to summarize their advertising stories here, placing emphasis on the lessons each learned. I believe their advertising experiences are typical of craft sellers everywhere, so you can avoid the pitfalls they encountered and capitalize on things that worked well for them.

What was interesting to me when I first interviewed these advertisers was the fact that their full-color ads were all about the same size and all were attractively designed, yet the response each received varied from dozens of orders to absolutely none. I believe the information that follows will help you avoid disappointing and costly advertising and give you an entirely new perspective on how to find new wholesale buyers.

High-Priced Items. As a general rule, don't offer a high-priced item in a display ad unless it's a product many would deem collectible. For example, Charlene's ad featured limited-edition Santas carved from cypress knees, available in different colors and sizes, priced at $100. Her goal was to reach Santa collectors, and she did get eight orders, which was enough to cover her ad cost. She was satisfied with this response because she knew the magazine would be kept by many readers and, based on previous advertising experience, she knew she could also

expect to receive additional orders over the next year or two.

Susan, on the other hand, struck out with her ad for a Bargello needle-work pillow priced at $195. When she failed to receive a single response to her ad, she questioned whether the magazine actually had the 400,000 circulation it claimed. As a check, I called Corina, another advertiser whose ad appeared on the same page. Her ad featured a selection of pottery pieces priced from $10.50 to $29.50. Since this ad had generated more than enough orders to pay for itself, it offered proof that many people did stop to read that particular page of the magazine.

To me, the lack of response to Susan's ad suggested that this magazine's readers were unlikely to be interested in buying $200 items by mail, especially when many were probably women who did needlepoint as a hobby. I couldn't help but wonder how many needlepointers saw this particular ad and thought, "Wow! Look what I could get for my needlepoint if I offered it for sale." This kind of logic may be one reason why so many display ads fail. Remember: The fact that someone has advertised a product at a certain price doesn't mean it is actually selling at that price.

Tip

If you can afford only one ad to begin with, consider offering a unique product in the fall that's perfect for the Christmas season, priced between $30 and $50. If you offer a product priced higher than $50, you may cut your order response in half, and if you try to sell anything priced lower than $30, you will have a difficult time getting the cost of your ad back.

Patterns and Kits. Since we all see advertisements for craft or doll patterns in magazines, we might assume that everyone is selling them with success. But this is not necessarily true. As I learned from Donna, whose ad featured country dolls and patterns priced at $6.50 each, patterns can be difficult to sell in a display ad. Although Donna was successfully wholesaling her dolls at the time she placed this ad, the orders she received did not begin to pay for its cost. "I've run ads in other magazine-catalogs," she told me, "and I've concluded that the pattern market is much harder to break into than the product market."

The difference in response between the two patterns ads placed by Donna and Diane confirms that it's not just the price of a pattern that determines it salability, but the pattern design itself. The more unusual the design, the better. For example, Rhonda's half-page ad paid for itself in less than a month. It featured four whimsical fabric-doll patterns including an amusing faerie godmother named "Celeste" (pictured at right). Each pattern was offered at $7.50 each. Interestingly, although Rhonda advertised only patterns, about 20 percent of the people who responded to her ad wanted finished dolls instead of patterns. She agreed to make them at $50 each provided she could deliver them on her own time schedule. (One reason she got into patterns in the first place was to break away from the labor-intensive work of selling finished dolls at craft shows.)

Offering a Catalog or Brochure in Your Ad.

Although a good display ad will generate retail sales up front, many people will want to see your catalog or brochure before they order. Offering one can also increase your chances for breaking even on an ad. Ask $2 to $3 for it, or whatever amount you need to cover its print and postage cost, plus the time it will take you to process the order. (Since you may or may not get a good order response from it, you don't want to lose money as it goes out the door.)

Carolyn, whose display ad featured four angel pins with matching earrings priced from $6 to $12 each, offered a catalog for $2 (refundable with order). She said she got more orders for the catalog than sales, but one out of three catalog recipients eventually ordered something, so she didn't lose money on the ad.

Rhonda, whose ad featured four fabric-doll patterns, offered a color brochure priced at $2, free with order. You've noticed, I'm sure, that many ads say "Catalog, $2, refundable," which means the buyer can deduct $2 from the total of their first order. You might want to experiment with "Catalog free with order," however, to see if it works any better. I found Rhonda's logic sound: "I think they figure that if a catalog costs $2 and a pattern costs $7.50 and includes a catalog, it makes sense to just order a pattern to begin with."

Deena, whose ad featured a selection of country crafts and patterns, generated twenty requests for her brochure (offered for $1, refundable with order), but six of them "forgot" to send the dollar, which is about par for the course in my own experience as a mail order advertiser. Only one out of the twenty ordered anything. "I think one of the main problems with magazines like this is that many people who are reading them are other crafters like myself who are looking for new ideas for things they can make and sell at fairs," Deena concluded.

Tip

Crafters do buy magazines to get ideas, but the main reason some handcrafts don't sell well in display ads is because too many people are offering similar items at fairs. To succeed in mail order, you must offer products that are not readily available from any other source.

Estimating Ad Response. With a guaranteed circulation of 400,000 or more, you might think it would be easy to get 100 orders from a display ad, but it's not. What you must remember is that 500 advertisers or more may be competing for attention in the same issue. The biggest mistake the beginner in mail order makes is expecting too great a response to their advertising.

An experienced dollmaker once asked the readers of a doll magazine to estimate the number of responses they thought they might get from a color display ad in a consumer magazine with a circulation of 700,000. Some thought that one person out of a hundred would respond (or 7,000) while others guessed at least one out of a thousand (700) would order. The advertiser who posed this question went on to explain that when she offered a tested product with a color ad, her response rate was actually about one in ten thousand, or just 70 responses. The three-month run of her ad cost $2,500 and netted $350 worth of orders. "My biggest mistake was to believe that the odds were with me," she said.

It would take a very unusual product to get back the cost of a $500 ad from a single item retailing for less than $10. Offering a selection of several items in this price range, however, has worked for some advertisers. Diane figured that if she offered a pattern for $8.75, she would need to sell 70 patterns to break even on her ad. "And this covered every penny of the expense of putting the pattern package together," she emphasized. Instead of offering single patterns for $6 or $7.50 each (the price range today of most craft and doll patterns), Diane offered a set of three full-size cloth patterns (two dolls and a small wall quilt) for just $8.75 ppd. Her ad worked because she offered consumers a good buy on an unusual set of patterns that were perfect for the season. She got 150 orders from this ad, plus several new wholesale accounts.

Wholesale Inquiries. Just as craft fair sellers often get wholesale requests from shop owners who browse shows, wholesale buyers also read magazine ads to search out new suppliers for their shops or mail order catalogs. Randall Barr's ad for his "Time Flies" Birdhouse Clock (pictured in Chapter Four), offered clocks in three sizes and four different color accents, priced from $25 to $54 each. Because this product was so unusual, his ad paid for itself within ten days after the magazine hit the newsstands, and he was still receiving orders from the ads five months later, some of which were repeat orders from satisfied customers.

Of the 75 orders Randall got from this particular ad, most were not for the lowest-priced item as one might think, but for the two larger and more expensive clocks priced between $48 and $54 (prices that included shipping costs). But what I found most interesting about Randall's story was that the real benefit of his ad in a consumer magazine came in the form of wholesale business. "I would have gotten my money back from this ad just from the retail sales," Randall told me, "but the fifteen new wholesale accounts I gained made this ad extremely profitable. Many of those

The Crafter's Mail Order Song
by Barbara Brabec
(A humorous poem to be sung to the tune of "Hey, Look Me Over!")

Hey, look me over, see what I've got,
I think you'll like my products a lot.
Customers tell me they're really great!
They're one-of-a-kind and superbly designed
and I know you'll appreciate the fact that
I need to sell them, to people like you,
they're my bread and butter, they pay the mortgage, too.
So fill out the order form, write me a check
and be sure to mail it today . . .
look me over . . . send me your order,
I'll ship it right away!

accounts placed repeat orders right after Christmas." This emphasizes the importance of always being ready to field wholesale inquiries as soon as you offer any product in the retail marketplace.

Deena Nixon's ad offered a collection of country crafts—a hand-painted sign, a dried-flowers heart, and a couple of country wall hangings in three different forms: finished, as a kit, and as a pattern. She sold only a couple of kits, half a dozen patterns and a few finished products, earning back less than half the cost of her ad. Six months later, however, the ad finally paid for itself when a couple of wholesale orders came in.

"More important than the orders I got from my display ad were the new wholesale doors it opened for me, "says Carolyn, the angel pin seller. "It led me directly to other people who are now showing my line in wholesale markets in Dallas, Atlanta, Chicago, New York and Los Angeles. The color flyers I use have made all the difference in getting my products into shops across the country."

Donna, the country doll pattern seller, said her ads in various magazines had consistently generated many inquiries from wholesalers that helped her move into a more profitable area. Rhonda also got several new wholesale accounts from her doll pattern ad, making it extremely profitable. By the time her second ad had appeared in the magazine (featuring new patterns), she was getting reorders from many individuals and quilt shops who had ordered from her first ad. "Once you connect with a new shop, you can usually count on getting repeat orders on a regular basis."

Adds Corina, the pottery advertiser, "We received a lot of wholesale inquiries along with retail sales, and most people who requested a brochure placed good-sized orders. We've found that you have to keep running an ad to make it pay off. We're now in our third year of advertising in the *Country Sampler* catalog, running six ads a year."

Tip

You may wish to check out *Country Sampler* magazine as a possible place to advertise your crafts (see Resource Chapter). This unique "catalog-magazine," in print since 1984, offers rates affordable to serious artists and craft sellers. Their 400,000+ distribution on newsstands and to paid subscribers guarantees a large national audience. Advertisers receive expert photography, ad creation, copy editing and more.

800-Numbers and Credit Card Sales. Although you are likely to sell more if you accept credit cards and include an 800-number in your ad, many mail order advertisers enjoy success with ads that simply ask for payment with order. Some advertisers take credit cards, but do not have an 800-number. If you are advertising in craft consumer magazines, however, my research suggests that if people really want what you offer, they will gladly pay the cost of a telephone call to place a credit card order, or send you a check if you don't take credit cards. Of all the advertisers mentioned above, only Carolyn (angel pins) published an 800-number in her ad (which barely broke even), and only Randall (clocks) and Corina (pottery) offered VISA and MasterCard privileges.

Telephone Tips. Don't advertise your phone number in a national magazine unless you're going to be available to answer the phone. Shortly after their ads were published, I was unable to reach several advertisers who had placed ads in *Craft Showcase*. In some cases, the phone rang off the wall, and no answering machine clicked in. Once, a young child answered the phone. (Not a good way to impress prospective buyers.) I left two detailed messages with a couple of advertisers saying I wanted to interview them for this book, but they never called back.

Many home-business owners run a business off their personal telephone line, which is not only unprofessional, but likely to be in violation of local telephone regulations. Generally, a personal phone number may not legally be advertised anywhere. Even when you have an answering machine, many callers will hang up rather than leave a message, particularly if your recording isn't professionally done.

Tip

When you prepare a message for callers, don't say "Hi, we're not here. You've reached (telephone number) . . . leave a message," but answer with your full name so callers will know they've reached the right number. (To avoid problems with your telephone company, do not answer using your business name unless you have a business telephone number.) In your message, be specific about what callers should do. Voice mail is more professional than an answering machine, and its great benefit is that messages from several people can be received at the same time.

293

In Summary

In revising this chapter in 2001, I had to ask myself whether marketing on the Web was going to eventually replace most of the mailings small business owners used to make, and I think the answer is yes. After selling by mail for twenty-five years, I finally got out of the book selling business because it was taking entirely too much of my time to plan and create direct mail pieces (leaving me with little time for writing), and the increasing cost of postage and labor involved in sending thousands of brochures or catalogs to my lists ultimately became too much work for Harry and me to handle. And then there was the matter of keeping thousands of names on my mailing lists updated, when each mailing would return two or three hundred mail pieces with new or undeliverable addresses.

Clearly, marketing electronically is less expensive and faster than marketing by mail, and Carol Carlson's experience sums it up nicely. For years, Carol has sold a line of hang tags for crafters by advertising her mail order catalog in magazines and regularly sending new catalogs to her entire customer list. Now, however, she says it has become too expensive and time consuming to mail a three- or four-ounce catalog to so many people. "I am so used to the Internet now that direct mailings seem to be an extremely slow process. The last mailing of my new catalog to all my regular customers took about two weeks, day-in and day-out! Everything else got backlogged during that period and I could have used that time for

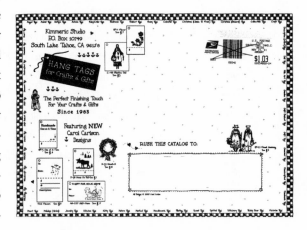

Get more punch from your mailings by printing interesting copy on your envelopes. Carol Carlson's interesting 9 x 12 envelope always does a nice selling job for the hang tags catalog it contains.

so many other things. I'm sure I will send out occasional reminders in the future, using postcards or small fliers, but I can no longer justify mass mailings of my catalog."

Before reading this chapter, you may have thought that advertising in a major consumer magazine would practically guarantee sales. Now you understand it doesn't work that way. While your association with a prestigious magazine will always be good for your professional image, sales success will depend on how well you have matched your products and prices to that particular audience.

Although the Internet has reduced the need for small businesses to send direct mailings, it will never replace the need for print advertising to attract new mail order buyers. Classified and display ads remain the best way to generate new mail order business, only now most of these ads are directing interested buyers to both a toll-free number and a Web site for more information.

One secret to selling successfully by mail is not to follow the trends so closely. Be more creative. Set your prices high enough to yield a true profit but don't overprice them in an attempt to get your ad costs back. If mail order shoppers find an item that is truly unique, they may be willing to pay anything to get it. If what you are advertising is something the average consumer can find at a local crafts fair or shop, however, they won't pay an inflated price merely for the convenience of buying it by mail.

Chapter Fourteen

Your Printed Professional Image

Good printed materials make a difference to buyers, but few crafters realize the direct connection between sales and the type and quality of their printed materials.

*I*f you have no printed materials at all, you are telling the world that you're an amateur seller. If your printed materials are of poor design or printed quality, prospective buyers may question the quality of your products. For maximum success in selling directly to consumers in person or by mail, you need high quality printed materials. Besides bringing in more orders, attractive printed materials enhance your professional image, make you feel good about your business and enable you to charge higher prices than the competition.

The primary focus of this chapter is not on how to design printed materials, but rather how and when to use certain printed materials to make sales, get reorders, attract a following and impress buyers. The specific printed materials under discussion are stationery, business cards, hang tags, designer labels, flyers, brochures, postcards and mail order catalogs.

If you don't have a computer, ask a friend to design your printed materials for you and then take the original "art" to any copy shop to be printed. If you have a computer and inkjet or laser printer, you can easily design and print outstanding stationery, business cards and brochures using regular paper or some of the exciting preprinted and scored papers available from paper suppliers included in the Resource Chapter. These papers are not inexpensive, but when you really want to make an impression on a few prospective buyers or customers, they do the job beautifully. The best thing is that you can print as few or many as you wish, buying stock in boxes of about a hundred sheets at a time.

Stationery: What It Says about You

A well-typed letter on business stationery suggests a degree of professionalism and stability no handwritten note on tablet paper can convey. No matter how small your crafts enterprise, one of your first expenditures should be for stationery and matching envelopes. Besides helping you in business, printed stationery will make you fell less like a hobbyist and more like the professional craft seller I know you want to be.

Years ago, when I emphasized in one of my "Selling What You Make" columns that professional crafters should type all letters on business stationery, a reader complained that not everyone could afford business letterheads or typewriters. "Perhaps concentrating not so much on the professional look but on the legibility and correctness of handwriting and grammar would have been more kind and gotten your point across as well," she said.

While I try never to be unkind, I do have a responsibility to my readers to be truthful, even if the truth sometimes stings a little. I do not see it as kind to let people think that legible handwriting and good grammar are enough when the letter's purpose is to secure supplies at wholesale prices or get one's foot in the door of a prospective buyer. If you're trying to get the attention of buyers and suppliers, you must present yourself as a business person,

The above examples show the different approaches used by creative people to create business stationery. There are no rules for creating a letterhead. Use whatever typefaces, colors and images that please you and reflect well on your business.

299

and typed letters on business stationery help achieve that image.

By "typed," I do not necessarily mean "on a typewriter." In fact, typewriters are now considered archaic equipment in most offices, having been replaced by inexpensive computer technology. If you have a home computer with word processing software that corrects spelling and grammatical errors, all you really need are a couple of fingers to hunt-and-peck great-looking letters. Space in this book does not allow for a discussion of why homebased businesses should embrace computer technology, but this topic has been discussed at length in my book, *Make It Profitable.*

Business Cards: How They Boost Business

The primary purpose of a business card is to help people remember who you are and how they can find you when they want you. Most business cards are rectangular and measure 3½" × 2", but cards used by artists and craftspeople come in all sizes, shapes and colors. Like hang tags (see next section), they are sometimes folded. If you want to stand out in a crowd, one way to do this is with a clever or unusual business card. But before you decide on the design details of your card, ask first what you really want a business card to do for you (or *not* to do for you).

The business cards on the adjacent page offer ideas on how to create a unique card for your own business.

A. Playing on her business name of "Golden Touch Crafts," Susan Larberg chose to print her card on gold metallic card stock. This card does double-duty by serving as a hang tag. (Note how copy is laid out so the card can easily be folded and punched to add a tie string.

B. "TC" Ferrito printed her own card on colorful preprinted stock (see resource chapter for such supply sources).

C. Rebekah Rowe's attractive card is printed on pale lavender stock, with a shaded design in the background and design touches that have a silver glitter to them.

D. Cathryn Peters has used her attractive business logo on her business card, stationery and envelope, printing with brown ink on ivory stock.

E. Trish Bloom's card is printed in black ink on white stock, with the moons and stars all in blue.

F. Susan Young designed a colorful card by finding clip art on the Internet and using her graphic arts software program to bring everything together. She had the card printed commercially as this was less expensive than printing color cards on her inkjet printer.

G. Most business cards are printed only on one side, but Christine Zipps' photo card of one of her floral creations has contact info printed on the back.

A

Susan
Larberg

(352) 796-7522
27271 Hickory Hill Road
Brooksville, FL 34602

Golden Touch
Crafts

C

heart of glass studios
rebekah rowe
★
art dedicated to
enhancing self esteem and
peace of spirit ★
2176 lockwood chapel rd.
dover, de 19904   ★
♡ 302-492-8915 ★
tinlizzie@worldnet.att.net
★
ART FOR LIFE!

B

TC's Sew What?
Polar Fleece Hats & Garments,
Clothing Alterations & Repair,
Sewing Instruction, Home Decor...Whatever!

Patricia "TC" Ferrito
440 Gordon Street
Angola, NY 14006-9749
716 549-1493
tcsewhat@a-znet.com

E

TRISH BLOOM

ONCE IN A

B.L.OoMOoN

CREATIONS

BLOOMOONCREATION@AOL.COM

D

THE
WICKER
WOMAN
EST.1975
Cathryn Peters
Original Design, Contemporary Deer Antler Baskets
Open by Chance or Appointment
531 Main St. • P.O. Box 61 • Zumbro Falls, MN 55991
(507) 753-2006 • E-mail: Wickrwoman@aol.com

F

PEACH KITTY STUDIO
Arts, Crafts & Gifts
7256 Wall Triana Hwy
Madison, AL 35757
(256) 722-0839
www.peachkittystudio.com

CZCreations

Wedding
Floral
Preservation

G

CZCreations
Turn your bouquet into a lasting keepsake!

• 100% Money Back Guarantee of Satisfaction
• Lots of Keepsake Design Styles
Call Now to Reserve Your Date!

CHRISTINE ZIPPS
Owner & Designer   **720-350-2404**
www.czcreations.com • cris@czcreations.com
PMB #113 • 4255 South Buckley Rd. • Aurora, CO 80013

Because every business book advises new business owners to order business cards, this is often the first printed item an artist or crafter buys. But if your printing budget is severely limited, invest first in hang tags, fly-ers and price lists. Handing out business cards to everyone who stops by your craft fair display is not only costly but unlikely to generate follow-up orders, says author and fiber artist James Dillehay. In his book, *The Basic Guide to Selling Arts & Crafts,* James reports that in his first two years of selling, he handed out nearly 1,000 cards to craft fair buyers and got no sales, phone calls or leads from any of them. Now he hands out cards only to store owners who give him their card in exchange, and he suggests that craft fair sellers could save money and accomplish as much by making their own business cards using rubber stamps. "There is a small expense in the self-made card and a card with an old-fashioned, hand done look is a sales plus, especially at craft shows," he says.

Content Suggestions

Be careful what information you put on your business card, such as your home address and telephone number. As discussed in Chapter Thirteen, there are many good reasons to protect your privacy with a P.O. Box address. If you invite mail orders, then you certainly need an address on the business card you hand out at fairs. If not, then a phone number, e-mail and Web site address (if you have one) would be sufficient, given the fact that so many people now communicate electronically.

A reader in El Paso reported an unusual business card experience. Instead of calling the city to see if she needed a permit to operate a busi-ness in her home, she first ordered business cards with her home address on them. On checking with city officials, however, she learned that El Paso regulations prohibit the use of a home address on a business card. She was upset because she had to dump the cards and have them reprinted with-out her address before the city would grant her a permit to work at home.

One crafter told me that she omitted the address from her business card because many people thought nothing of just dropping by her home to see if she would let them in to see what she had for sale. "This interfered with my work schedule and all that visiting proved to be very wearing," she said. Artists who work with gold, silver and other precious materials rarely put their home address on a card because they don't want to invite thieves to their home. It's a mistake, however, to print your telephone number without an area code. You may exhibit only at local shows, but many people outside your area may attend such shows.

If you invite wholesale inquiries when you do a retail crafts fair, you might consider using a photo business card. A homebased photographer told me about her friend who scouts for new mail order products at shows and fairs, saying: "She complains that she has to write product descriptions on the backs of business cards, but even then she can't always remember the products. Business photo cards would be an excellent visual marketing tool for wholesale buyers like her."

Hang Tags: Great Image Tools

As consumers, we have all been educated to read hang tags and labels on commercial merchandise because it is here that we find the designer's or manufacturer's name, guarantee, care instructions and other special features of a product. It makes sense, then, that handcraft buyers also look for and appreciate the special tags and labels on handmade products. Many buyers think a product is worth more simply because it carries this professional touch, so a tag that costs only a few cents could enable you to raise the price of your handcrafted items by several dollars.

One craft seller told me her sales increased 15 percent after she added hang tags to her products. Other crafters have reported an increase in sales simply because products displayed in craft shops bore an attractive hang tag. You would be surprised at the number of shop owners who browse competitor shops in search of suppliers. When they spot an item they'd like to sell, they look for a hang tag so they can call for wholesale information. One seller told me that her first $99 investment in professionally printed hang tags for music boxes and ornaments displayed in one shop quickly led to $2,000 in orders from other retailers.

For each of her one-of-a-kind wearables, Sherrill Lewis creates a hang tag that tells a story about the piece, writing the text by hand in one of her blank cards shown at right. The card (shown here in reduced size), measures 2-3/4 x 4-1/4 in. when folded in half. This particular pin, titled "Come Play With Us!" stars a whale carved in ivory, with a "supporting cast" of carved shell and stone critters and semi-precious and glass seed beads. The "story" reads:"Gliding effortlessly in his aquatic world, the whale calls to his friends and playmates playing tag in the coral and seaweed. Later, the guiding star will lead them all home."

Text Speak

Eximiously Yours!

Pins with a Story

Let me tell you a Story ...

It began in time before mind, when the earth God created was new...

Pretty rocks, fire-dancing glass and sparkling beads talk??

Not quite... yet every rock or fused glass cabochon suggests a story by its innate design. Using her God-given artistic talent, Sherrill "reads" the implied theme, then draws on an extensive palette of beads, semi-precious stones, crystal, vintage glass, and silver to expand on the suggestion.

Each piece, be it woven, fused or embellished, like its story, is a classic ~~ one-of-a-kind wearable t.

May you wear it with joy!

Title:

Star:

Supporting cast:

Story:

Tip

Some shop owners automatically remove tags that include a seller's complete address. That's because they want to encourage customers to buy additional products in their shop, not by mail directly from their suppliers. Thus, on merchandise wholesaled to shops, many professional crafters use tags containing only their copyright information, crafts business name, city and state. Because they have a business telephone number anyone can obtain through information, this is all that's needed to get additional sales from other wholesale buyers. (The next time you visit a shop, check product hang tags to see how other sellers handle this problem.)

Copyrighting and Design Tips

First decide whether you will use a simple two-sided tag or one that is folded to reveal four separate areas where art or messages can be printed. Select a size that is appropriate to the size of a product. While miniature items may call for a tiny, one-inch tag, larger items could use a larger, folded tag. (Tags need not be square or rectangular, but other shapes will require hand cutting or extra print shop costs.)

Since a hang tag is an image product, you should incorporate your logo if you have one or use the same special design or typeface used on your business cards or stationery. Use calligraphy, artistic hand-drawn letters or computer-generated typesetting to create a tag that looks as professional as those found on commercial gift items. The copy you put on a hang tag depends on who you are, what you do, what kind of products you make, what's special about them and how they should be cared for. Some products need their own special tags while other products can share a common hang tag. When writing copy for the inside and back of the tag, ask yourself what you would like to know about each of your craft products if you were in the buyer's shoes. Consider such information as colorful details about your business, traditions involved with your craft, special materials used and other things that make you or your products unique.

For example, the weaver who spins and dyes her own wool could mention this fact on her hang tag while the potter who digs his own clay would use that as a selling point. The woodworker who carves only the burls from trees on his property in Missouri would pass such interesting information along to buyers. The dollmaker whose dolls are perfect replicas of antiques . . . the toymaker who sells unfinished products for safety's sake . . . all would use such information to their advantage on a tag.

Sherrill Lewis designs and creates distinctive beaded and fused glass jewelry and adornments, selling in several art and craft shows. Her "Heartspeak Pins" include a hangtag that reads like the opening of a book, with a title line, star, supporting cast, and story. (See illustration, left.)

Printing Tags

If you do not have a computer and software to print your own hang tags, you can buy commercial tags from a supplier such as Kimmeric Studio or E & S Creations (see Resource Chapter). Some crafters create tags using rubber stamps, or make copies on inferior photocopy machines at the local drug store. While such tags may be better than nothing if you're selling directly to consumers at shows, they are not suitable for merchandise sold through shops. Here is information on how to print professional-looking hang tags economically.

After you have designed a tag, duplicate it several times to fill a page that can be reproduced on lightweight card stock on your inkjet or laser printer, or printed by a quick print shop or copy center. If you already have your stationery and cards, use the same colors and type styles on your hang tags so all your printed materials have a coordinated look. If copies are printed on a commercial photocopy machine rather than by the offset process, cost may run no more than five to twenty cents a sheet depending on the stock selected. To save money, buy an inexpensive paper cutter and cut the hang tags yourself. Punch holes, add a nice cord, and you've got a great selling tool for just pennies apiece.

Designer Labels: An Impressive Sales Aid

I have previously discussed labels that are required by law on textile products and items made of wool (see Chapter Three). Designer labels are something extra you can add to impress buyers of such handmade items as garments, toys, teddy bears and decorative accessories. They convey a professional message that a product has been exclusively designed, is one-of-a-kind, one in a series of collectibles, handcrafted or fashioned by a specific individual. Since consumers have been educated to the value of originally designed items, they expect to pay more for them. Thus, the crafter who uses designer labels can get higher prices than the average seller. As you look for certain brand names when you shop, so, too, do craft consumers look for designer labels they recognize.

Several companies will create designer labels (like those shown below) at a modest cost and in small quantities any crafter can afford. Stock designs are offered, but for a small extra charge, you can design your own label, incorporating whatever images and words you want. (Check craft magazines to find advertisements from label suppliers such as Charm Woven Labels, GraphComm Services, and Widby Enterprises.)

Flyers: How to Use Them Effectively

Flyers are not the greatest selling tool, but they are an inexpensive form of advertising that has its place. They're great when you want to announce an open house or holiday boutique in your home to people in your neighborhood, and they're perfect for distribution at any kind of meeting. They also work well as bag stuffers at a crafts show, and as a supplement to a mail order catalog when you want to put extra emphasis on a particular item. If you're trying to sell something, be sure to include an order form at the bottom of the flyer so people can tear it off and send it with a check.

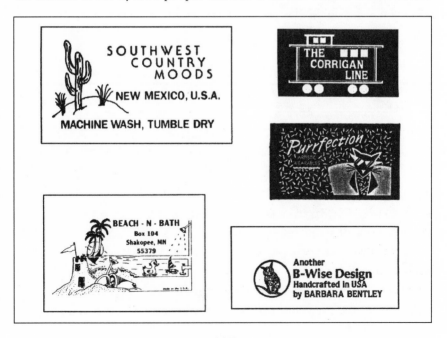

(And be sure that your address appears on the part of the flyer they will keep for their own records.)

In my own mail order business, I always used flyers when I didn't want to waste expensive printing on a mass audience that might or might not be interested in buying my books. Many times when I distributed flyers at home-business conferences, I received no response at all. What I never knew, however, was how many of those people were influenced by my flyer to purchase one of my books in a bookstore, or check it out from their library.

Flyer Content and Distribution

If you're aiming for follow-up sales, select one of your most popular items, something that is easy to pack and ship by mail or UPS. Make a flyer for that product, including a picture or illustration of it. Also create a descriptive price list that can be tucked into packages along with your special promotional flyer. After returning home, some shoppers may regret that they didn't purchase a particular item, or maybe they now wish they had purchased two instead of one. By including a flyer and order form with every item you sell, you will be encouraging mail order sales.

Tip

Each flyer you create should focus on one or two related items. If you try to sell more than one thing on a flyer, you're asking people to make two decisions instead of one: whether to buy at all, and which one to buy. Make it easy by telling them what to do: "To order, clip and mail the handy order form below." Place the order form either in the bottom right-hand corner of the flyer or run it clear across the bottom. (If you need to include a lot of "sell copy," print on both sides of the flyer and put the order form on the back.)

The right color of paper can increase response. Studies have shown that advertising messages printed on yellow paper generate a greater response than white paper. To convey business messages, a better response may be gained by using subtle colors such as tan, gray or ivory. If you're promoting a holiday boutique, however, try bright yellow, green or pink paper to attract attention. Avoid the use of red paper because the black ink on red is very hard to read. Experiment with colors to see if one is more effective than the other. Instead of the standard paper colors, try some of the "hot" paper colors that are currently popular.

Tip

There is no sense in advertising if you're not going to monitor the effectiveness of each promotion. To monitor sales results of flyers you distribute, either code individual batches of printing or use different colors for different events. You might also stamp something on the back or corner of the order form that tells you where a flyer was distributed.

To promote an event, post flyers on community bulletin boards, distribute them to groups or tuck them into door handles, but never place them in mailboxes, because this is a violation of postal rules. It is generally a waste of time and money to stick flyers under windshield wipers of cars in parking lots because nothing you're promoting is going to be of interest to everyone.

Brochures: Good for Your Business

Many craftspeople use flyers with success, but a brochure is more professional, and it will do a better selling job for you. Because brochures are more expensive to print than flyers (estimate 20 to 50 cents each), they should be distributed on a selective basis. When you make a sale, include a brochure to encourage a follow-up sale by mail. Give copies to friends who offer to tell others about what you do. Include them with promotional mailings to the media. When sending a brochure by mail, either to an individual or wholesale buyer, always include a sales letter that focuses on the benefits of ordering from you now. If you have a mailing list of satisfied customers from craft fairs, send them your brochure with a note telling them when you'll be in their area again, reminding them that you have several new items in your line.

Content and Printing

Like flyers, brochures should focus on only one or two related products or services. (To market a complete line, use a catalog.) Brochures come in all sizes, shapes, textures and colors, but the simplest brochure begins with 8½" × 11" inches or 8½" × 13". The first folds nicely in thirds, while legal-sized paper allows for folding in fourths. If you're going to have an offset printer or copy shop print your brochure, ask for paper samples and illustrations of different ways a brochure can be folded since this has everything to do with how copy should be placed on each fold of the page.

Tip

Always get more than one printer's estimate since prices can vary dramatically depending on a printer's specialty or the type of equipment used. For your first brochure, print as few copies as possible because you will want to make changes to it long before your supply is exhausted. Printers will encourage larger press runs for economy's sake, but beginners who follow this advice are often stuck with thousands of pretty brochures that don't produce sales. By starting with a small run of 500 brochures, you will automatically limit your loss in case the new brochure doesn't pull orders or has to be changed because of a mistake.

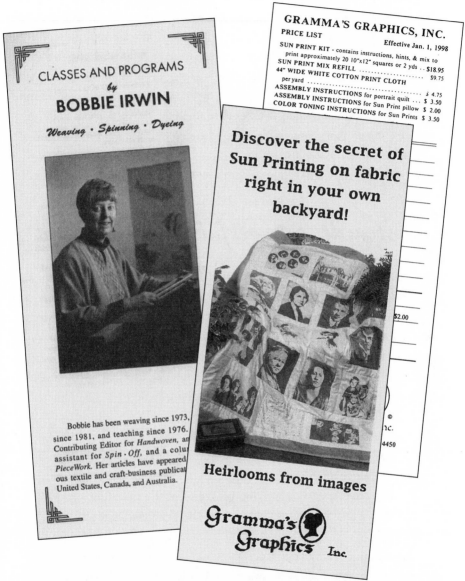

CLASSES AND PROGRAMS
by
BOBBIE IRWIN
Weaving · Spinning · Dyeing

Bobbie has been weaving since 1973, since 1981, and teaching since 1976. Contributing Editor for *Handwoven*, and assistant for *Spin·Off*, and a colu... *PieceWork*. Her articles have appeared... ous textile and craft-business publica... United States, Canada, and Australia.

GRAMMA'S GRAPHICS, INC.
PRICE LIST
Effective Jan. 1, 1998

SUN PRINT KIT - contains instructions, hints, & mix to print approximately 20 10"x12" squares or 2 yds .. $18.95
SUN PRINT MIX REFILL ....
44" WIDE WHITE COTTON PRINT CLOTH $9.75
per yard ....
ASSEMBLY INSTRUCTIONS for portrait quilt ... $ 4.75
ASSEMBLY INSTRUCTIONS for Sun Print pillow ... $ 3.50
COLOR TONING INSTRUCTIONS for Sun Prints $ 2.00
$ 3.50

Discover the secret of Sun Printing on fabric right in your own backyard!

$2.00

©
...c.
...4450

Heirlooms from images

Gramma's Graphics Inc.

These well-designed brochures have been printed on 8-1/2 x 11 inch paper and folded in thirds for mailing inside a business-size envelope. Using this format, you can print separate price lists or other information of a changing nature and insert them into the brochure before mailing. If a quantity of brochures are needed, it may be less expensive to have them printed commercially. If only a few copies are needed at a time, printing on your laser or inkjet printer may be most practical, particularly if yours is a full-color brochure, such as the Gramma's Graphics brochure shown above.

Insert sheets can always be added to a brochure to announce new items, but it doesn't look professional to start writing in price changes and other corrections. One way to avoid this problem is to include only descriptive information in the brochure and print a separate price list that will fit inside the brochure (the size of one brochure panel). Then, if prices change, all you have to do is reprint the insert. You'll know it's time to design and print a new brochure when you begin to feel embarrassed about your current one. Since many buyers base their buying decisions on the quality of a seller's printed materials, it's far more expensive (in terms of lost business) to use old materials than to print new ones.

Postcards: A Powerful Marketing Tool

Postcards are inexpensive yet powerful marketing tools that can be used in many ways to publicize or sell products and services. Currently, to receive the lowest rate, postcards must be at least 3½" high and 5" long, but no more than 4¼" high and 6" long. If you have a laser or inkjet printer and occasionally need special postcards, check the colorful postcard papers offered by the paper companies listed in the Resource Chapter. Here are five ways to use postcards as a selling tool:

1. Announce upcoming appearances at craft shows and fairs or new shops and malls that now feature your products.

2. Announce a new product, slanting your message to people who may have special gift-giving problems at the time (e.g., graduation gifts, weddings, baby showers, teachers, Mother's Day, etc.).

3. Announce a holiday special—your best offer for Valentine's Day, Easter, Halloween, Christmas, St. Patrick's Day, etc.

4. Invite people to your open house, boutique or home party.

5. Send a thank-you to a valued customer—good image advertising for small businesses. You might remind people that you offer custom design services and can help them solve special gift-giving needs.

Full-color post cards are used by many professional crafters today, and available from a number of sources (read ads in crafter magazines to find them). Below left, Christine Zipps' photo postcard matches her business card. A good sales message is included on the back. The card to the right, used by Yvonne Ward for her Country Garden Designs business is a bit larger than the average postcard, with plenty of room on the other side for including both a personal message and address information.

Catalogs: Building a Mail Order Business

Once you have a growing line of products, a catalog will make your selling job easier. One advantage of a catalog is that it is a self-mailer that does not require an envelope. Although it will cost more per unit to print only

500 catalogs instead of a thousand, you might want to keep your first print run short. As soon as it comes off press, you're likely to find yourself wishing you had "done this instead of that." Most small businesses use a 5½" × 8½" stapled catalog with 10 to 12 pages, including the cover (five or six sheets of 8½" × 11" paper folded in half). Use a sturdy paper for the cover so your catalog will travel well through the mail.

Tip

Make sure your printer gives you a dummy copy to weigh before you print it so you can keep the weight under one ounce. More than one business novice has printed a thousand catalogs only to find they couldn't be mailed without the addition of extra postage. Also check with the post office to make sure that the size and style of your catalog are acceptable for mailing. In particular, ask which direction the address area must run to meet postal requirements.

On the inside front cover of your catalog, you might write a personal note to your customers about who you are, what you do, and why you can serve them well by mail. A photograph of you working at your craft or selling at a fair would build confidence and probably increase sales. For added customer confidence, offer satisfaction or money back.

Professional photos of your products will also increase sales, but many crafters just beginning in mail order don't feel they can afford the extra cost of photographs, so they use line drawings and artistic hand-lettering instead. To make your catalog less "folksy," use computer typesetting instead of hand lettering. (Most communities now have "quick printers" who offer inexpensive computer typesetting. Just take a dummy of your catalog to them and they'll do the rest.)

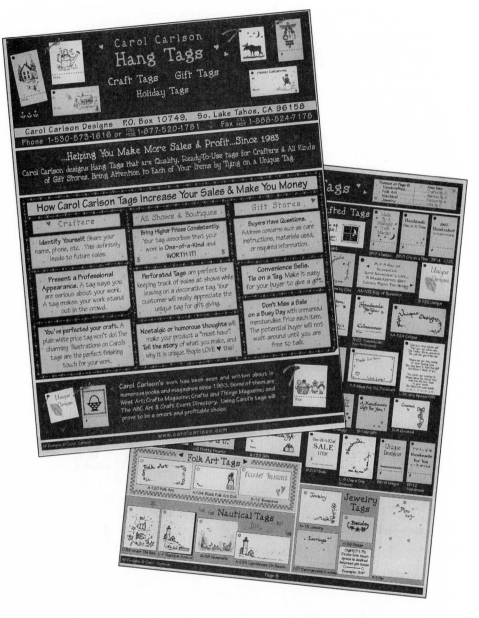

Carol Carlson's very impressive 12-page full-color Hang Tags Catalog measures 8-1/2 x 11 inches, and is stapled in the left-hand corner. She saved a fortune in printing costs by taking classes at her local community college to learn how to design and lay out catalog pages using PageMaker software. She then shopped around for the best printing price and sent camera-ready art for printing. Her cost for printing 5,000 copies of this 12-page catalog was about $700, plus shipping.

315

PLASTIC CANVAS LOVERS CATALOG
from Designs by Joan Green

Dear Fellow Needlepointers,

Needlework has been a major part of my life for over 40 years now, but my very favorite is Plastic Canvas Needlepoint—in fact, I work full time creating designs for this exciting and fun to do craft!

Since designing is my main job, my catalog is not large or printed in color, however it is chock full of great products which you may have trouble locating elsewhere. One of the reasons I started a mail order catalog over 10 years ago was fellow needlecrafters like you who told me you could not find many of the products called for in patterns.

So, although my catalog may look plain compared to the slick colored catalogs from the large companies, what you WILL receive from me are great coupon specials, rebates and free patterns, not to mention some of the best but hardest to find products for plastic canvas! Your order and your satisfaction is very important to me— your order will be given personal attention and will be filled promptly (many orders are shipped within 1-2 days after they are received!)

Please feel free to contact me if you have problems locating anything for your plastic canvas work, and I will try to help out. Since I am a one woman show with a home based business and have no other full time employees, I prefer that you write, FAX or e-mail me with any questions or comments you may have. Thanks for requesting my catalog—I look forward to helping you find everything you need for your plastic canvas projects—HAPPY STITCHING!

Sincerely,

Joan

Joan Green

Professional Needlework Designer • Writer • Consultant

3897 Indian Ridge Woods, Oxford, OH 45056-9481
Phone: 513-523-0437 • FAX: 513-523-1520 • E-mail: designsjg@aol.com

The best (most effective) handcraft catalogs feature a letter on the inside front cover or first page that gives a little story about the company and the people behind it. Often, business owners include a photograph of themselves or their family at work on the business.

This catalog by needlework designer Joan Green will give you ideas on how to write warm, personal, trust-building copy for your own catalog or brochure.

Tip

To make your own line drawings, first take snapshots of what you want to picture in your printed materials. Buy some clear plastic sheets (the kind used for photos or business documents) and place your snapshots under them. Using a fine tip black pen, trace the outline of your product, adding just enough detail to make the picture interesting. When satisfied with your sketches, use the reduction or enlargement options on a photocopy machine to make illustrations in the sizes desired. For sharper printed copies, take your "plastic art" to a local copy shop and ask them to give you prints on slick white paper, or simply scan the image into your graphics art program to further enhance it.

Make the last page of your catalog an order form the customer can tear out and mail back to you with payment. You will get a larger order response if you can take charge card orders. If you plan to mail more than 200 catalogs at a time, save money by mailing at bulk rates. (Your postmaster will tell you what you have to do to get this savings.)

Finally, will you be selling at retail to individuals only or wholesale to shops and stores? A single catalog can do double duty if you print a separate wholesale price list to tuck into the catalog before it's mailed to a shop owner. In approaching shops, however, it would be more professional to send the catalog in an envelope with a cover letter and a color photograph of some of your best items. If you don't hear from a shop you are particularly interested in selling to, follow up with a telephone call three or four weeks later to determine level of interest.

Chapter Fifteen

Making Transitions

From time to time, we all need to ask ourselves if we are living life the way we really want to, and when that life includes a business at home, the questions become more pointed.

Crafters have much in common with writers. To be a good writer, you must be able to express thoughts clearly, arrange sentences into paragraphs, then smoothly link those paragraphs to create an article, story or book.

This linking process is called "making transitions," and it's like shifting gears on an automobile. Writers who do not take the time to learn how to make good transitions will probably remain amateurs forever, while those who study their craft and learn how to put everything together properly will have the elements of success at their fingertips.

Like writers, crafters must learn to make regular transitions if they are to grow as part-time craft sellers or full-time craft professionals. Sometimes

319

this means arming yourself with new information, other times it means taking a step into unknown territory. Often, it requires a bit of courage that seems hard to muster at the time. One of my jobs as a crafts writer is to help people shift gears at the right time. I try to point them in new directions while offering encouragement, ideas, information and resources.

Shifting gears does not always mean going forward, of course. Sometimes we have to back up before we can go on, and sometimes we just need to idle in neutral for a while. This chapter is designed to make you think twice about whether you want to go forward, backward, or just stay where you are for the time being. Now is a good time to pour a cup of tea or coffee and relax a bit.

Moving From Hobbyist to Professional

I've tried for years to figure out just what it is that motivates some people to move from the hobbycraft stage into the professional world of business, but it's not easy to pinpoint. Mostly it seems to be a matter of things falling into place at the right time or getting the right information at the right time.

"After reading about the successes of others, I'm going to try my luck at my own home business," one of my readers told me. "It doesn't seem such a far-fetched idea to me anymore." Another wrote to thank me for the encouragement and information I had provided adding: "I'm jumping into the craft business with both feet, going from a hobby seller to a full-fledged home business owner."

Perhaps the biggest mistake beginners make is their failure to buy specific information that could benefit them. They often look at the cost of a book or subscription as an expense they cannot afford. The purchase of business information, however, is not an expense but an investment. True, it's an expense because it is tax-deductible if you're presently making money from your craft, but in truth, information is always an investment in your future. Everything you learn about business today can help you earn more money tomorrow.

If you want to get ahead in life, I cannot emphasize enough the importance of reading and self-study. Reading makes us aware of things we did

320

not know before, giving us a broader perspective on a wealth of topics. Reading is especially beneficial when it forces us to ask questions. Only by asking new questions and seeking answers to them can we hope to keep growing. Phil Jackson, NBA coach and a bookworm and spokesperson for the Literacy Foundation, puts it this way: "You have to assimilate. If you read you're letting someone else say something to you. And you have to refute it, assimilate or dispute what the person has brought to your consciousness."

The Secret to Big Profits

Based on surveys I've taken of my newsletter and column readers through the years, I've learned that the average *hobbyist* who sells at fairs and boutiques on a part-time basis makes about $1,000 a year. More aggressive sellers in this category may generate sales of $2,500 to $5,000 a year. While the average part-time *craft business* may gross between $20,000 to $30,000 a year, full-time craft businesses may quickly reach the $50,000 to $100,000 level. Some of my readers have reported gross incomes of half a million dollars from a craft business based at home.

As I've explained in earlier chapters people who want to make big money from crafts soon realize that the greatest profits are not in one-of-a-kind crafts, but in fashionable lines that can be wholesaled or sold through multiple retail outlets, such as rent-a-space shops and craft malls. Professional crafters must step into the world of serious manufacturing and marketing if they want their business to grow. They will arm themselves with computers and sales reps, advertise with high-quality printed materials and make a concerted effort to learn more about business practices. They will read business periodicals, attend conferences and business workshops, network with other business owners and work hard to stay ahead of the competition. They will stay in tune with the times and check out new methods of marketing. In addition to selling products, many craft professionals ultimately branch out into writing, designing, speaking, teaching, consulting or publishing.

On second thought . . . maybe you've just decided that you don't want to get *that* serious about a craft business. If so, let me give you a gracious "out." You may identify with the crafter who told me that my comments had made her realize the importance of reevaluating herself and her craft ambitions.

"I now realize that I am not cut out to be a producing, selling craftsperson," she said. "Actually, I really never wanted to be one, but my friends and acquaintances sort of pressured me into it. To be absolutely truthful, I hate to part with the things I make, and maybe subconsciously that is why I price everything so high. Everything I make, I love fiercely. Sometimes after finishing a project I can't keep away from it. In the middle of the night I get up and have to look at it to see if it's still there and to reassure myself that I really did make it and not imagine that I did."

I've had similar feelings myself, and if you also identify with this crafter maybe you're not cut out to be a professional craft seller either. There is an easy way to find out for sure. Ask yourself this question: "Do I view my finished craft objects as an expression of my inner self, and therefore find them magnificent?" If you answered yes, that's wonderful! But it also means you're going to have trouble when it comes to selling your work.

Individuals who work at their craft full-time cannot afford to be emotionally attached to the things they make. As craft professionals, they must view their work impersonally, look at it from a commercial standpoint and be able to say that perhaps it isn't perfect after all, that it needs a bit of redoing before it will be a good, marketable item. Until you can do that with your work, you won't be thinking like a professional, and this is important because professionals are the only ones who make sizable amounts of money from crafts.

I hasten to add that you do not have to sell full time to be seen as a professional. In fact, that is really the whole point of this book. My wish is that even part-time hobby sellers will strive for professionalism in the way they approach their moneymaking activity, make products, keep records, and display, package and sell what they make.

A Little Retirement Business

Maybe all you really had in mind when you bought this book was a little retirement business that would add some fun and extra profit to your life. Great! Let's talk about that.

You may be years away from retirement right now, but it is never too early to start thinking about what you will do when you reach the "autumn of your life." Many older people are interested in starting, or have already started, part-time craft businesses they expect to operate full-time once they retire from the work force. If you're already at this point in life, you may find yourself wishing for additional income to supplement Social Security. Senior crafters who do not need extra income may want a deeper involvement with crafts because they know it will add interest and enjoyment to their later years. Instead of rocking away time in front of the television set, thousands of energetic seniors across the country have something special to get up for every morning, thanks to a beloved crafts hobby.

In summarizing the benefits gained from crafts, a senior crafter explained, "Crafting is therapeutic and builds confidence. It provides supplemental income, keeps my thought processes active and enables me to make new friends." This woman told me she was selling Valentine wreaths, flower arrangements for weddings and special calligraphy documents. She was also teaching a crafts class at a local community service facility, regularly donating small items to a local nursing home for Bingo prizes and making gifts for family and friends.

"I'm slowing down," says a woman in her sixties, "but I hope to leave a few dolls, signed and dated, that might end up in someone's collection. At least I'm not one of those bored people who sit in front of a television set all day. I'm having fun!" Another dollmaker who didn't start selling until the age of seventy-two reported to me three years later that she had her dolls and crafts in eleven states and had just sent $1,000 worth of crafts to a friend who sold them in schools. Stories like this are inspiring to all!

The late Jerry Buchanan once shared this interesting view of ego, creativity and enthusiasm in his TOWERS Club USA, Inc., newsletter:

Gerontologists aren't exactly sure why, but they know that those of us who are artistically inclined . . . driven to create new and original concepts in music, art and literature past the age when the rest of us retire to rest on our oars . . . live decades longer. Perhaps this was the fountain of youth Ponce DeLeon was searching for. To create beautiful works is to earn the praise of the multitudes. Praise feeds the ego. An ego that is continually fed is one that generates enthusiasm for the next project. And also it seems to me that the three form a magic ring of longevity. Ego, creativity, and enthusiasm feed upon each other to form a kind of perpetual motion of the Life Force.

Learning Invites Change

Jacqui Collins-Parker started a ceramics business in 1981 after learning the basics of hobby ceramics from her mother and sister. In 1998, when I first met Jacqui by mail, she gave me a chuckle when she wrote, "Like many pursuits that start as hobbies, over the years my ceramic ventures took on a life of their own. It has been profitable, enjoyable, and has taxed my creativity to its limits. (And my husband's patience to his!) Everything in the house has a veneer of clay dust . . . as does the dog if he sleeps in one place for too long."

In that same letter, Jacqui also shared her concern about the changing ceramics market. Seeing her steadily declining sales as a signal for change, she decided to learn a new craft—glass beadmaking—picking up on a suggestion I'd put into my *Creative Cash* book:

> "The secret to marketing any craft is constructing an item that few other people are willing to attempt."

"I began the learning process by buying how-to videotapes and a manual on glass beadmaking," Jacqui explains. "Through perseverance and practice, and using design and color skills I'd acquired through years of producing ceramics, I was producing high-quality glass beads within three months. This was the most exciting craft I'd ever delved into! And this experience taught me an important lesson, too. I learned that hanging on to a dying business doesn't make financial sense, and that it's okay to start to let go of something that just isn't working anymore. Folks around me thought I was crazy to start anew after so many years of making and selling ceramics, but I figured then that if glass beadmaking wasn't going to be the answer I was looking for, I'd just research some more, read some more, learn some more and try some more. In truly accessing my situation, and adapting to it, I've not only gained more self-esteem, but have developed a more successful business in the process."

Always remember that your road to success in crafts is not one big highway running straight from here to there, but a circuitous road with many forks and interesting side roads along the way that you might explore. Few of today's most successful artists and crafters are still doing today what they did when they started their creative journey, so if you ever begin to feel like you're in a rut, don't just sit there . . . get on a new road!

Other Ways to Profit from Your Creativity

Many people with skill in an art form or craft have narrow vision when it comes to making money. Instead of exploring other ways to profit from years of creative experience and know-how, they limit themselves to making products for sale. While this can be great for a long time, it can also be physically exhausting. In the life of every serious craft seller there will come a day when he or she says, "Whew! I'm tired of this. There has to be an easier way to make money than this!"

In addition to—or instead of—selling handmade products only, give some thought to the following crafty income suggestions. One or more of them may put you on a new road of discovery, and all of them are less physically stressful than making and hauling carloads of craft products from one show or craft mall to another. Due to space limitations, my discussion of these moneymaking ideas must be brief, but I have devoted

Selling Original Designs

You don't need to copyright a design before you sell it to a magazine editor, but you need to understand the rights you are selling when you offer one of your designs for publication. Basically, if you sell "all rights" to a magazine editor, you are literally giving them the right to profit from your design in the future, and you can never turn it into a kit or put it in a book of collected designs or anything. Many magazines insist on buying all rights because they want to protect their readers who are likely to make a project and sell it at craft fairs. This may limit your opportunities, but if you're a prolific designer, you might sell only selected designs outright and keep the best ones for your own special uses.

Browse local magazine racks or the library to find specific magazines that feature how-to projects. To learn what individual editors want, request a "Writer/Designer's Guidelines" sheet from each magazine of interest. Rank beginners need not be afraid to submit an idea because craft editors do buy from beginners if they are professional in their approach and offer original designs and projects of the right type. (This means sending typed query letters and project instructions.) Do not send a sample of your work unless it is requested, but do include a couple of photographs with your initial letter.

Editors rarely explain why they don't want a particular design because you're expected to know this through a study of a magazine's contents. Read several issues before contacting an editor to make sure you understand the type of projects they buy, and pay particular attention to the type of supplies and raw materials used in each project. Many editors want projects that use the kind of supplies the average reader can buy in a local craft supply shop, while others may want scrap craft projects or things that can be made from nature's bounty.

Remember that designs submitted for publication must be truly original, not adapted from, inspired by or "lifted" from another source. Although an editor might not realize that your design isn't original, upon publication the original designer might see elements of her copyrighted work in your published project and bring a copyright suit against you and the magazine.

326

whole chapters to these topics in my *Creative Cash* book. You will also find additional information in books mentioned in the Resource Chapter and in some of the articles on my Web site.

Sell How-to Projects to Craft Publishers and Manufacturers

Not everyone can write well or design original how-to projects, but history has shown this to be a profitable possibility for many. In fact, most of the how-to projects in leading craft consumer magazines today are created by individuals (mostly women) who were once hobbyists themselves. The editors of craft, needlecraft, hobby and handyman magazines buy how-to craft and needlework projects every month, paying from $25 to $350 per design or project, depending on the design, one's reputation as a designer, and the magazine's budget.

Some crafters earn extra income by demonstrating at industry trade shows or doing project sheets. Manufacturers in the crafts industry often use one-page idea or project sheets to help them move their products in shops. These sheets are either offered free to dealers or sold at very low cost. Shops then give or sell these sheets to consumers. If you've done an original project using a particular raw material or commercial art/craft supply item, contact the company that manufactures this merchandise and ask if they'd be interested in buying project sheets from you. Payment for such ideas is usually on an outright basis and may range from $25 to $200, depending on the designer's experience and the manufacturer's budget.

After joining the Society of Craft Designers (a move that literally launched her career as a professional crafts designer), Lisa Galvin began to sell her how-to projects to magazines such as *Craftworks*. One thing soon led to another and now she regularly designs for leading manufacturers and publishers. (See sidebar, "Be Patient!")

"At the first SCD seminar I attended, I met with several editors and quickly sold five projects," says Lisa. "I have since designed project sheets and crafting kits for kids for a major plastics manufacturer, as well a wooden materials company, and I've been approached by other manufacturers who would like me to work with them in this area as well."

Besides selling project ideas to magazine editors, professional designers often work with manufacturers or publishers in the crafts and needlework industry doing pattern leaflets or design books. Diane Williams finally found her perfect work after years of involvement in the crafts industry. "When my crafts and doll business began to slow down, I began to look for a new way to make money while also soothing the creative beast inside me," she says. "I was still selling my craft patterns by mail when I sent my first package of glossy photos of cross stitch designs to Leisure Arts. After two months, I got a polite letter of rejection. Not being a quitter, however, I began designing again and later sent a second proposal to them in 1998. Shortly afterward, they said they wanted to buy my work and were going to do a designer profile on me in their magazine, *For The Love of Cross Stitch.* Shortly after that, I did my first leaflet for them.

"At that point I made a decision I've never regretted. I decided to throw myself entirely into cross stitch design. Ever since, I've worked as a free agent, selling both individual designs and collections to Leisure Arts." (Diane creates her patterns using *Pattern Maker for Cross Stitch* from Hobbyware.com.)

Write a Book for a Crafts or Trade Publisher

If you've ever browsed the book rack in a shop that sells fabric, needlework or craft supplies, you've noticed the many colorful booklets and leaflets that offer patterns and designs. Other design and pattern books will be found in any bookstore. If you've ever opened one of these books and thought, "Why, I could have done this," then you ought to contact the publisher to see if they would be interested in publishing your designs.

Your profit potential here will vary dramatically, depending on the kind of publisher you work with (craft industry or trade book publisher), how the book will be marketed (craft and needlework shops or bookstores), and your degree of skill, reputation and ability to negotiate a contract. For "floppy books" normally found in craft and needlework shops, a beginner might be offered a flat fee of as little as $250 for a single design, or as much as $2,000 for a collection of designs. Royalties might range from 5 to 15 percent of the wholesale price of a booklet or leaflet. Trade book publishers who sell mostly to bookstores work with writers and designers on a royalty basis that varies from publisher to publisher.

After years of selling her weaving, Bobbie Irwin realized that her greatest talents lay in the area of writing and teaching. After publication of her first book, *Twined Rag Rugs* (Krause Publications), she followed up with *The Spinner's Companion* (Interweave Press). Today, in addition to her teaching, Bobbie continues her regular editorial assignments with Interweave Press and contributes occasionally to other textile publications (more than five dozen articles since 1986, in thirteen journals in three countries). "I tell people that my first book took 51 years; the second took two months," Bobbie jokes. "I was afraid that when my first book was published no one would ask me to teach that topic again because they'd have the 'how-to' right in front of them. Instead, the demand for my workshops has increased, and I'm able to make a lot of book sales to workshop attendees besides."

In addition to a terrific boost to one's ego, there are many benefits in being a published author. You immediately have instant credibility in the eyes of many, and fan mail can often spark new ideas. As a result of getting an e-mail from a reader of her book, *Knitting for Fun & Profit* (Prima), Shirley MacNulty became interested in designing with qiviut, a yarn new to her at the time. "I thought qiviut was an interesting idea," she told me, "so I queried the editor of *INKnitters*, a new knitting magazine and sold an article. Shortly afterwards, I was invited to become a regular columnist for the magazine."

As a result of working with a plastics manufacturer, Lisa Galvin got the idea for a book, *Plastifoam Fun for Kids*, which was published by Grace Publications. "I spoke with other designers who had written books to get a clearer idea of how to begin the whole process, what I needed, and how to present it, which was very helpful to me. Looking back, the book wasn't nearly as intimidating as I thought it would be," she says.

Publish and Sell Your Own Book

Today, anyone with a computer can easily format a book that can be printed by an offset printer or a publisher who specializes in books. Many crafters have seen the profit potential of adding this kind of item to their line and are now selling them through classified ads, publicity, at craft shows, and on their own Web sites. There is also growing interest today on the part of crafters to publish information and patterns electronically, and many such books will now be found on the Bizymoms.com Web site.

Perhaps you'd like to publish a collection of how-to tips on your favorite art or craft topic, or compile a directory of all the special supply sources you've spent years tracking down. (The more specialized, the better.) Most people, however, are more likely to be interested in your "inside information" on how you've succeeded in a particular endeavor. For example, in an earlier chapter, you read about Opal Leasure's self-published party plan book, based on the success she had in presenting this type of home show.

Margaret Huber has been creating floral keepsakes since 1987. After customers showed an interest in creating their own, she wrote and published a 36-page illustrated book titled *How to Preserve Your Bridal Bouquet.* Margaret sells the book to both florists and individuals and now has a Web site for the book and her Everlasting Words and Flowers business.

Many self-publishers have done so well selling their own books that they become "in demand" by trade publishers. A good example is Mary Mulari (see sidebar, "Start Small, Keep Growing!"), whose books are now published by Chilton, a major crafts book publisher.

After twenty-one years in business, grandmotherhood was the trigger that turned Sue Johnson into an author. Sue and her daughter-in-law, Julie (both former teachers), wrote a book to help grandparents relate to their grandchildren. "*Grandloving: Making Memories with Your Grandchildren* is the book I wanted and couldn't find when our first grandson was born on the other side of the country," says Sue. "We wanted to be part of his life despite the distance. Julie and I began the book project with a questionnaire to 350 families worldwide who shared what had worked for them. We wrote the book back and forth by e-mail, had offers from three publishers, and sold it to Fairview Press at the proposal stage. We've now purchased back the rights, as we knew we had a super book and wanted to make it even better."

The latest edition of *Grandloving* is published by Heartstrings Press, the new division of Gramma's Graphics, Inc. (see "Design and Sell Kits" below). The book has won three national parenting awards and other honors to date.

Never say you can't write a book because you're not a writer. Network with other authors, and pick up some books at the library on writing and publishing, which is how I and many others got their start as authors. Remember that it is real-life experience—not writing skill—that prepares most people to write their first book, and a good content editor can easily fix writing that is informative, yet lacking in finesse. If you decide to self-publish and want your book to be as good as possible, invest a little money in your project and hire an editor to check your manuscript before you send it to the printer. (This is a service I now offer to writers, in fact.)

Design and Sell Kits

Can you supply hard-to-find raw materials such as wheat for weaving or dried nature items such as pine cones for wreaths? People who won't buy your finished products might be interested in buying a supply kit to do it themselves. (Remember Joan Green's success as a mail order seller of plastic canvas supplies in Chapter Thirteen?) If offering craft kits, don't duplicate your regular products as a kit, but create a different design and make the item smaller than something you make for sale. Price your kits lower than the finished product, yet high enough to make a good profit. (Commercial kit manufacturers figure a kit should cost no more in materials than one-fifth of its retail price.)

If kit manufacturing is of interest to you, begin with the idea that you will sell your own kits, either by mail or on your Web site, or as a sideline product at craft fairs and other retail outlets. Don't expect anyone to buy your craft kit idea on a royalty basis. Manufacturers either have their own in-house designers or they work exclusively with professional designers such as those who are members of the Society of Craft Designers.

Many crafters are now finding it easy to sell kits on their Web site. Rochelle Beach is enjoying success with her "Cinnamon Clay Kit" that allows crafters to make their own cinnamon-scented dough dolls. Remember Marj Bates from earlier chapters? In addition to making glass beads and jewelry, she offers a line of lampworked glass drawer pulls and lamp finials. Her profitable "Make-a-Knob" and "Make-a-Finial" kits were added when other artists began to ask how they could make them, too.

Offering a product not easily found anywhere else is one key to success as a kit manufacturer. In 1978, when Sue Johnson's "gramma" reached her 100th birthday, Sue turned to her quilting and the new use of an antique process known as blueprinting to create a "Centennial Quilt." The resulting one-of-a-kind gift featured family photographs printed onto squares. Everyone who saw the quilt wanted to know how to make one like it, so Sue started a mail order business called Gramma's Graphics, Inc., offering her popular "Sun Print Kits" and related items.

Although computers have now made it possible to scan photos and print them to fabric, Sue's kit continues to sell to crafters who appreciate the antique heirloom quality and the softness of these prints not possible with computerized technology. This traditional craft method also allows crafters to create unique shading that only the sun can impart. Some of the old photographs produce prints that resemble the old-fashioned woodcuts unobtainable through modern technology.

Though the computer can't produce the artistic prints that blueprinting can, Sue has found it to be a marvelous means for networking and selling kits on the Web. "It was through our modest Web site that Better Homes and Gardens Craft Book Club discovered our Sun Print kits and ordered them wholesale by the thousands for years," says Sue.

Some kits, particularly needlework kits, may find a good wholesale market in selected mail order catalogs. Plastic canvas designer Joan Green has enjoyed success in selling kits of her original designs to The Stitchery Catalog because they include the right-size plastic canvas and specialty yarns that are now difficult for the average needleworker to find. "Most of my kits have sold only in the 50 to 75 quantity," she says, "but one of my kits—a set of three Christmas quilt hang-ups worked in regular and metallic floss, with glitter hangers and pearl cabochon beads—went gangbusters, resulting in more than a thousand orders from its first run in the catalog."

Although Joan says she is not yet a famous designer, she has been published internationally and her name is becoming more recognizable with the consumer, which is important to her because her unfulfilled dream for well over a decade has been to write a full-length book on her favorite topic.

Sell Your Patterns and Designs

If you have a collection of your own original craft patterns or designs that you're ready to retire (no longer interested in making and selling them as finished crafts), offer them to other crafters who aren't creative enough to design their own projects. This is as easy as drawing them neatly on sheets of paper, adding neatly typed how-to instructions, and having them printed. If you have a computer, scanner, word-processing software and inkjet printer, this kind of work is now "a piece of cake."

When selling to shops, most crafters package patterns in Ziploc bags, adding an attractive, lightweight cardboard header or cover sheet with a color photograph to give the package a professional look. Such pattern packs make good mail order items and are also the perfect solution for craft fair shoppers who say they'd rather make it themselves. A pattern kit might cost only a dollar to produce, but could retail for between $4 and $8. Check local craft and needlework shops for ideas on how others are packaging patterns.

Offering patterns is an alternative way to make money when you're involved in a labor-intensive craft. As a dollmaker once told me, "When I was selling my $34 dolls at fairs, I figured the most I could earn a day was a hundred dollars because I couldn't make more than three dolls in one day. Now that I have a pattern business, however, I sometimes get orders for $300 worth of patterns in a single day, and I spend only two or three hours filling the orders."

If you happen to sell cloth doll patterns, check out Lisa Risler's site, DollHeaven.com, as a possible market for patterns you can wholesale. (You'll recall reading about Lisa's success as a Web entrepreneur in Chapter Twelve.)

Teach Craft Classes Locally

Many creative people teach part time in addition to running their regular art or craft business. In addition to being paid for teaching, classes and workshops can be a good way to sell your own books or a line of supplies. (See sidebar, "Teaching to Sell Supplies.") Some people teach at home while others teach at local craft or fabric stores, at craft conferences, in adult education or senior retirement centers, or on the Internet (see sidebar). Fees vary greatly for this type of work, from so much per student to so much per hour or per day. Contact local colleges and adult education centers for a catalog of programs to learn what's currently offered in your area and call local craft and fabric shops to see if there is a need for classes you might offer.

In addition to running her alterations and custom sewing business, TC Ferrito also teaches at sewing conventions and in different sewing stores in her area. "Arrangements at each place are different," she says. "Jo-Ann stores always seem to be looking for instructors for all kinds of arts and crafts, sewing, quilting and home decor items because these classes help them move more product."

At Jo-Ann stores, one can either teach for the store itself, getting a percentage of student fees and discounts on supplies, or for the sewing machine dealers that lease space in these stores. While working with a sewing machine dealer at one store, TC got 75 percent of whatever fee the students paid. "Class fees for students range from $15 to $50," she says, "so the more students you teach, the more money you can make. I got a discount on any supplies I needed to make the class samples, and could have gotten all supplies free if I had let the store keep the samples. I was also offered a 20 percent instructor discount from the sewing machine manufacturer, which is a nice discount for anyone who is interested in buying a new machine or accessory items."

Before moving to San Luis Obispo, Joyce Roark had worked as an instructor at Michaels in Baton Rouge, so she naturally introduced herself to the Michaels store manager after moving to her new home in California. To her surprise, she was offered the part-time job of Event Coordinator at

Teaching to Sell Supplies

Denise Lipps has a burgeoning rubber stamp business that consists of teaching the art of rubber stamping at home workshops and group meetings. She has associated herself with one of the major rubber stamp manufacturers from whom she buys supplies at wholesale for profitable resale to her students. She teaches both in her own home and in others' homes, but the norm is others' homes or other locations.

"In my home I do special 'stamp camps' for previous hostesses, or good customers, or to generate future bookings," she explains. "I often teach at church retreats or for women's groups. I charge nothing for my two-hour classes because I make my money from selling stamps and accessories from the manufacturer's catalog. I teach using the materials from the catalog, so those are the materials students want. I have perhaps $1 per student invested in consumable materials, and I average approximately $100 gross profit per workshop. It's a good part-time business.

"Every new workshop I present leads to additional workshops. The student sees what I do at a workshop, and they want to learn more and invite their friends, so they book a workshop in their home. Some need a speaker at their ladies' group, or they have a scout troop to entertain, or they're responsible for getting speakers at their church retreat, so they book me to teach. Additionally, I leave catalogs at schools or in waiting rooms, and I e-mail potential hostesses. But seeing me in action is my best advertisement."

the store, where she is now in charge of all classes, instructors, events, the monthly calendar and more.

"I used to subscribe to many craft magazines," she says, "but now I have them available all the time and it doesn't cost me anything. I'm able to keep up on all the new products and techniques, get a discount on store merchandise and, best of all, I get paid for it! All the knowledge about products and resources I got while running my business is now being passed on to Michaels' customers, and I have become known as 'the source' for just about any information one might need. What a dream job

Teaching on the Internet

Electronic teaching—or "distance learning" as it is now being called—is a new industry that's growing by leaps and bounds as this book goes to press. Crafters were among the first to discover the profit potential of this kind of teaching, but all kinds of information providers are now finding ways to conduct classes on the Web.

Quilters and authors Myrna Giesbrecht and Sylvia Landman both offer classes through QuiltUniversity.com. Here, lessons are posted and students use a password to visit the class as often as they like, 24 hours a day. "These online workshops offer students a chance to work at their own pace, using their own supplies in their private studios," says Myrna. "It is especially wonderful for working persons, busy mothers, those who live in out of the way places, and those with handicaps that make it difficult for them to attend regular classes. It works like a charm without the stress of managing and credit cards." Adds Sylvia, "It's truly a fascinating experience for one who does not mind working from home without much opportunity to see the outside world."

QuiltUniversity collects all fees and does all organizing of classes, and teachers get 80 percent of student fees. "Teaching this way is the most exciting thing I have ever done, and the pay is very satisfactory," says Sylvia. "I love it!" Some of Sylvia's classes have included "Fine Hand Applique," "Making Money with Quilts," and "How to Teach What You Know." Myrna has offered such quilting technique classes as "Triangle Tangle," and "Press for Success." Check the Web sites of both authors (see Resource Chapter) for more information about all their books and classes, online and off.

Home-Business Classes. A growing number of eBook authors whose how-to home-business books have been published by BizyMoms.com now offer four-week classes on this site. All classes cost $60, and teachers receive 40 percent of the tuition. After registration, students receive weekly lesson handouts via e-mail, which they can study at their convenience. There are no set meeting times for classes, and all questions, comments, and homework are handled by e-mail.

"Internet learning is the great geographic equalizer," says Sandra Miller-Louden, coordinator of the BizyMom online classes. "No longer are physical miles a deterrent for the wonderful process we call education."

this is!" This work still leaves Joyce enough time to continue wholesaling her jewelry and music boxes. And, as a certified Pergamano Parchment craft instructor, she also teaches parchment classes in her home in the evenings or on weekends.

Many art and craft teachers will agree with Marj Bates, who says, "I love meeting people and I learn a lot from my students. Introducing creativity to others is an important part of my crafts life, and it's my passion to see others experience their 'ah-ha!' moment when they've created something special."

Teach or Speak at Conferences and Other Events

Another way to teach is through speaking at art or craft conferences, conventions, guild meetings and so on. Many professional artists and crafters present workshops or seminars on special techniques or business aspects of their art or crafts. In most cases speakers are invited to sell their books or other products they may offer, such as special tools, kits, patterns, etc. Small groups might pay a beginner only $50 to $100 for a short talk, but experienced speakers can command $1,000 or more plus expenses, so this is worth working for. In my experience, one speaking engagement always led to another. If you make a good presentation, word will get around quickly.

To promote yourself as a speaker, design a brochure that includes your picture, some background information (your credentials), a description of your talk and its intended audience. Add testimonials as soon as you can get them. Subscribe to a variety of craft periodicals to learn about upcoming art or craft conferences that might offer speaking opportunities and learn to use the power of the Internet. Also consider the benefits of having a Web site to promote yourself as a teacher.

Weaver Bobbie Irwin taught on a local basis for many years before going on the road to present workshops on weaving, spinning, teaching and writing throughout the United States and Canada. "At first I taught at just a

337

few weavers' conferences in the summer. Since I got e-mail, however, I've greatly expanded my teaching for local guilds, shops and schools from coast to coast. E-mail makes it easy to organize teaching tours (I've done a couple of three-week tours), and the one mailing list I subscribe to increases my visibility and access. Like most lists, The Weaving List doesn't allow blatant advertising, but I am allowed to say that 'I'll be teaching in such-and-such region in April,' and that brings more inquiries. Plus, my frequent posts offering helpful advice help to establish my reputation as a teacher. And it never hurts when someone who has taken one of my classes posts a note to the whole list saying how much they enjoyed it!"

Demonstrate An Old-Time Art or Craft

Large fairs and festivals often hire individuals who can demonstrate old-time craft skills such as spinning, weaving, woodcarving, blacksmithing, candlemaking, pottery making, basketry, cornhusk crafts, tatting, lacemaking, folk painting, dollmaking and so on. Product sales may or may not be part of such arrangements. Subscribe to show-listing periodicals to learn about such events months in advance.

Mary Lou Highfill has built a business around the sale of sunbonnets made from old bonnet patterns in her collection and from drawings she has made of bonnets in museums and historical societies. Her growing reputation as an expert on sunbonnets has naturally led her into public speaking on her favorite topic. Her programs are popular at historical societies, museums, churches, heritage societies and reenactment events.

Cathryn Peters has demonstrated basketry and seat weaving at numerous Pioneer, country, and Victorian festivals or shows sponsored by historical societies, country fairs, garden clubs, arts councils and various other organizations. She dresses in a period costume and entertains visitors while also educating them on her craft.

"Sometimes I have been allowed, and even encouraged, to sell my wares, but many times I have participated as a demonstrator only," she says. "Frequently I have used these events as a no-cost way of advertising to let the public know that my craft of seat weaving and basketry is still being done and that if they need repairs made to their chairs, I'm the person to do it for them. I always have my business cards at hand and also a professional looking photograph album of the 'before and after' work I have done. Prior to every demonstration, I have called all the local TV stations and sent out news releases and pictures to all the surrounding newspapers. Since I also belong to many trade organizations like basket guilds and art groups, they, too, would get the news release information. Many a time I have landed on the evening news programs just because of a well-placed telephone call!"

Cathryn is one of only a few craftspeople in the nation who still does natural rush seat weaving on a regular basis for hire, so she is always interesting to the media. At one demonstration for an annual Threshing Bee event, she and her apprentice got a seven-minute feature on the local TV news. (Imagine what seven minutes' advertising on television would cost and you begin to see the value of this kind of publicity.)

Offer Business or Marketing Services

Many crafters need help in designing business logos, stationery, cards, brochures, and other promotional materials. Others need bookkeeping or mail list services, photography, slide presentations, ads or logos designed, news releases written, etc. Lately, with more crafters getting on the Internet, I'm seeing a growing need for service providers who can enhance photographs for the Web (resizing, fixing colors, brightness, or making them download faster).

Often, creative people also wish they had someone to do their selling for them, so if you're a natural salesperson, you might represent several artists or craftspeople at major trade shows, or act as a sales representative to present their work to retail outlets. A sales commission of from 15 to 20 percent is common.

If you have writing skills, consider offering your writing services or desktop publishing skills to local art, craft and needlework shops and other businesses that might need a print newsletter or someone who would write an e-mail newsletter for them.

Start Small, Keep Growing!

Mary Mulari has been helping women discover their creativity since 1983, when she first offered to share her ideas in a community education class. The overwhelming response she received encouraged her to develop many new designs and, before long, she had enough for a book. Since she had no publisher connections, she took a chance and published *Designer Sweatshirts* herself, cautiously printing only 300 copies. It wasn't a fancy book—pages were hand-lettered and illustrated with designs and sewing directions—but all 300 copies sold within two months. Encouraged, Mary published a second book.

By helping others learn how to create designer sweatshirts, Mary helped herself to financial success. Even after she began to use a computer in her publishing business, she continued to letter and illustrate her books by hand. "This became my trademark," she says, "and the response to it was very positive."

Now in demand by trade book publishers, Mary no longer publishes her own books, although four of them are still available and she uses them in her sewing seminars, along with the four books she has written for Chilton/Krause Publications. "Although the profit margin is much higher in self-publishing, at this point in my career I like having the publisher promoting and selling my book with me just collecting the royalty check. I still believe in the power and possibilities of self-publishing as a way for an unknown writer to get into the marketplace, however. The promotion and marketing efforts I learned and exercised to sell my books are valuable to me even now as an author for a trade publisher. I also know that teaching and promoting my own books (both self-published and trade published) makes a huge difference in the number of books sold. There's a magical power about having your name on a book as the author. It gives you instant credibility and expertise. Having more than one book helps, too."

A frequent guest on television shows, Mary presents seminars across the United States and is always up to something new. She has produced her own instructional videotape based on her first book, and also designed four embroidery/applique cards for computerized sewing/embroidery machines. "This is a new and advanced aspect to sewing, and it's growing," she says. "It expands the possibilities and earning potential for me since I also receive royalties from sales of these cards."

Serendipity and Creativity

Now that you've seen how other people have accomplished their goals, I hope you feel more confident and adventurous, and are ready to capitalize on your creativity. As the creator of the Bartles & Jaymes commercials once said: "Creativity is just doing what other people don't do. We have two choices in life. We can dissolve into the mainstream, or we can be distinct. To be distinct, we must be different; we must strive to be what no one else but us can be."

If you make things with your hands, you are a creative person whether you can design original projects or not. In the book *Living Your Life Out Loud,* the authors state, "The difference between creative people and those who are not is purely a matter of self-perception. If you perceive yourself as creative, you are, and if you don't, you won't be." If you're striving to unlock your natural creativity, this book will help.

The one thing all creative people have in common, says PBS host Bill Moyers, is that they are infinitely curious. "They never take for granted what they're told. They take risks, take advantage of the unexpected and are not fearful of being wrong."

Moyers's research shows that, often, creative people have been touched and moved by another person at some point in their lives. "That person has communicated to them a sense of 'you matter' and made them aware of their own intrinsic worth as a human being."

The desire to do something special with your skills and talents and a positive "I can do it" attitude will take you in exciting new directions if you can only muster the courage to try something new. As a crafter once pointed out to me, "Some people weakly try positive thinking and when it doesn't work, they become discouraged, stop believing and quit. My favorite word is serendipity," she said. "To me, serendipity is the plan, idea or event that unfolds while making other plans, only to find the accidental happening better than the intended."

This word also means to "dip" into life with "serenity." I've learned that serendipity walks hand in hand with creativity, often playing a role in the creation of a new and original piece of craft work. Serendipitous things

341

Be Patient!

"When I first began this career of mine, I often thought, 'Why can't this happen NOW!' But the longer I'm in business, the more I realize that many times the best answer to this question was that I simply wasn't ready then.

"There are times when we need to sit back and take the slow road and times when we need to jump in feet first and swim. Deciding which step you're at with every obstacle can be the hardest thing. But when you begin talking and networking with others in your field—some of whom you may have admired for a long time—and listen to them tell their story, most will let you know they made mistakes in their careers, some which may have cost them dearly. But when they stopped fearing to make mistakes and began counting them as 'lessons to learn from,' they began to succeed. And with time, patience and effort, so can we all."

—Lisa Galvin, Crafts Designer, Flora Decker Products

also happen where business is concerned. For example, you might set out to get publicity in one place, but through a chance meeting with someone, you will get it in another. Or you may try to market one way and in the process accidentally discover a new way that works better.

A serendipitous connection with one special person could literally change your life, so always stay open to the idea that life will naturally lead you in new directions when you least expect it. You will get involved in one thing, sometimes accidentally, and before you know it, you'll be off and running in a new direction, meeting new people, doing new things, achieving new goals. You will find yourself zigzagging here and there until one day—*voila!* You suddenly realize that you've found work you want to do for the rest of your life. And how exciting it is when you also learn that you may be able to make a living doing what you love most.

In closing, I would like to share a success secret that took me far too many years to discover. Remember to thank God for the artistic and creative talents with which you have been blessed, and don't hesitate to lean on the Lord when you need support and encouragement in either your personal or home-business life. From experience I have learned that if we will simply put our faith in God and give Him an opportunity to work in our lives, He will lead us in the right direction and reveal wondrous things we never could have discovered on our own.

In Summary

As you continue your efforts to acquire the necessary skills and information needed for a profitable homebased business, remember to step back from time to time to give yourself and your ideas a critical analysis. Make sure you're building on an idea or concept others have already proven successful. If not, you may end up wasting valuable time and money pursuing a dream that can't be realized. Not every hobby can be turned into a profitable business, but this does not mean that you cannot profit from what you know by doing something else. All you have to do is have the courage and good sense to make necessary changes.

If you ultimately decide that your favorite art or craft activity is never going to be very profitable, consider getting interested and involved in something else related to it. Remember that you are capable of loving more than one thing, and with time and experimentation, you may find you have enormous talent for some other art or craft in which your moneymaking opportunities will be far greater.

Everyone I've ever written about in my books or articles has made an effort to get acquainted with me, and you're invited to contact me, too, with information about what you do. This could lead to publicity for your crafts business on my Web site or in one of my articles or books.

Although I welcome mail from my readers, due to the volume I receive every day, I do not give crafts marketing or business advice by e-mail. However, I'm alway happy to refer readers to one of my books or some other source that will answer their questions. You'll find a table of contents for each of my books on my personal domain at www.BarbaraBrabec.com, and e-mail may be sent to me at Barbara@BarbaraBrabec.com. (Please indicate a subject line of "HFP Feedback." Thanks!)

Resource Chapter

"Some of us spend so much time wishing that things were different, and thinking up alibis for why things aren't different, that we overlook all of the advantages and the opportunities open to us right where we are."

—*Billy Graham*

Use the helpful print and Web resources in this chapter to develop your craft business. Don't just wish for success, make it happen!

Section I: Books

Section II: Periodicals

Section III: Internet Resources

Section IV: Organizations

Section V: Government Resources   359

Section VI: Suppliers

Section VII: Web Sites of Individuals Quoted in This Book   361

Section I: Books

All of these books are available in bookstores, online from Amazon.com or BarnesandNoble.com, or directly from the author's Web site if one is included in the listing. Your library will also have most of these books on their shelves, or can obtain them for you through their Inter-Library Loan program.

Craft Business "Bibles"

The Basic Guide to Selling Arts & Crafts by James Dillehay (Warm Snow Publishers; www.Craftmarketer.com).
The Basic Guide to Selling Crafts on the Internet by James Dillehay (Warm Snow Publishers; www.Craftmarketer.com).
The Complete Idiot's Guide to Making Money with Your Hobby by Barbara Arena (Alpha Books).
Crafter's Guide to Pricing Your Work by Dan Ramsey (Betterway Books).
Crafting as a Business by Wendy Rosen (Sterling).
Crafting for Dollars—How to Establish & Profit from a Career in Crafts by Sylvia Landman (Prima; www.Sylvias-Studio.com).
The Crafts Business Answer Book & Resource Guide by Barbara Brabec (M. Evans; www.BarbaraBrabec.com).
Creative Cash: How to Profit from Your Special Artistry, Creativity, Hand Skills and Related Know-How (6th ed.) by Barbara Brabec (Prima; www.BarbaraBrabec.com).
Make It Profitable—How to Make Your Art, Craft, Design, Writing, or Publishing Business More Efficient, More Satisfying, and More Profitable by Barbara Brabec (M. Evans; www.BarbaraBrabec.com).

How-to Guides (Specific Craft or Business Topics)

The Apron Strings Lady Did It . . . So Can You! A Guide to Party Plan Selling by Opal Leasure. (www.CraftMark.com/apron/home.htm).
Candlemaking for Fun & Profit by Michelle Espino (Prima).
Cart Your Way to Success—A Guide to Pushcart Merchandising by Gail Bird (www.GailBird.com).
Craft Sewing for Fun & Profit by Mary Roehr (Prima).
Decorative Painting for Fun & Profit by Susan Young (Prima).
Getting Publicity by Tana Fletcher and Julia Rockler (Self Counsel Press).
How to Get Happily Published (5th ed.) by Judith Appelbaum (HarperPerennial).
How to Show & Sell Your Crafts by Kathryn Caputo (Betterway Books).

347

Internet Marketing for Less Than $500 a Year by Marcia Yudkin (Independent Publishers Group).

Jewelry Making for Fun & Profit by Lynda S. Musante & Maria Given Nerius (Prima).

Knitting for Fun & Profit by Shirley MacNulty (Prima).

Make Your Quilting Pay for Itself by Sylvia Landman (Prima; www.Sylvias-Studio.com).

Making $$$ at Home—Over 1,000 Editors Who Want Your Ideas, Know-How & Experience by Darla Sims (Sunstar Pub.).

Pricing Guidelines for Arts and Crafts by Sylvia Landman (iUniverse.com; www.Sylvias-Studio.com).

Pricing Your Craftwork by James Dillehay (Warm Snow Publishers; www.Craftmarketer.com).

Quilting for Fun & Profit by Sylvia Landman (Prima; www.Sylvias-Studio.com).

Rubberstamping for Fun & Profit by Maria Given Nerius (Prima).

The Self-Publishing Manual by Dan Poynter (Para Publishing).

Small Time Operator—How to Start Your Own Business, Keep Your Books, Pay Your Taxes, and Stay Out of Trouble by Bernard Kamoroff, CPA (Bell Springs Publishing).

Soapmaking for Fun & Profit by Maria Given Nerius (Prima).

The Woodworker's Guide to Pricing Your Work by Dan Ramsey (Betterway Books).

Woodworking for Fun & Profit by Jeff Greef (Prima).

Writing Effective News Releases—How to Get FREE Publicity for Yourself, Your Business or Your Organization by Catherine V. McIntyre (Piccadilly Books).

Your Guide to EBook Publishing Success by James Dillehay (Warm Snow Publishers; www.00ebooks.com).

Motivational Guides

Living Your Life Out Loud—How to Unlock Your Creativity and Unleash Your Joy by Salli Rasberry and Padi Selwyn (Pocket Books).

What Are Your Goals? Powerful Questions to Discover What You Want Out of Life by Gary R. Blair (Blair Pub. House).

What to Say When You Talk to Yourself by Shad Helmstetter (Pocket Books).

Sourcebooks & Directories

The Crafts Supply Sourcebook (4th ed.) by Margaret Boyd (Betterway Books).

Directory of Grants for Crafts—And How to Write a Winning Proposal by James Dillehay (Warm Snow Publishers; www.Craftmarketer.com).

Section II: Periodicals

Craft Business Magazines

Country Sampler, 707 Kautz Rd., St. Charles, IL 60174. An ad-based magazine and guide to where to buy country accessories. (Many crafters advertise here to reach a national consumer audience.) For ad rates, call 1-630-377-8000. Subscription information: 1-386-447-6034, or subscribe to this and other country magazines in the publisher's line at www.Sampler.com. Also available on newsstands.

Craftrends, P.O. Box 1180, Skokie, IL 60076. A trade magazine for craft retailers, available only by subscription. Visit the Web site at www.Craftrends.com to find news and information for businesses involved in the creative marketplace.

The Crafts Report—The Business Journal for the Crafts Industry, Box 1992, Wilmington, DE 19899, 1-800-777-7098; www.CraftsReport.com. Check this site's archives for a collection of crafts business articles by the author, and read "Are Craftspeople Making Money on the Internet?" at www.CraftsReport.com/january01/2000artistresults.html to get the first-ever statistics on online craft sales among craft artists.

ProCrafter—Ideas & Information for Today's Professional Crafter, 700 E. State St., Iola, WI 54990; www.Krause.com. A national trade magazine for professional crafters, formerly known as *Craft Supply Magazine.*

The Professional Quilter, 22412 Rolling Hills Ln., Laytonsville, MD 20882; www.ProfessionalQuilter.com. A quarterly business journal for quilters, designers and teachers interested in a career in quilting.

Sunshine Artist, 2600 Temple Dr., Winter Park, FL 32789. 1-800-597-2573; www.SunshineArtist.com. A monthly magazine with timely articles and detailed descriptions of over 2,000 art/craft events throughout the country, with critiques of shows from working artists and crafters.

Show Listing Publishers (Print & Online)

The ABC Art & Craft Event Directory, P.O. Box 400, Walland, TN 37886-0400. 1-800-678-3566; www.theABCDirectory.com. A national show listing guide.

Art & Craft Show Yellow Pages, Choices, P.O. Box 484, Rhinebeck, NY 12572. 1-888-918-1313; www.CraftShowYellowPages.com. Quarterly issues include show listings for CT, MA, NJ, NY, PA and VT, plus show reviews. In addition, this site contains a good archive of craft business articles, tips, resources and craft business links.

Arts & Crafts Show Business, P.O. Box 26624, Jacksonville, FL 32226-0624. 1-904-757-3913; www.ArtsCraftsShowBusiness.com. A monthly that includes articles and listings of shows, festivals, trade shows and competitions in FL, GA, NC, and SC.

Craftlink—www.Craftlink.net. Initially a western Canadian trade publication, *Craftlink* now serves subscribers in both Canada and the U.S. The magazine is edited for artisans, craft manufacturers, show promoters, wholesalers and independent retailers. For U.S. subscription information, write to Craftlink, #586 - 200 West 3rd, PO Box 8000, Sumas, WA 98295-8000. In Canada, mail to 35410 Anderson Ave., Matsqui, BC V3G 1N4.

Craftmaster News, P.O. Box 39429, Downey, CA 90239, 1-562-869-5882; www.CraftMasternews.com. Published monthly, each issue lists upcoming events for the entire West Coast six months in advance.

The Crafts Fair Guide, P.O. Box 688, Corte Madera, CA 94976. 1-800-871-2341. A show-listing periodical for craftspeople on the West Coast. Features in-depth reviews and critiques of shows by exhibiting artists and craftspeople.

Mid-Atlantic Craft Show List, P.O. Box 161, Catasauqua, PA 18032-0161. 1-610-264-5325; www.CraftShowList.com. Publishing monthly, featuring shows in PA, NJ, NY, MD, DE and VA.

Midwest Art Fairs, P. O. Box 72, Pepin, WI 54759. 1-800-871-0813, www.MidwestArtFairs.com. A regional guide to over a thousand shows in MN, WI, IA, ND and SD.

SAC Newsmonthly, P.O. Box 159, Bogalusa, LA 70429. 1-800-825-3722; www.SACNewsmonthly.com. A monthly featuring national news and listings of art and craft shows; available in both print and Web versions. (Many regional show listing publishers advertise in this national newspaper.)

The Ronay Guides, A Step Ahead, Inc., 2090 Shadowlake Dr., Buckhead, GA 30625-2700, 1-800-337-8329. Three different volumes list hundreds of art and craft shows in Georgia, in the Carolinas, and in Virginia and around the South. See related Web site at www.Events2000.com.

Section III: Internet Resources

The following Web sites, recommended by the author or her book contributors, are just a small sampling of those you may find helpful. Most of them offer a free newsletter or e-zine that will help you keep learning more about the topic discussed on the site. To find other sites related to your particular art or craft interest, type appropriate key words in your browser's search engine box.

Crafts Marketing & Home Business Web Sites

About.Com—www.about.com. This is a large network of rich content sites dedicated to specific topics, including arts and crafts. Begin by visiting William T. Lasley's pages at http://ArtsandCrafts.about.com to find a wealth of crafts business information, articles, and resources, and to network with other crafters in a chat room or forum. Also sign up for Lasley's free newsletter. From this site you can link to several other art/craft sites in the About.com network that discuss jewelry making, candles and soap, knitting, quilting, sewing, cross stitch, beadwork, and needlepoint. All sites feature articles, forums, chats and a free newsletter.

Auntie—www.Auntie.com. This doll-oriented site offers an e-zine, several informative crafts business/marketing articles, and a nice collection of original clipart by site owner April Millican that can be used on craft products.

Barbara Brabec's World—www.BarbaraBrabec.com. The author's personal domain. It features all of her books, with a table of contents, reviews and reader feedback on each title, plus a variety of articles on home business, "Computertalk," writing, publishing and personal reflections.

The Basket Connection—www.theBasketConnectionInc.com. This site offers a choice of four business plans that will teach you how to develop a successful gift basket business.

BizyMoms—www.BizyMoms.com. An organization and Web site for moms and dads in homebased businesses of all kinds, with chapters in many states that offer local networking support. BizyMoms also publishes home-business eBooks and offers eClasses on a variety of home-business topics. The site features chats and a message board, a directory of home-business ideas, FAQs, warnings about scams, and a good collection of articles.

Color Marketing Trends—www.ColorMarketing.org. The Web site of the Color Marketing Organization. Click "Press Releases" to read about the latest color and design trends.

Coomers—www.commers.com. Coomers is the nation's largest retailer of American handmade crafts, gifts, and decorations for home and offices. This site explains how to get started selling in Coomers craft malls, and also allows current mall sellers to check their craft mall sales at any time. to receive information by mail, call toll free, 1-888-362-7238.

Craft Business News—www.Bluebonnetvillage.com. Nora Creeach publishes this very informative e-mail newsletter each month, sharing crafts business and marketing information along with answers to questions submitted by her readers. Check her Web site to find back issues and subscribe there or by sending an e-mail to CraftBusinessNews-subscribe@yahoogroups.com.

Craftmarketer—www.Craftmarketer.com. This site features the books of crafts author James Dillehay and includes many valuable business resources, articles and links to craft fair information online. A special "Toolbox" department also lists free software programs and business aids James has personally checked out.

Craft Sayings—www.CraftSayings.com. Check this site if you're looking for copyright-free sayings that can be safely used on craft products for sale. Includes one-liners, original poems by site owner, Shirley Thomas, and a list of project ideas to make using sayings on her site.

John Dilbeck—www.JohnDilbeck.com. A good information resource for artists, crafters, and others who manage a small business and want to market their products over the Internet.

Dover Pictorial Archive Books—www.DoverPublications.com. Your source for print books containing copyright-free designs that can be incorporated into craftwork for sale. (Type "Pictorial Archive" into the site's search engine.)

Ebay—www.eBay.com. "The World's Online Marketplace," and a great place to sell selected art/craft items, as discussed in Chapter Twelve.

HomeBiz Advice—www.HomeBizAdvice.com. This site, founded by the author in March 2000, is now owned and managed by the National Craft Association. It features a wide variety of home business articles—many of them from the author, who is now a contributing editor here—plus craft business news, tips, resources, links and a free e-zine.

The Professional Crafter—www.Procrafter.com. This site, one of the first on the Web for professional crafters, contains business articles, crafting tips and shortcuts, and a bulletin board.

Quilt University—www.QuiltUniversity.com. Check out this site if you want to learn quilting techniques from the experts, or are interested in teaching this topic on the Web.

The Wicker Woman—www.WickerWoman.com. Cathryn Peters owns this informative site, which contains basketry FAQs and links to several basketry suppliers. She also recommends the following sites, which offer information about guilds, other basketry sites, suppliers, and events calendars:
Basketry Information—www.ulster.net/~abeebe/basket.html

Baskets, Etc. -www.Bright.net/~basketc/
Susi Nuss' Basketmakers—www.basketmakers.org
Virtual Basketmakers—http://home.sprynet.com/~cpantrim/
Weave Net—www.Weavenet.com

Mailing Lists and Discussion Groups

There are more mailing lists and discussion groups on the Web than anyone can count. The best ones, however, have good word-of-mouth advertising. Here are some recommendations from business owners quoted in this book.

A CraftBiz Connection—http://groups.yahoo.com/group/acraftbizconnection. "This Yahoo group, sponsored by the National Craft Association, is fantastic in giving advice for people who are in the craft business." —Lisa Risler

David Collins' Weavers Words—http://groups.yahoo.com/group/weaverswords (recommended by Cathryn Peters)

Delphi Forums—www.delphiforums.com. "Go to hobbies or crafts and look for forums named Primitive and Rustic and another one, named Black Sheep. These forums are made up of primitive crafters who range from professional to gals who just do a show here and there. They discuss everything from how their latest show went to what is going on in their personal lives. If you're looking for business info you can sort through all the ramblings and get a pretty good idea of how things are going throughout the U.S. in the crafting business." —Linda Kindle

eBay Feedback Forum—www.eBay.com. (Click on "Community.") "Lots of information exchanged here, although there's also a lot of crabbing and complaining about eBay! Just sift through the junk to find the stuff that's useful to you." —Jacqui Collins-Parker

The Friendly Painters Club—http://clubs.yahoo.com/clubs/thefriendlypaintersclub. "This is my favorite painting club online. They offer tips, pattern and painting exchanges, chats, and friendship." —Suzanne Lloyd

The Professional Crafter's Mailing List—a one-stop resource for all of your professional crafter needs. To subscribe, send a blank e-mail to professionals-crafters-subscribe@egroups.com.

Sunshine Artist—www.sunshineartist.com/forum/index.php. "For shows to avoid or try, or general discussion regarding any aspect of this crafts/arts adventure, the Sunshine Artist forum is full of good information. (There is nothing like another artist to give info and opinions beyond what the promoters are telling us!)" —Sherrill Lewis

The Weaving List—To subscribe to this list, recommended by Bobbie Irwin, e-mail to majordomo@quilt.net with no subject, but with a body message of subscribe weaving <your e-mail address>.

Yahoo Mailing Lists—http://dir.yahoo.com/Arts/Crafts. You'll find more than thirty crafts categories on Yahoo's Web site. Click categories of interest to you to find a list you might like to join for networking purposes.

Crafts Web Site Design & Hosting Services

CraftMark, P.O. Box 799, Azle, TX 76098. 1-800-335-2544; www.CraftMark.com. This organization will design Web pages for you for as little as $10 a month or more (depending on features selected) for a minimum period of six months, payable in advance. This will buy you space in CraftMark's online catalog, reportedly the largest catalog of its type. (Your domain name here would be under CraftMark's URL.) To accept credit card sales on this site, you must first have your own system in place. Many crafters, however, simply include order forms that customers can print out and mail with a check or money order.

The National Craft Association (NCA), 2012 E. Ridge Rd., #120, Rochester, NY 14622. 1-800-715-9594. NCA can put your crafts business online within ten business days for between $129 and $149 for a year (includes design and layout of home page, product pages and order form with hosting for one year). This will buy you some attractive space on NCA's Web site in one of four shopping malls under their URL. If you want your own domain name and merchant card account, the cost will be higher, yet still reasonable and affordable to professional crafters. (See "Merchant Account Providers" below.)

Individual Web Site Designers

The following individuals—all business friends or associates of the author—can be trusted to do a good job in designing a Web site for you at a reasonable price. Or, if you are trying to do your own Web site and merely need some extra technical assistance or guidance with this job, one of these professionals can help you. Explain your needs by e-mail and ask for a quote, mentioning Barbara's name in your message.

John Dilbeck, Dilbeck Consulting, www.JohnDilbeck.com. This expert programmer, a craftsman himself, offers computer consulting and Web site development services at affordable rates. See his site for details.

Chris Maher, www.ArtWebWorks.com. At no extra fee, above the cost of registering your domain name, Chris will handle this detail for you and also find the best and most affordable Web server for your particular needs. Or, if you need to move your site to another server but don't have control of your domain name, Chris will "do battle" for you for a modest fee. Chris and his partner, Larry Berman, also offer expert Web site design services. Together, they have built nearly a hundred Web sites for artists and craftspeople, and you can link to several of them from their Web site to get ideas for design elements you'd like in your own site.

Susan Scheid, www.SmallBizCommunity.com, offers professional Web development specifically designed for home businesses on a limited budget. Prices range from $9.95 for a Web template to $325 for a full five-page custom site with shopping cart that can be modified as needed. (For more information, click Webtools/Services" on her site.)

Steve Maurer, www.Steve.Maurer.net, offers Web design services and assistance in adding new features to existing sites. From his site, you can link to other sites he has designed.

Do-It-Yourself Web Site Design/Development Tools

Refer to Chapter Twelve for additional comments about some of these service providers.

www.AddMe.com—This site lets you submit your site or URL to the top 20 search engines and directories for free. Also includes dozens of articles on the techniques of Web site design and management—great for beginners.

www.BigNoseBird.com—Over 300 pages of tutorials, reference materials, and other free resources located on this site–everything you need to create a great Web site, including HTML tricks, free graphics, scripts, software tools and more.

www.GlobalScape.com—Your link to the "CuteSiteBuilder" software mentioned in Chapter Twelve.

www.NewbieClub.com—The Newbie Club is a great source of help and information for Internet beginners, offering inexpensive resources to help one learn, such as a "First Website Builder Course," a guide to using Windows, and an eBook on computer key shortcuts. Sign up for the free newsletter, and check out the low-cost Newbie Club membership where you can get answers to technical questions from experts.

www.Trellix.com—A multi-page Web site authoring tool that does not require a knowledge of HTML or other Web languages.

www.Tripod.com—With tools on this site, you can build a free Web site with ads or, for a small monthly amount, a site free of ads.

www.WebMonkey.com—Excellent Web developer's resource, with a library of how-to articles, a JavaScript library, "HTML Cheatsheet," color codes and much more.

www.WilsonWeb.com—The Web's largest source of key information about doing business on the Net, with hundreds of articles and thousands of links to resources on e-commerce and Web marketing. This site also offers three free e-mail newsletters on Web marketing, eBiz and eCommerce.

Merchant Account Providers

The following sites all charge a varying percentage of sales and some also have either a one-time setup charge or fixed monthly fee whether sales are made or not. Study the information on each company's Web site and compare monthly costs to see which might work best for your site's expected sales volume. Pay particular attention to the discount rate and transaction fee, how and when you will receive money from sales, what chargeback fees are, and how you can terminate your account should you wish to change services later on.

www.ClickBank.com—This company will handle the processing of credit card orders but only one item can be purchased at a time, which is why it is often used by electronic publishers selling reports or books. Currently, the charge is $1 per transaction, plus 7.5 percent of the sale. This program also includes an affiliate program, in case you want to sell your publications through other dealers on the Web.

www.CCnow.com—This quick-and-easy shopping cart solution for new Web site owners offers secure transaction processing for all major credit cards with no extra charge for international orders. No startup costs or monthly fees; just a straight 9 percent commission on sales.

www.CraftAssoc.com—The Web site for the National Craft Association. Its members have access to an excellent, low-cost merchant account program, whether for craft show sales or sales on the Web. See the Web site for more information or call 1-800-715-9594 to explain your needs and get a recommendation for the best and most affordable solution for your business.

www.GoEmerchant.com—Another e-commerce solution, but the $49.95 monthly fee makes this service too costly for most beginners. Probably best for established/growing Web sites with sales of $1,000 a month or more.

www.PayPal.com—Perfect for beginners who have no sales track record yet, because fees occur only when sales are actually made. (Currently, the cost is thirty cents per transaction for sales under $15; for items $15 and more, the cost is thirty cents plus 2.2 percent of the sale.) The downside of PayPal is that some shoppers who aren't already registered with PayPal may not take the time to open their own account there (which is necessary before they can buy on a PayPal site).

www.ProPay.com—Similar to PayPal, except that shoppers do not have to register before making a purchase. This service provider claims to be 55 percent less expensive than other merchant account providers and is easy to set up. Currently, the fee is 3.5 percent of the sale, plus thirty-five cents per transaction.

Shopping Cart Systems (for Web Sellers with Merchant Accounts)

www.ait2000.com/index.htm—Mal's E-Commerce offers a free e-commerce service to small business owners who have their own merchant account. You can use this service to collect orders for later processing. Customers click on a "Buy Now Button" link on your site, and you are notified whenever an order is received. You then go to the administration area of the site to retrieve the secure credit card info stored there and complete the order process. This service is free, but you can upgrade to a premium account later if you want to do online payment processing.

www.Americart.com—Americart is a cost-effective shopping-cart system that can be added to any Web site for a flat annual rate of $249. You can use this system in conjunction with PayPal or your own merchant account system, or mail orders payable by check or money order.

Section IV: Organizations

Art/Craft Organizations

American Craft Council (ACC), 72 Spring St., New York, NY 10012. 1-800-724-0859; www.CraftCouncil.org. This organization offers a broad range of insurance plans, including group health insurance and a Studio Policy that protects against loss to both unfinished and finished works, at home or away. Members receive *American Craft* magazine.

Hobby Industry Association (HIA), 319 E. 54th St., Elmwood Park, NJ 07407. (201)794-1133; www.HIAshow.org. This trade organization sponsors the world's largest trade show for craft and hobby supplies. HIA's companion Web site for consumers, at www.I-Craft.com, features a Craft Library and projects for seniors, kids and teachers (a good place to find projects you can use in your craft classes).

357

International Guild of Candle Artisans, 867 Browning Ave. So., Salem, OR 97302. Members have access to workshops, the national IGCA convention, round-robin groups and a subscription to *The Candlelighter.*

The Knitting Guild of America (TKGA), P.O. Box 1606, Knoxville, TN 37901-1606. 1-800-274-6034; www.CraftYarnCouncil.com/join.html. Membership includes the quarterly journal, *Cast-on,* and opportunities to exhibit in retail markets and the annual National Convention and Knitting Market.

National Craft Association (NCA), E. Ridge Rd. #120, Rochester, NY 14622. 1-800-715-9594; www.CraftAssoc.com. An information and resource center for artists and crafters from beginner to seasoned professional. Members have access to insurance programs (including a good liability insurance policy), discounts on business services and products, merchant card and Web site design/hosting services, and the *NCA Arts & Crafts Newsletter*, available both in print and online. NCA's Web site includes business articles; Internet Tools to help crafters learn how to do business on the Web; sources and links to craft and trade show information and wholesale suppliers; a chat room, bulletin board and more. (See also "Crafts Web Site Design & Hosting Services" in this chapter.)

National Quilting Association, Inc., P.O. Box 393, Ellicott City, MD 21041. 1-410-461-5733; www.NQAquilts.org. Membership benefits include workshops at the annual quilt show and subscription to *The Quilting Quarterly.*

Society of Craft Designers (SCD), Box 3388, Zanesville, OH 43702-3388. 1-740-452-4541; www.CraftDesigners.org. A professional organization for craft designers, writers, book and periodical publishers, editors, teachers and others who wish to sell in the crafts and needlework industries. The Society's newsletter and annual educational seminar enables beginners to learn from the experts and make valuable editorial, publishing and manufacturing contacts.

Society of Decorative Painters, 393 No. McLean Blvd., Wichita, KS 67203-5968. 1-316-269-9300; www.DecorativePainters.com. This organization holds an annual convention and publishes an annual directory. Members receive a quarterly, *The Decorative Painter.*

Home-Business Organizations

The American Association of Home-Based Businesses (AAHBB), P.O. Box 10023, Rockville, MD 20849. 1-800-447-9710; www.AAHBB.org. This national organization has chapters across the country. Its members have access to merchant status, discounted business products and services, prepaid legal services and more.

Home Business Institute, Inc., P.O. Box 301, White Plains, NY 10605-0301. 1-888-DIAL HBI; www.HBIweb.com. Offers merchant card services and a group health insurance plan. Members receive *Inside Home Business* newsletter.

National Mail Order Association, 2807 Polk Street NE, Minneapolis, MN 55418-2954. www.NMOA.org. This organization offers information on starting a mail order business and using mail order and direct marketing techniques to advance one's business.

Section V: Government Resources

Bureau of Consumer Protection, Division of Special Statutes, 6th & Pennsylvania Ave. NW, Washington, DC 20580. Information on labels or tags required by law for items made of wool or textiles. Ask specifically for these booklets: *Textile Fiber Products Identification Act* and the *Wool Products Labeling Act of 1939*.

Consumer Product Safety Commission, Washington, DC 20207. Information on safety standards for toys and other products designed for children. Call 1-800-638-2772 to get a menu of several extensions you can punch to order publications of interest. Ask for booklets on the *Consumer Product Safety Act of 1972* and *The Flammable Fabrics Act.* The Web site at www.CPSC.gov includes a "Talk to Us" e-mail address where you can get answers to specific questions.

The Copyright Office, Register of Copyrights, Library of Congress, Washington DC 20559. Information on how to register and protect your original designs and patterns. Request all free publications, particularly those on how to file a copyright claim, protect your rights under current copyright law and investigate the copyright status of a work. To hear recorded messages on the Copyright Office's automated message system, call (202) 707-3000, or get the same information online at www.loc.gov/copyright.

Federal Trade Commission (FTC), 6th St. & Pennsylvania Ave. NW, Washington, DC 20580, www.FTC.gov. Information on trade practice and labeling rules. Ask specifically for booklets on *The Fabric Care Labeling Rule* and *The Wool Products Labeling Act of 1939.* The FTC also enforces trade practice rules and labeling requirements applicable to specific industries, so you may need to read one of these FTC booklets as well: *Guide for the Jewelry Industry, The Hand Knitting Yarn Industry,* and *The Catalog Jewelry and Giftware Industry.* If you plan to sell crafts by mail, also request the FTC booklets, *Truth-in-Advertising Rules* and *Thirty-Day Mail-Order Rule.*

Internal Revenue Service (IRS). Call 1-800-829-1040 or visit www.IRS.gov to get tax forms and free booklets and other tax information such as *Tax Guide for Small Business* (#334); and *Business Use of Your Home* (#587).

Patent & Trademark Office, U.S. Department of Commerce, Washington, DC 20231, www.USPTO.gov. Information about patents and trademarks. Call (800) 786-9199 to hear various messages about patents and trademarks, or to order booklets, *Basic Facts About Patents* and *Basic Facts About Trademarks*. (If you live in northern Virginia, you must call (703) 308-9000 instead of the toll-free number above.)

The U.S. Small Business Administration (SBA). Call 1-800-827-5722 to reach the SBA's "Small Business Answer Desk" and access a variety of prerecorded messages. A wealth of free information and publications is available on request. The same information may be accessed on the Web at www.SBA.gov.

SCORE (Service Corps of Retired Executives). Call 1-800-634-0245 to reach SCORE's main office, where you will be directed to your nearest local chapter for free assistance with your particular business problem or question. Thousands of SCORE volunteers are available to help small business owners, and e-mail counseling is also available via the Internet at www.SCORE.org.

Section VI: Suppliers

Craft Hang Tags

Cranberry Junction Designs, E&S Creations, P.O. Box 68, Rexburg, ID 83440; www.CranberryJunction.com

Kimmeric Studio, P.O. Box 10749, South Lake Tahoe, CA 96158; www.KimmericStudio.com

Wood Cellar Graphics, 87180 563rd Avenue, Coleridge, NE 68727; www.WoodCellarGraphics.com

Fabric Labels

Charm Woven Labels, 2400 W. Magnolia Blvd., Burbank, CA 91506. 1-800-843-1111; www.CharmWoven.com

GraphComm Services, P.O. Box 220, Freeland, WA 98249, 1-800-488-7436.
Widby Enterprises, P.O. Box 53253, Knoxville, TN 37950-3253;
www.WidbyLabel.com

Office & Paper Suppliers

The following companies offer quick shipment by UPS. Request their catalogs to compare prices of basic computer supplies, shipping labels, and other office-related products.

Office Depot 1-800-685-8800 (free delivery)
OfficeMax 1-800-788-8080 (free delivery on orders of $50 or more)
Quill 1-800-789-1331 (free delivery on orders of $50 or more)
Viking 1-800-421-1222 (free delivery on orders of $50 or more)

If you own a computer and a laser or inkjet printer, you can print your own promotional printed materials by adding copy to colorful preprinted papers. The companies below offer a wide variety of papers for stationery, flyers, business cards, postcards, presentation folders, labels and much more. Request samples or a catalog by calling these toll-free numbers:

Great Papers, 1-800-287-8163, www.PaperShowcase.com
Paper Direct, 1-800-A-Papers, www.PaperDirect.com

Insure your computer system with an inexpensive insurance policy from Safeware, The Insurance Agency, and enjoy coverage at 100 percent of your system's replacement value. 1-800-848-3469; www.Safeware.com.

Section VII: Web Sites of Individuals Quoted in This Book

Barbara Arena, National Craft Association, www.CraftAssoc.com
Marj Bates, Glass Things, www.GlassThings.com
Rochelle Beach, Cinna-Minnies Collectibles, www.Cinna-Minnies.com
Gail Bird, www.GailBird.com
Barbara Brabec, www.BarbaraBrabec.com
Carol Carlson, Kimmeric Studio, www.KimmericStudio.com
Jacqui Collins-Parker, Angel Craft Studio, www.AngelCraftStudio.com
John Dilbeck, Metalsmith, www.JohnDilbeck.com
James Dillehay, Craftmarketer, www.Craftmarketer.com

Myrna Giesbrecht, www.Press4Success.com

Joan Green, www.JoanGreenDesigns.com

Tammy Hodson & Shirley Harrison, Mother & Daughter, LLC, www.MotherDaughterSoap.com

Sue Johnson, Grammas Graphics, www.bubblink.com/donnelly; Heartstrings Press, www.Grandloving.com

Linda Kindle, Porhouse Primitives, www.PorhousePrimitives.com

Sue Krei, Wood Cellar Graphics, www.WoodCellarGraphics.com

Sylvia Landman, Sylvia's Studio, www.Sylvias-Studio.com

Susan Larberg, Golden Touch Crafts, http://clix.to/larberg

Opal Leasure, www.Craftmark.com/apron/home.htm

Gwen Taylor Lord, Things of Joy, www.ThingsofJoy.com

Chris Maher, Art Web Works, www.ArtWebWorks.com

Cheri Marsh, The SoapMeister, www.Soapmeister.com

Mary Mulari, www.MaryMulari.com

Liz Murad, Calligraphy, Ink, www.Inkybiz.com

Elaine Obidowski, The Laurel Tree Cooperative, www.geocities.com/laureltreebutler/

Cathryn Peters, The Wicker Woman, www.WickerWoman.com

Marsha Reed, Craftmaster News, www.CraftmasterNews.com

Lisa Risler, Interior Matters, www.DollHeaven.com

Bill Ronay, A Step Ahead, www.Events2000.com

Rebekah Rowe, Heart of Glass, www.geocities.com/heartofglassstudios/home.html

John Schulte, National Mail Order Association, www.nmoa.org

Debbie Spaulding, Puppet Patterns, www.PuppetPatterns.com

Susan Young, The Peach Kitty Studio, www.PeachKittyStudio.com

Christine Zipps, EZ Creations, www.picturetrail.com/czcreations

Index

363

Disney characters, 65-66
display ads. *See* advertising
donations, of crafts, 147, 151, 227, 239, 240, 241
Dunn, Barbara, 51
Durham, Dessie, 240

eBay, 58, 264-269
eBooks, 12
eCommerce Web site
    design/hosting services, 251-252, 259, 260, 354
    design/development tools, 254, 355
    designers, 253-254, 354
    domain name, registration, 249
    maintenance costs, 258
    sales, 270-271
    shopping cart, 261, 263, 264, 357
    site design software, 254, 256, 257, 259
    See also merchant account providers; Web site
e-mail, 136, 269-270
e-mail signature, 271
E&S Creations, 306, 360
excuses checklist, 15
expenses. *See* business expenses; selling expenses

failure, benefits of, 15
fairs. *See* craft fairs and shows
fear, fighting, 15, 30
federal regulations, affecting craft sellers, 41-42
Federal Trade Commission, (FTC), 42, 285
Ferrito, TC, 226, 300, 301, 334
festivals. *See* craft fairs and shows
fictitious name, 36-38
financial goals, 16, 32-33, 85
financial tips, 128-129

flea markets, 108
floral shops, as markets for crafts, 223
flyers. *See* printed materials
food, selling, 100
freebies, promotional, 49, 93, 123, 153, 285
freight charges, 217

galleries. *See* art and craft galleries
Galvin, Lisa, 327, 329, 342
garments, labels required by law, 41
Gearing, Susan, 100, 130, 207, 210, 213-214, 265-266, 271
Giesbrecht, Myrna, 336, 362
goals, setting, 16, 18, 20-21
Goldberg, Ellen, 38
government agencies. *See* U.S. Government
GraphComm Services, 307, 361
Green, Joan, 277, 316, 331, 332-333, 362
greeting cards. *See* note cards

Haddow, Irene, 125, 211
Hall, Denise, 229
handling charges, 95
hang tags, 52, 125, 187, 303-306
    copywriting and design tips, 305
    illustrations, 96, 304
    suppliers, 306, 315, 360
Harrison, Shirley, 96, 153
Heavey, Stephanie, 239
Highfill, Mary Lou, 338
Hirschmann, Susan Fox, 149-150
hobby income, 31-32, 35, 321
Hobby Industry Association (HIA), 2, 4-5, 86, 357
hobby sellers, 31, 35, 40, 69, 212, 319-322
hobby, tax definition of, 35
Hodson, Shirley, 253
Hodson, Tammy, 96, 153-154, 203, 247, 253, 261, 271, 362